Fighting with the Empire

STUDIES IN CANADIAN MILITARY HISTORY

Series editor: Andrew Burtch, Canadian War Museum

The Canadian War Museum, Canada's national museum of military history, has a threefold mandate: to remember, to preserve, and to educate. Studies in Canadian Military History, published by UBC Press in association with the Museum, extends this mandate by presenting the best of contemporary scholarship to provide new insights into all aspects of Canadian military history, from earliest times to recent events. The work of a new generation of scholars is especially encouraged, and the books employ a variety of approaches – cultural, social, intellectual, economic, political, and comparative – to investigate gaps in the existing historiography. The books in the series feed immediately into future exhibitions, programs, and outreach efforts by the Canadian War Museum. A list of the titles in the series appears at the end of the book.

CANADIAN WAR MUSEUM
MUSÉE CANADIEN DE LA GUERRE

Fighting with the Empire

Canada, Britain, and Global Conflict, 1867–1947

Edited by Steve Marti and William John Pratt

UBCPress · Vancouver · Toronto

27 26 25 24 23 22 21 20 19   5 4 3 2 1

Printed in Canada on FSC-certified ancient-forest-free paper (100% post-consumer recycled) that is processed chlorine- and acid-free.

Library and Archives Canada Cataloguing in Publication

Fighting with the empire : Canada, Britain, and global conflict,
    1867–1947 / edited by Steve Marti and William John Pratt.

(Studies in Canadian military history)
Includes bibliographical references and index.
Issued in print and electronic formats.
ISBN 978-0-7748-6040-6 (hardcover).—ISBN 978-0-7748-6041-3 (softcover).—
ISBN 978-0-7748-6042-0 (PDF).—ISBN 978-0-7748-6043-7 (EPUB).—
ISBN 978-0-7748-6044-4 (Kindle)

1. Canada—History, Military—19th century—Case studies. 2. Canada—History, Military—20th century—Case studies. 3. Great Britain—History, Military—19th century—Case studies. 4. Great Britain—History, Military—20th century—Case studies. 5. Canada—Military relations—Great Britain—History—19th century—Case studies. 6. Canada—Military relations—Great Britain—History—20th century—Case studies. 7. Great Britain—Military relations—Canada—History—19th century—Case studies. 8. Great Britain—Military relations—Canada—History—20th century—Case studies. 9. Imperialism—History—19th century—Case studies. 10. Imperialism—History—20th century—Case studies. 11. Case studies. I. Marti, Steve, editor II. Pratt, William J., editor III. Series: Studies in Canadian military history

FC226.F57 2019   355.00971   C2018-905831-5
                                                               C2018-905832-3

Canadä

UBC Press gratefully acknowledges the financial support for our publishing program of the Government of Canada (through the Canada Book Fund), the Canada Council for the Arts, and the British Columbia Arts Council.

Publication of this book has been financially supported by the Canadian War Museum.

UBC Press
The University of British Columbia
2029 West Mall
Vancouver, BC V6T 1Z2
www.ubcpress.ca

Contents

Acknowledgments

THE SUCCESS OF any edited collection rests on the contribution of its authors. This collection is no different. The editors offer their most heartfelt appreciation to the author of each chapter in this book for trusting us with their research. We also want to acknowledge those colleagues who offered to produce a chapter but, owing to the workload placed on early-career academics, found themselves unable to contribute. Much of the credit for the conception of this edited collection goes to Tyler Turek. Tyler stepped away from the project to pursue opportunities beyond academia, but his energy and enthusiasm shaped and sustained the project in its earlier days.

The editors extend their gratitude to the generous support provided through the Canadian War Museum's Studies in Canadian Military History series. We also wish to thank the anonymous reviewers, whose constructive suggestions strengthened the chapters, and to the acquisitions and production staff at UBC Press. Emily Andrew provided valuable advice in preparing the proposal. Darcy Cullen proved thoroughly efficient while guiding the collection through peer review and endlessly patient in answering the editors' technical questions during the production process.

Fighting with the Empire

Introduction

Steve Marti and William John Pratt

> *"Britons" means us; it means all we stand for in Canada; it means French-Canadians and German-Canadians and it means magna charta.*
>
> – CANADIAN HOUSE OF COMMONS DEBATES, MAY 7, 1942[1]

IN MAY 1942, Douglas Ross rose briefly in Parliament to interject in the debate over sections of the War Appropriations Bill. Ross had been a critic of the government's failure to promote martial music across the Dominion, so it might have come as no surprise that the Conservative member of Parliament for St. Paul's, Ontario, added emphasis to his speech by reciting two verses of the patriotic standard "Rule Britannia!"[2] After reading out the famous line "Britons never will be slaves," Ross explained that the title "Britons" applied to all Canadians.[3] Such inclusivity might have struck his colleagues in the House of Commons as novel. Twenty-five years earlier, when Canadians rallied to support Britain's effort against the Central powers, the title "Britons" had been reserved for those Canadians who could trace their heritage to the British Isles. Ross's inclusion of German Canadians and French Canadians presented a stark contrast to his own party's actions during the Great War. Not only had the Conservative government sanctioned the internment of immigrants born in the German, Ottoman, and Austro-Hungarian empires as enemy aliens, the rhetoric of its pro-conscription election campaign of 1917 had made a scapegoat of French Canada's lagging enlistments.

The expanding definition of "Britons" reflected the need to mobilize Canadians for another global war. Ross offered his vision of inclusivity to Parliament in the wake of a referendum on conscription, during which strong opposition in French Canada had led Prime Minister Mackenzie King to delay the implementation of conscription until absolutely necessary. Having learned from the social divisions wrought by policies enacted during the Great War, King chose to conciliate French Canadians rather than alienate them from the war effort against the Axis powers and adopted some relatively selective criteria for the detention of German and Italian immigrants. The future prime minister John Diefenbaker also rose in the House in 1942 to call upon Quebec ministers to mobilize their constituents for war. He stated, "The challenge to us to-day as

Canadians, without regard to race or creed, is to unite in a common dedication to our way of life and our national life itself. If there is one thing that has done more to undermine this Dominion and its unity ... it is the fact that we as Canadians are too prone to hyphenate our citizenship."[4]

The sweeping internment of Japanese Canadians earlier that year, however, revealed that exclusion and division persisted in Canada. Internment operations did not distinguish between recent immigrants and second-generation Japanese Canadians, but the dispossession of Canadian-born Japanese summarily deprived them of their rights as British subjects – protections that traced their origins to the Magna Carta. The abhorrent treatment of Asian immigrants in Canada reached its apex under the rationale of wartime security. Mobilizing for war against the Axis powers pushed statesmen such as Ross and Diefenbaker to call for a more inclusive version of Canada, but how far were Canadians willing to stray from the British template? Canada's participation in a series of imperial wars in the first half of the twentieth century revealed incremental adjustments not only to the imagined boundaries of their nation but also to their bonds to the British Empire.

Canadian historians have long grappled with the complexities of identity inspired by Carl Berger's landmark book *The Sense of Power*, which demonstrated how ideas of British imperialism were integral to Canadian nationalism before 1914.[5] The familiar master narrative of Canadian history has long traced a seemingly inevitable historical trajectory towards national independence, but this course was punctuated and, at times, ironically accelerated by collective action with the British Empire. The Dominion of Canada's earliest military engagements provide the most prominent examples of such imperial efforts. Historian Philip Buckner frames Canadian enthusiasm in support of Britain's war against the Boers in South Africa – a conflict that served British interests far more than it benefitted the Dominion – squarely in terms of Canadians' imperial nationalism.[6] The role of imperial sentiment in motivating the Dominion's commitment to imperial defence remains undeniable, and Canadian historians have pointed to the complementary goals of nationalism and imperialism to explain why Canadians participated so willingly in Britain's wars.

This volume examines how Canadians imagined their relationship with Britain through the experience of war. Nation and empire may have been inseparable in the minds of Canadians, but they were never one and the same. The Dominion supported Britain's war in South Africa out of imperial loyalism, but Canadians celebrated the exploits of their soldiers on the veldt to emphasize the inherent difference between Canadian militiamen and British regulars. For veterans, the war strengthened their devotion to imperial defence but also created a desire to see a larger, contiguous, Canadian-commanded expedition operating as part of a larger British-led army.[7] Fighting with the Empire as part of an imperial force strengthened sentimental attachments to Britain, but Canadians also fought with the Empire at the negotiating table to better define their place alongside the other Dominions. Canada remained a part within the whole, and the ways Canadians imagined this relationship changed over time. Each time war loomed on the horizon, Canadians recalibrated the equilibrium of national imperialism to determine why and how they would join a British war effort.

Fighting with the Empire delves into Canada's relationship with Britain and the Empire by focusing on the history of conflict and diplomacy. By exploring how Canadians responded to the threat of war, this volume examines how allegiances and identities were constructed in different social and strategic contexts. This relationship alternated most visibly between the opposing poles of imperial entanglements and national autonomy, but ties to Britain and the Empire require a more nuanced calculus. Military or diplomatic cooperation with Britain often advanced the national interest while also making a display of imperial solidarity. Many Canadians felt a strong connection to Britain because of their ancestry and were ready to fight in defence of the Empire, but travelling overseas highlighted the cultural differences between Britain and Canada. Indigenous peoples, French Canadians, and Asian, African, or continental European immigrants did not share this British lineage, but many were nevertheless ready to take up arms for Britain to claim the legal protections promised to British subjects, such as religious freedom or enfranchisement.[8] Canada's participation in a series of imperial wars highlighted the tensions between nation and empire. The essays here examine the ways that the malleable relationship between Canada and Britain was shaped and reshaped through the experience of conflict and the conduct of diplomacy.

In exploring Canadian attachments to the Empire in wartime, this volume includes case studies that demonstrate how race and ethnicity factored into this imagined relationship. The study of the British world as a cultural phenomenon has highlighted the imagined continuity between Britons throughout the Empire, but this focus on "Britishness" often neglects the role of race or ethnicity in the construction of nationalism in the Dominions.[9] The status of British subject extended beyond those who originated from the British Isles, and this distinction highlighted the contradictions of a British Canada. The threat of war helped draw out these contradictions. French Canadian, Indigenous, African, and Asian or continental European immigrants and their diaspora mobilized in support of the war effort to protect or assert their rights as British subjects. Their inclusion in the process of national mobilization helped strengthen Canada's contribution to an imperial war effort, but their participation also produced a more diverse war effort, one that challenged the imagined homogeneity of Canada as a British nation.

To bring to light the experiences and motivations that compelled Canadians to participate in, or prepare for, the defence of the British Empire, this volume relies on new methods to explore the boundaries between nation and empire. The contributors examine how Canadian attitudes towards the imperial relationship were shaped and reshaped in response to, or in anticipation of, Canada's participation in British imperial wars. As case studies, the chapters reveal how different communities in Canada grappled with the complementary or competing categories of nation and empire. Together, they provide narrative stepping stones that reveal how wartime mobilization forced Canadians to examine and confront the tensions between nationalism and imperialism.

The study of the British world centres on exploring the persistence of Canada's cultural ties to the Empire, particularly after the Second World War. Due largely to the efforts of Philip Buckner and R. Douglas Francis, this field of research addresses themes of migration, identity, and transnational connection, which tied Great Britain to its Dominions until the 1960s. Only a few of the nearly sixty chapters in Buckner and Francis's three edited collections on the British world address the impact of war and conflict on Canada's relationship to Britain.[10] These chapters demonstrate that war and peace were central to discussions regarding Canada's place in the Empire from the late nineteenth century to the mid-twentieth century, yet the impact of these conflicts played only a minor role in explanations of Canada's sudden break from empire in the 1950s and 1960s.[11] We share the "British world" approach to exploring the legacy of British identity and transnational connections in Canada, but we place a greater emphasis on qualifying the meaning and limits of Britishness in Canada. More importantly, the chapters in this volume provide a closer examination of the dissolution of imperial bonds through the experience of warfare.

Amid the recent centenary of Vimy Ridge and the sesquicentennial of Confederation, as well as the upcoming centenary of the Treaty of Versailles, *Fighting with the Empire* sets out to reassess the impact of conflict and diplomacy on Canada's relationship to Britain and the Empire. Canada dispatched its largest overseas military deployments in the years between Confederation and the end of the Second World War. During this period of intermittent global conflict, the Dominion of Canada aspired to negotiate and assert its status as a nation within the British Empire. This volume draws a closer connection between the impact of war on Canadian society, international relations between Canada and Britain, and the imaginary bonds between nation and empire. In particular, individual chapters focus on the periods between watershed moments, such as the ones marked by centenary commemorations, to understand how the experience of war changed Canadian attitudes towards Britain and the Empire.

Even before the bittersweet triumphs on the battlefield or the incremental constitutional concessions won over a series of imperial conferences, the prospect of participating in an imperial war pushed Canadians to question the place of their nation within the Empire. Together, the contributions to this volume reassess both formal and informal ties between Canada and Britain and explore how participating in an imperial conflict challenged the comfortable notion of imperial nationalism in Canada. By examining the experiences of soldiers, officers, statesmen, and civilian actors over the first eighty years of Confederation, the chronological scope of this volume offers a longitudinal analysis of the evolving ideas of nation and empire in Canada. Nationalist narratives of Canada's military history focus on the battlefield to examine the impact of war on Canada's relationship to Britain. Military victories such as Vimy Ridge are held up as moments of national awakening while the appointment of Canadian officers to command Dominion forces serve as benchmarks on the constitutional progression towards national autonomy. The contributions to this volume look beyond battlefield narratives to explore the subtler ways that warfare changed Canada's relationship to Britain.

When battlefield narratives are not explicitly constructing a patriotic edifice stretching from colony to nation, they often serve as an allegory for intellectual or cultural constructions of Canada's imperial relationship.[12] The study of home fronts or soldier's experiences can show how the bonds of empire were recast through broader experiences of war. Several Canadian historians have examined how imperial attachments shaped how Canadians understood their participation in Britain's wars. Historians of the Canadian home front have considered the importance of imperial sentiment in wartime mobilization. Ian Miller's *Our Glory and Our Grief* (2002) and Robert Rutherdale's *Hometown Horizons* (2004) both show that the mobilization of the home front offered Canadians an opportunity to make imaginary ties to Britain and the war overseas concrete through patriotic demonstrations at home.[13] Building on his description of Toronto as one of the great imperial cities, Miller argues that imperial sentiment drove wartime enthusiasm: "Torontonians were devoted to supporting Britain, defending the Empire, and achieving victory."[14] While the 1931 Statute of Westminster, which restricted the imperial government's power over the dominions' affairs, is sometimes seen as a legal and symbolic watershed between an imperial past and a colonial future, scholars have noted that many Canadians in 1939 still felt that when Britain was at war, so too was Canada.[15] For historian Serge Durflinger, ties to "British working-class political culture and social identity" made Verdun, Quebec, "uncommonly patriotic in the defence of British, and therefore Canadian, interests" during the Second World War.[16]

The experience of Canadian soldiers and nurses stationed overseas during times of conflict has inspired scholars to explore the impact of these journeys on understandings of empire, nationalism, and their place within this network. Cynthia Toman has examined how gender and race shaped the national identity of military nurses in the First World War, expanding on the work of Katie Pickles, who revealed the centrality of maternal themes to female imperialism.[17] Toman suggests that Canada's nursing sisters showed a "fluidity of identity" in their awareness of their own distinction from British nurses while at the same time identifying with white, British femininity and British cultural traditions.[18] Jonathan Vance expands on this approach to examine the broader experiences of Canadian soldiers posted in Britain during the world wars, revealing that Canadian soldiers identified themselves as "colonials" who were also "colonizing" enclaves of the imperial metropole by establishing training bases and rest homes throughout Britain.[19] Robert Engen has recently argued that Canadian infantry in the Second World War showed no "feelings of patriotism, nationalism, or of 'fighting for Canada'" but, at the same time, they took great pride in their separateness from the British.[20] By studying wartime mobilization or mobility, such works expose Canada's imperial ties and reveal how personal experiences can shed light on the nuanced relationship between Canada and Britain.

Race, ethnicity, and indigeneity have generally been examined as categories of exclusion in Canadian studies of war and society. Histories of wartime internment, which focus on the experience of minorities who were classified by the Canadian state as enemy aliens during times of conflict, have illuminated how the outbreak of war deepened existing divisions of race and ethnicity in Canada.[21] The internment of suspected enemy aliens in Canada presents an accurate but incomplete study of the experience of non-British minorities in wartime. These marginalized communities made repeated attempts to overcome exclusive policies by participating in the national and imperial war efforts. James Walker's research on recruiting in the Canadian Expeditionary Force and Lyle Dick's study of Japanese Canadians' military service – and the commemoration of their service – both demonstrate that race and ethnicity were constructed into formidable, though permeable, social barriers in Canadian society.[22]

The growing body of research on Canadian Indigenous peoples' wartime experience highlights how constructions of race and indigeneity shaped Canada's military history. The Canadian government's sustained campaign to assimilate Indigenous peoples into settler society by attacking the basic structures of their culture – such as removing Indigenous children to residential schools to undermine Indigenous language, family structure, and attachment to the land – also set the framework through which Indigenous peoples contributed to the imperial war effort. Historian Robert Talbot, for example, has shown how Indian agents extended these "civilizing" policies by soliciting the participation of Indigenous communities in the war effort; he also illuminated the extent to which Indigenous communities resisted these interventions.[23] The symbol of the British Crown plays an important role in power relationships between settlers and Indigenous peoples in Canada. Scholars such as P. Whitney Lackenbauer, Katherine McGowan, and Timothy Winegard have highlighted the importance of historical ties to Britain, whether through treaties or alliances, in shaping Indigenous peoples' perceived relationship with the Canadian settler state in wartime.[24] Winegard suggests that First Nations communities declared loyalty to both Canada and the Crown in 1914 but that returning veterans were disappointed by the lack of improvement in their position in Canadian society.[25] R. Scott Sheffield has shown that government resistance to changing assimilative policies remained after the Second World War, despite the varying ways in which First Nations people were perceived by bureaucrats and the public during the conflict.[26] First Nations peoples' arguments against their conscription by the government ranged from the Six Nations arguing that they remained allies of the Crown (and not British subjects) to other nations pointing out the contradiction of fighting for a state that did not grant them the rights of citizenship. Such debates emphasize the complicated nature of the relationship between Indigenous peoples and the Crown and Canada, and they beg further study of how identities were constructed and negotiated along ethnic lines.

A new wave of scholarship in Canadian international history is working to highlight how constructions of race influenced both Canadian foreign policy and Canadians' perception of their place in the British Empire and the world. John Meehan has highlighted the importance of race and exoticism in shaping Canadian missions to Shanghai in the first half of the twentieth century. John Price's *Orienting Canada* places race at the centre of Canadian foreign policy towards the "transpacific" after 1945. These latter studies reveal that race was central to British Canadian identity, as practices of colonization and policies of exclusion were motivated by ideas of racial hierarchy and racial purity: Britishness was implicitly constructed in terms of whiteness. Essays in the recent edited collections *Within and Without the Nation* and *Dominion of Race* explore how constructions of race shaped Canadians' perceptions of their place in the wider world across a wide chronological and geographical scope, though less than a handful of them explore Canadian experiences in the context of global conflict.[27]

The chapters in this volume extend the methodologies of the new imperial and new international history to the study of war and society in Canada. The contributors present a series of case studies that examine how the process, or promise, of wartime mobilization forced Canadians to consider how they defined their place in the nation and the Empire. Part 1, "Mobility and Mobilization," examines how the process of wartime mobilization and the movement of people forced members of the British diaspora in Canada to confront the duality of imperial nationalism. For intellectuals or idealists, the development of a strong British nation in Canada complemented British imperial ambitions. The mobilization of Canadian contingents to fight as part of an imperial army, however, highlighted the competing interests underlying these supposedly complementary efforts. The Boer War marked the first deployment of Canadian soldiers overseas, but their integration into a larger imperial force prompted elaborate discussions on the qualities that distinguished Canadian soldiers from their British counterparts.

Amy Shaw's chapter examines newspapers and soldiers' correspondence to explore the careful construction of Canadian soldiers as embodiments of an idealized archetype of British manhood who also exhibited the unique traits of Canadian frontier masculinity. The experience of colonial warfare in South Africa forced Canadian soldiers to confront their role as agents of empire as well as the more unsavoury realities of their frontier identity. The outbreak of war in 1914 prompted a much greater mobilization of human and material resources to support the imperial war effort, yet these combined efforts led volunteers to question whether they should devote themselves to support national or imperial war efforts. Steve Marti's chapter on the patriotic work of the Imperial Order Daughters of the Empire (IODE) considers how wartime mobilization pulled apart the strands of the IODE's ideals of imperial citizenship. The desire to take a leading role in maximizing voluntary patriotic work in Canada prompted an expansion of the organization's membership, which ultimately compromised the IODE's idealized imperial sisterhood in favour of Canadian demographics. The lengthy deployment of Canadian soldiers overseas during the Second World War strained individual morale and unit cohesion as soldiers longed for the comforts of home. Though many English Canadian soldiers thought of Britain as an ancestral home, William Pratt's examination of censors' reports during the Second World War uncovers a shifting preference among Canadian soldiers for North American consumer goods and a growing distaste for British products. In each case, Canadian participation in an imperial war effort highlighted the growing divergence between nation and empire and unravelled the comfortable logic of national imperialism.

Part 2, "Persons and Power," explores the impact of individual officials as figureheads or representatives of the Crown or Dominion government. These prominent persons wrote, enacted, or assented to policies that defined or redefined Canada's constitutional status within the Empire; however, outside the halls of power, these statesmen acted as a relatable personification of the state for the public. The Canadian public's ability to relate to these representatives reflected an idealized version of the imperial relationship. Eirik Brazier's chapter examines the role of imperial officers in the pre-1914 militia and criticisms that they alienated Canadian politicians with their attempts at reform. Brazier challenges this assessment of senior British officers seconded to the Dominion of Canada by highlighting their role as public representatives of the Crown. In their ceremonial role, imperial officers embodied the ideals of uniformity and shared military traditions among British colonial forces; they symbolized organic continuity between the Canadian militia and the British army.

Robert Talbot's chapter delves into the politics of the Department of Foreign Affairs during the interwar years. In the aftermath of the First World War, William Lyon McKenzie King appointed a slate of civil servants that shared his goal of an Anglo-French rapprochement in Canada. Under their guidance, Canadian foreign policy responded to the various international crises during the 1930s by cultivating public consent, particularly in French Canada, as a precursor to any imperial or international commitments. Claire Halstead's chapter re-examines the royal tour of 1939 to focus on the response of ordinary Canadians to the arrival of the royal couple. The tour anticipated the outbreak of another European war and sought to rekindle Canadians' emotional attachment to Britain and the Empire in the event of another major war. While Brazier shows that imperial pageantry implied conformity within the Empire, Halstead reveals that Canadians' often welcomed the monarchs as "their own." Statesmen, whether civil servants or imperial figureheads, represented the power structures of the British and Canadian states. These appointments encouraged participative exercises of imperial loyalty that relied increasingly on winning public approval before committing the Dominion to imperial entanglements.

Part 3, "Hardly British," examines the meaning of the British Empire to communities in Canada that did not trace their ancestry to the British Isles. The rhetoric that tied Canada to Britain and the Empire often relied on the sentimental ties and common heritage of the dominant British diaspora. British settlement on Indigenous lands, the incorporation of French settlers into Confederation, and the reliance on immigration from continental Europe, Asia, and the Caribbean to sustain demographic growth all worked to disprove the rhetoric of a racially homogenous British Canada. The cultural and racial diversity of the British Empire, as well as its liberal ethos, necessitated a legal definition of the British subject to unite disparate populations into a single category. The difference between a British subject and the – still undefined – Canadian citizen highlighted the tensions between racial and legal conceptions of citizenship, particularly as the onset of war raised issues of loyalty, security, and the obligation to perform military service. Geoff Keelan's chapter highlights French Canadian perspectives on Canada's participation in the First World War. While generally supportive of Canada's involvement in the war at its outbreak, the attitude of French Canadian *nationalistes* shifted when Ontario's Conservative government implemented Regulation 17 and when conscription was enacted in 1917. Both developments contradicted the traditional freedoms of British liberalism. Mikhail Bjorge's chapter explores the rash of illegal strikes in collieries at the outbreak of the Second World War. Led by committees of xenophobic miners, these strikers demanded the dismissal of recent European immigrants, playing on the threat of sabotage by enemy aliens. Bjorge situates these strikes in the longer narrative of nativism in the Canadian labour movement, which helped define its membership in terms of race, and the Canadian state's reluctance to correct this intolerance. The demands of the war effort and the need to maximize the Dominion's industrial output, however, required the Canadian state to uphold the rights of European workers in miners' and manufacturers' unions.

In the final chapter, R. Scott Sheffield surveys the contributions of First Nations communities to the Canadian war effort during the Second Word War. While band councils often framed patriotic gifts in terms that honoured their relationship to the Crown, the implementation of conscription after the 1942 plebiscite heightened the need to clarify the relationship between First Nations communities, the Crown, and the Canadian government. Much as First Nations communities contributed to the Canadian war effort by enlisting or donating funds, these contributions were often intended to leverage their status as allies of the Crown in negotiations with the Dominion government. Although imperial wars were often described in terms of a familial obligation, as is in shown in Part 1 of this volume, this rhetoric of race patriotism held little relevance outside of Canada's British diaspora. Securing the participation of First Nations, French Canadian, or continental European communities in Canada's war effort necessitated a legal rather than a racial definition of Canadian citizenship that often drew on British conventions. Ironically, this pluralism, based on British legal conventions, helped dispel British race patriotism in Canada and facilitated the inclusion of a larger proportion of the population in the Canadian war effort.

Canada's participation in three imperial wars during the first eighty years of Confederation expedited a transformation in Canada's relationship to Britain.

The contribution of Canadian lives, funds, and resources to an imperial war effort was leveraged to achieve a constitutional transition from colony to nation, but the considerations of wartime mobilization forced a more fundamental transformation in the popular perception of Canada's relationship to Britain and the Empire. Alongside the martial accomplishments of Canadian victories on the battlefield and the collective grieving for lives sacrificed in the name of nation and empire, mobilizing a national contribution to an imperial war effort disrupted the comfortable logic of Canadian national imperialism, whose contradictions were so easily reconciled in peacetime. Contributing to the imperial war effort brought Canadians to fight alongside British and other imperial soldiers, but it also highlighted the growing divergence between Canada and Britain. *Fighting with the Empire* explores the middle ground between narratives that celebrate the emergence of a Canadian nation through warfare and studies that equate Canadian nationalism with British imperialism. This volume examines how the paradox of raising a national effort to fight in an imperial war forced Canadians to reconsider their relationship to Britain and to one another and the gradual changes that transformed that relationship over time.

Notes

1 Canada, House of Commons, *Debates*, 19th Parl., 3rd Sess., May 7, 1942, 2225.
2 For his criticism of the government's failure, see ibid., 19th Parl., 1st Sess., July 8, 1940, 1425.
3 These were the lyrics sung by Douglas Ross, as recorded in *Hansard*. The editors acknowledge that versions of this patriotic staple vary between "Britons never *will* be slaves" and "Britons never *shall* be slaves."
4 Canada, House of Commons, *Debates*, 19th Parl., 3rd Sess., June 15, 1942, 3334.
5 Carl Berger, *The Sense of Power: Studies in the Ideas of Canadian Imperialism, 1867–1914* (Toronto: University of Toronto Press, 1970).
6 Philip Buckner, "Canada," in *The Impact of the South African War*, ed. David Omissi and Andrew S. Thompson (Basingstoke: Palgrave, 2002), 234.
7 Ibid., 241–42.
8 We use the term "Indigenous" when discussing broader, often transnational patterns in settler-Indigenous relations. The term "First Nations" is used when referring specifically to Indigenous peoples in Canada, separate from the experiences of Métis and Inuit. The term "Indian" is only used when referring to historical terminology, such as "Indian agent."
9 "Britishness" refers to more than diasporic ties to Britain; it defines a synthetic identity based on shared cultural values. As Linda Colley explains in her groundbreaking study on the emergence of British nationalism in the nineteenth century, a common British identity emerged out of a period of protracted war with France. Importantly, Colley demonstrates that the idea of Great Britain appealed to residents of England, Scotland, Ireland, and Wales because it provided valuable – if sometimes intangible – benefits. The promise of economic and social mobility for the enterprising or intrepid Scots, Irish, or Welsh turned England's burgeoning empire into a British concern. See Linda Colley, *Britons: Forging the Nation, 1707–1837* (New Haven: Yale University Press, 1992).

10 See chapters by Patrick Brennan and Jeffrey Grey in *Rediscovering the British World*, ed. Philip Buckner and R. Douglas Francis (Calgary: University of Calgary Press, 2003), and the chapter by Wesley C. Gustavson in *Canada and the British World: Culture, Migration, and Identity*, ed. Buckner and Francis (Vancouver: UBC Press, 2006).

11 Similar criticisms can be levied against the debate between José E. Igartua and C.P. Champion. See Igartua, *The Other Quiet Revolution: National Identities in English Canada, 1945–1971* (Vancouver: UBC Press, 2006) and Champion, *The Strange Demise of British Canada: The Liberals and Canadian Nationality, 1964–1968* (Montreal/Kingston: McGill-Queen's University Press, 2010).

12 For challenges to narratives of colony to nation in the Canadian Expeditionary Force, see Mark Osborne Humphries, "Between Commemoration and History: The Historiography of the Canadian Corps and Military Overseas," *Canadian Historical Review* 95, 3 (September 2014): 384–97; Terry Copp, "The Military Effort, 1914–1918," in *Canada and the First World War: Essays in Honour of Robert Craig Brown*, ed. David Mackenzie (Toronto: University of Toronto Press, 2005), 35–61; and Jeff Keshen, "The Great War Soldier as Nation Builder in Canada and Australia," in *Canada and the Great War: Western Front Association Papers*, ed. Briton C. Busch (Montreal/Kingston: McGill-Queen's University Press, 2003), 3–26.

13 Robert Allen Rutherdale, *Hometown Horizons: Local Responses to Canada's Great War* (Vancouver: UBC Press, 2004), 48–87.

14 Ian Hugh Maclean Miller, *Our Glory and Our Grief: Torontonians and the Great War* (Toronto: University of Toronto Press, 2002), 197–99.

15 Jack Granatstein, *Canada's War: The Politics of the Mackenzie King Government, 1939–1945* (Toronto: University of Toronto Press, 1990), 19, and Jeff Keshen, *Saints, Sinners, and Soldiers: Canada's Second World War* (Vancouver: UBC Press, 2004), 12.

16 Serge Durflinger, *Fighting from Home: The Second World War in Verdun, Quebec* (Vancouver: UBC Press, 2006), 4.

17 Cynthia Toman, "'A Loyal Body of Empire Citizens': Military Nurses and Identity at Lemnos and Salonika, 1915–17," in *Place and Practice in Canadian Nursing History*, ed. Jayne Elliott, Meryn Stuart, and Cynthia Toman (Vancouver: UBC Press, 2008), 8–24, and Katie Pickles, *Female Imperialism and National Identity: Imperial Order Daughters of the Empire* (Manchester: Manchester University Press, 2002).

18 Cynthia Toman, "'Help Us, Serve England': First World War Military Nursing and National Identity," *Canadian Bulletin of Medical History* 30, 1 (Spring 2013): 146.

19 Jonathan A. Vance, *Maple Leaf Empire: Canada, Britain, and Two World Wars* (Toronto: Oxford University Press, 2011).

20 Robert Engen, *Strangers in Arms: Combat Motivation in the Canadian Army, 1943–1945* (Montreal/Kingston: McGill-Queen's University Press, 2016), 21, 81.

21 See, for example, Franca Iacovetta, Roberto Perin, and Angelo Principe, eds., *Enemies Within: Italian and Other Internees in Canada and Abroad* (Toronto: University of Toronto Press, 2000); Bohdan S. Kordan, *Enemy Aliens, Prisoners of War: Internment in Canada during the Great War* (Montreal/Kingston: McGill-Queen's University Press, 2002); and Martin F. Auger, *Prisoners of the Home Front: German POWs and "Enemy Aliens" in Southern Quebec, 1940–46* (Vancouver: UBC Press, 2006).

22 James W. St.G. Walker, "Race and Recruitment in World War I: Enlistment of Visible Minorities in the Canadian Expeditionary Force," *Canadian Historical Review* 70, 1 (1989): 1–26, and Lyle Dick, "Sergeant Masumi Mitsui and the Japanese Canadian War Memorial," *Canadian Historical Review* 91, 3 (2010): 435–63.

23 Robert J. Talbot, "'It Would Be Best to Leave Us Alone': First Nations Responses to the Canadian War Effort, 1914–18," *Journal of Canadian Studies/Revue d'études canadiennes* 45, 1 (2011): 90–120.

24 P. Whitney Lackenbauer and Katharine McGowan, "Competing Loyalties in a Complex Community: Enlisting the Six Nations in the Canadian Expeditionary Force, 1914–1917," in *Aboriginal Peoples and the Canadian Military: Historical Perspectives*, ed. P. Whitney Lackenbauer and Craig Leslie Mantle (Winnipeg: Canadian Defence Academy Press, 2007), 89–116.

25 Timothy Winegard, *For King and Kanata: Canadian Indians and the First World War* (Winnipeg: University of Manitoba Press, 2012), 7.

26 Scott Sheffield, The *Red Man's on the Warpath: The Image of the "Indian" and the Second World War* (Vancouver: UBC Press, 2004).

27 See John Price's chapter on Asian Canadians during the First World War, Francine McKenzie's chapter on Robert Borden at the 1919 Peace Conference, and P. Whitney Lackenbauer's chapter on encounters between African Americans and Indigenous peoples during the Second World War in *Dominion of Race: Rethinking Canada's International History*, ed. Francine McKenzie, David Meren, and Laura Madokoro (Vancouver: UBC Press, 2017); Kristine Alexander's chapter on internationalism in the Girl Guides movement during the interwar years is framed in the context of the legacies of the First World War. See "Canadian Girls, Imperial Girls, Global Girls: Race, Nation, and Transnationalism in the Interwar Girl Guide Movement," in *Within and Without the Nation: Canadian History as Transnational History*, ed. Karen Dubinsky, Adele Perry, and Henry Yu (Toronto: University of Toronto Press, 2015), 276–92.

Part 1
Mobility and Mobilization

1

Fathers and Sons of Empire
Domesticity, Empire, and Canadian Participation in the Anglo-Boer War

Amy Shaw

THE ANGLO-BOER WAR was the first time Canadians went in significant numbers to fight overseas. The conflict brought forward, often passionately, varying interpretations of the responsibilities of nationalism and imperialism and exacerbated French-English divisions in the country, linking the conflict firmly to later wars of the twentieth century. It is also an understudied period in Canadian history.[1] This is unfortunate because focusing on the stories of the men who went overseas, and how their doing so affected their families, can, among other things, help us understand much about how imperialism was experienced on an individual level.

One step towards resolving this is to use their letters and diaries to discuss how Canadian soldiers fighting in South Africa recognized their domestic and familial duties – as sons, fathers, husbands, or brothers – and reconciled them with their sense of imperial and national responsibilities. As with participation in later overseas wars, service in South Africa disrupted the family life of many Canadians. The letters help us understand these disruptions and how these men perceived their gendered responsibilities to their children, wives, and parents. That the turn of the twentieth century saw a so-called crisis of masculinity, during which masculine identity and behaviour was a topic of public concern, increases their relevance. This correspondence illuminates the intersections between domesticity and family life, along with the perceived national and imperial responsibilities of masculine citizenship.

The war in South Africa, more properly the Second Anglo-Boer War (known in South Africa as Vryheidsoorlog, or the War of Freedom) lasted from 1899 to 1902, much longer than anyone expected.[2] It is generally divided into three phases. The first, a period of heavy British losses, culminated in "Black Week" in December 1899. The second was a period of reorganization and reinforcement that ended with the capture of Bloemfontein and Pretoria – the capitals of the Orange Free State and South African Republic. Everyone assumed these victories would mean the end of the war. There was, however, another two years of virulent guerrilla warfare, during which British frustration with the "bitter-enders" led to Lord Roberts' scorched earth campaign and his creation of concentration camps to house those believed to be aiding them.[3]

When the South African republics declared war on Britain in October 1899, there was considerable pressure in Canada to send a tangible demonstration of support to the mother country. Some of the pressure came from Britain and British representatives in Canada. The colonial secretary, Joseph Chamberlain, for whom imperial unity was key (especially the fostering of closer relations between Britain and the settler colonies) wanted an enthusiastic colonial initiative. Neither the War Office nor Chamberlain believed that colonial troops would actually be needed. What the Colonial Office wanted was a clear, symbolic, and official colonial demonstration of support.

While more cynical thinkers pointed to the gold deposits in the Boer territories, the avowed purpose for the declaration of war was the grievances of the Uitlanders, the mainly British non-Boers who had immigrated to the Transvaal upon the discovery of gold in the Witwatersrand in 1886. The Uitlanders faced limitations on their franchise rights, high taxes, and education. Britain, according to this argument, had a duty to redress wrongs done to its subjects.[4] In September 1899, the *Globe and Mail* printed an extract from a letter sent by Canadians resident in the Transvaal. It asserted that "the Uitlanders are justly entitled to these rights ... as British subjects and white men."[5] That Britain justified war to protect the entitlement of their male white subjects to a political voice meant that the motivations for war were themselves explicitly gendered and racialized.

Demands for a tangible expression of support also came from within Canada. The prevalent rhetoric of the time saw the war as a moral imperative. Although popular, and loud, support for the war was not a universal Canadian response. As in Britain, there were voices in Canada who viewed the war as motivated more clearly by the gold in the Transvaal than by the need to redress the wrongs done to British subjects there. This perception was most visible among Québécois, many of whom found themselves identifying more with the religious, rural Boers, surrounded by expansionist English, than with the rest of the British Empire.

Canada's duty to Britain during the War in South Africa was often expressed in family terms. In speeches, editorials, and poetry, the image of Britain's children – with Canada as the eldest, rushing to help – was rife. One poet wrote:

Where'er that brave old Banner flaunts our Triple Cross on high,
Where'er the Lion's cubs are reared, rings out the stern reply, -
"We hear thy voice, great Mother, and we answer to thy call,
The offspring of they mighty loins, spread over the seagirt ball.[6]

Lion cubs were frequent symbols in war poetry and posters of the day. That Queen Victoria, well loved and often portrayed in a maternal way, was the head of that empire, strengthened the sense of colonial sons rushing to defend their mother.

Connected to the strong sense of imperial family in terms of the outbreak of the war and the sending of volunteers, there is also a sense of Canada growing to manhood in the discourse of the war. The minister of militia, Frederick Borden, put this forward in his speech to the First Contingent at their departure from Quebec: "At last the people of Canada have realized their responsibility and the debt they owe the Empire. Canada has thrown off her swaddling clothes and stands forth as a full grown member of the family which makes up the Empire."[7] Canadian soldiers took on an important role during the Boer War as representatives of the colony's coming of age and ascent into adulthood. It was a perspective encouraged by Britain. In discussion of reactions to the Battle of Paardeberg, the first major British victory of the war, and a battle in which Canadians played a part, Annie Melish proudly quoted the theatrical claim of a *Times* reporter that it was "the insistence of Canada" that "broke down Roberts's reluctance" and persuaded him to send "the men of the oldest colony ... in the small hours of Tuesday morning to redeem the blot on the name of the mother country."[8] Britain's praise of the deeds of colonial troops was fulsome, aiming (along with encouraging colonial participation) to showcase support to an international community generally critical of Britain's war against the South African republics.

Canada's responsibilities were often understood, on the national level, in family terms. Letters written home by soldiers offer insight into how imperial, domestic, and familial responsibilities were understood on an individual level. Three sons from the Rooke family of Manitoba went to fight in South Africa. Charles and Robert went first, joining Strathcona's Horse. They came back after their year was up and later re-enlisted with the Canadian Mounted Rifles, this time taking with them their younger brother, George. Robert, called Bert, sent a letter to his mother on February 11, 1900.

Dear Mother

I have a little rather interesting news for you. Charlie and I came into town on Wednesday from Selkirk having finished our job out there. On Thursday night we were along at Jim's and while talking, Jim asked me why I didn't join Strathcona's Horse and go to South Africa. Charlie spoke up and said "What do you say if we both go?" "Alright," I said, "I'm with you." So next morning we got a letter of introduction from a friend of Jim's to the captain, went up to the barracks, were examined, measured, sworn in and had 2 hours drill before night, and we leave for South Africa tomorrow afternoon. We will go from here to Ottawa to be fitted out and then to Halifax and thence to Cape Town.[9]

Bert was twenty-two years old and worked as a surveyor. In a general sense, his letters show that he was more drawn in by the imperialist and nationalist discourse of the war, with all its gendered ramifications, than were his brothers. His second letter to his mother, sent from Ottawa, indicated surprise at her apparently less-than-enthusiastic response to the sudden news of their joining up.

Dear Mother

I received your letter last night, & was surprised to hear that you felt our leaving so much. Of course it is quite natural that you should be so, but I thought that you would have been glad at the same time. I don't think that you could have felt very proud of the family if, out of 8 grown sons, you could not send a representative to the front when your country needs them. I am not in the least sorry at having joined, in fact, I am only sorry I did not get away before. All I hope is that we get there in time to have a finger in the pie. There is one thing, dear mother, if we do get there, & get snowed under, I hope it will be as a soldier should fall, with his face to the front.[10]

The farewell letter of his older brother, Charlie, to his mother was a little more emotional than Bert's matter-of-fact report, an indication of the differences in personality that come across in their letters. Charlie was twenty-four and gave his profession on his attestation paper as rancher. His letter, dated a day after his brother's, repeated the news of their impromptu enlistment and closed:

Well, good bye and God bless you, dearest mother, & if we return we will not be in Canada long before we make our way to Saltcoats. Give my love to the boys. We have left a lot of things with Jim and Stan which you might as well make use of, as we may never need them again. I saw George yesterday & he seems better, but we did not tell him we were going, as it might excite him. Good bye again & take care of yourself till we see you again.

Your affectionate son, Charlie

Bert's letter had likewise mentioned the fulfilling of family duties. A postscript informed his mother, "We're going up to see Dodo this afternoon. He was quite a bit better yesterday."[11] Bert and Charlie also gave their mother advice for the brothers still at home: "Tell Jack and Vic I think a spell of this life would help them & cure them of their unmethodical habits."[12]

Letters home often support the contemporary sense that the discipline and hardships associated with fighting in South Africa were a good thing in and of themselves.[13] In recommending enlistment as a means of masculine self-improvement, the letters drew on popular Victorian conceptions of the virtues of British imperial manliness. There is an interesting tension, though, in that the war also appealed to what might be termed a frontier masculinity, which connected Canadians to a North American identity that valourized a more rough-hewn independence and countenanced disorder, including violence, as a necessary means to an end.

When Bert Rooke referred to his motivations for going, he did so in the patriotic language of the time, which saw participation in the war as a necessary support for the values of the British Empire.[14] Thomas Bertrand Day, a twenty-four-year-old teacher from Grey County Ontario, also tried to reassure his father in somewhat different terms. After raving about how exciting his training was, he assured his father:

> Now I don't want you to think that because I like the soldiering that I never feel as if I would like to see you all again. I should like very much to see you once more before I leave this half of the world, perhaps forever. But I have no fears of the outcome. As you say, I know God can protect me as well in Africa as he has done in America. I hope to be able to do something for him in my own weak way.[15]

Day's hope "to do something for him" perhaps referred to the religious motivations for the war. The strong connection between Christianity and imperialism also coloured Canada's sense of the necessity of sending a contingent to South Africa. It is almost impossible to disentangle the missionary impulse from understandings of imperialism. While often portrayed as justifiable because it was a defensive war (the republics had declared war first), the War in South Africa was also read as a proselytizing opportunity. Even though the Boers were also Christians, in many Canadians' view, British soldiers were merely "missionaries togged in khaki, bibles on the end of guns."[16] A sermon by Rev. Norman McLeod, stated that the Canadian soldiers who died in the war did so to send "the gospel of Christ to an unenlightened people."[17]

Letters home spoke of imperial motivation interconnected at times with religious impetus. They also stressed what an imperial soldier looked like. Soldiers often wrote in detail about their new uniforms. Charlie and Bert both wrote to their sister Eva about them.

> We have been getting our kits the last day or two, and I will tell you it is a great outfit.
> There are:
>
> 2 khaki uniforms, riding breeches;
> 1 dark green serge dress uniform, long trousers;

> 1 dark green serge uniform with 2 pairs riding breeches; making 4 tunics and 5 pairs breeches.
>
> Our boots are lovely tan riding boots, laced front and side, with uppers as soft as kid, besides which we have heavy fatigue boots and canvas deck shoes.
>
> The hats are stiff-brimmed Stetsons and khaki forage caps.[18]

They were excited about how they looked in their new uniforms. The uniform conveyed authority. It distinguished them from civilians and from the British soldier, Tommy Atkins, who was associated with less admirable characteristics than those of the high-spirited cowboys that Canadians wanted to see in their volunteers. The Stetson hat and Strathcona boots were likewise assets, linking Canadian soldiers in the South African War to the North-West Mounted Police, a force whose own highly gendered mythology has been a key aspect of Canada's self-imagining.[19] Associated with this pride in their appearance as soldiers was an emphasis on getting their photos taken in uniform and sending them home to family.[20]

The Rooke family had three sons – Bert, Charlie, and George – who fought at various stages in the Boer War. Their letters to various family members offer insight into different relationships, and interrelationships, among family members. In his letters to his brother Jim, Charlie is more graphic and discusses a level of danger, both from fighting and sickness, than he is in his letters to his mother. On his second trip out, Charlie wrote to his brother from the SS *Victoria*, anchored in Table Bay:

> Here we are at last at Cape Town. We got in last night about midnight after a voyage of 23 days, flying the Yellow Jack, as we have four cases of smallpox on board, besides several cases of measles. I have had measles & only got back on duty yesterday. I was in hospital 8 days & was as weak as a cat when I came out. I am first-rate now though, & if I don't get smallpox, I guess I will pull through alright. It's just our luck to have this happen, & now we will probably be in quarantine for goodness knows how long.[21]

There was no mention of any quarantine or smallpox or even measles in his letters to his mother.

Having the letters of several members of a family also means having glimpses of sibling squabbling. Younger brother George joined the elder Rookes at the end of 1901. In a letter from Halifax, written just before he left for South Africa, he wrote, "My dear Mother, As Bert lost the letter he had from me for you, I thought I had better write to you before I heard from you again as you might think I had forgotten to write to you."[22] Family bickering is also evident in the frequent complaints of lack of mail. Thomas Bertrand Day wrote to his father from Nova Scotia in January 1902:

> Dear Father: I suppose you will have received my card before you read this. You say you only received one letter from me since I left. But if you did that is one more than I got until today and I have been here over three weeks. I got Art's beechnuts but no cake or word of any kind. You may be sure I was greatly disappointed in not receiving a line from some of you either [on] Christmas or New Years.

Things were mitigated somewhat by other relatives. "Auntie sent me a large box of cake, Maple Creams and good Home Made Taffy, all of which we all enjoyed for everything of that nature which comes is common property to the troop to which he belongs." But his family's apparent neglect clearly irked Day, as he came back to it at the end of the letter.

> I have not received a sentence from Flo yet though I wrote her as soon as I landed. You say in your letter that the rest are going to write but I fail to find any but yours. Think your letters must be lost before they leave. You might write more often than I do. Think of how many I have to write to. Then I think you might send me a paper once in a while especially those in which my letters are published then I would not be apt to write the same thing twice. Auntie sent me the Times in which my sendoff was reported and that is the only paper I have received. It seems to me if it were not for her I would fare pretty slim. ... Take my advice and answer the letter when you read them then you will fill the bill better.[23]

Complaints about a lack of familial attention are a consistent theme in letters home, and soldiers only rarely acknowledged other factors that might slow correspondence from half a world away and during wartime. Soldiering, particularly between battles, was boring, probably unexpectedly so. Soldiers felt it was their family's duty to maintain the connection, to write, entertain them, and maybe send a cake or something.

In contrast to homesick soldiers in later wars, those writing home during the Boer War were seldom particular in what they wanted sent to them. Will Pratt shows in his chapter in this volume that requests for Canadian food and cigarettes were common in letters home during the Second World War. The absence of similar requests in letters home from the Boer War is, perhaps, suggestive.

Such homely details offer potential insight into how nationalism and imperialism were understood on a personal level. The treats that soldiers wanted sent from home seem, along with their toothsome value, intended to maintain a connection to the allegiances of family more then to have abated homesickness for a faraway country.

If letters reveal a different sense of expectations from and responsibility for different family members, the soldiers' letters to children back home are most distinctive. Their tone is, predictably, lighter, and the focus is on the exotic elements of their new location: the strange animals, or the disappointing absence of strange animals, and the clothing of South Africans, especially black South Africans. Noble Jones wrote to his younger sister:

> Nellie I have seen some queer subjects & sights since the morning we left you at the station some comical & some sad we have a Cape Colony Baboon with our Batt as a mascot & you bet he is a comical gent and then to see the boys in rows on a still hunt on their shirts & under clothing myself with the rest they are as big & fat as little oxen.[24]

The shift in tone, from the boredom and disillusionment of earlier letters (one to his mother a week before had said, "If any of the boys around there ever think of coming out here discourage the Idea knock it out of their head some way if with a club") to the "comical gent" and the soldiers' battle against their diminutive enemy, body lice, is marked.[25] Jones, like other older brothers, recognized his duty to entertain.

There is also an element of status in these conversations, linked to the frequent promise to send home souvenirs. Thomas Bertrand Day wrote about his younger brothers: "I hope Leonard and Cam are better. I wish I could have kissed the dear boys before I left. Never mind I'll bring them a monkey from Africa if I can find one. The boys brought three home the last time. How does Ed like his school? Tell him to write."[26] Day had enlisted in the second contingent of the Canadian Mounted Rifles and was killed, at the Battle of Hart's River in April 1902, three months after this letter was written. The soldiers, whose send-offs were splendid affairs and whose enlistments were the pride of their local communities, understood that their relatives needed stories to tell and souvenirs to show their friends so they could share in the glamour of their relatives' journey to the other side of the world to fight for the Empire. They recognized their obligation to be a good story.

To understand the sense of familial relationships and responsibilities contained in the letters, it is necessary to broaden definitions of family. Robert Robinson wrote several letters to his friend Art Galoska. The letters, like others written by Canadians in South Africa, show a strong yearning for information from home: "How is everybody? Did Sandy and Bill Mathews or Joe Murphy row this year? Had the club any races or at-homes, etc.? How ever are Dave Burgess or Bobby Welsh? If it was not for homesickness I would stay in this country. A man could save easily fifty dollars per month at even labouring work such as mining etc."[27] Robinson gave his job on his attestation paper as "professional athlete," hence the talk of rowing and races.[28]

These letters never mention family of any kind. But there is still a strong sense of attachment – he is not going to stay because he is homesick. The end of the nineteenth century was a time of high immigration to Canada. Several volunteers were recent unattached immigrants.[29] Sometimes the family they tried to remain connected to was one of their own creation – a group of other unattached young men:

> Will have to write Sandy soon. I would like to know how the regatta came off, (I'll bet there were two or three surprises), and how the club is doing. I hope Ernie Morisette's [?] arm is right again. I often think of what old Jack Clarke said to me about being foolish for volunteering – especially when I was seasick or when doing guard or outpost on a cold night. But it much agrees with me, as I stand it all right and I weigh 165 lbs. – which is a lot more than I have ever done before. I am not sorry I came, but you can bet I'll never do it again.[30]

Robinson's insistence on his health is interesting partly because it follows so much in the vein of other letters home and because fighting in the Boer War was notoriously unhealthy. More soldiers died from disease, especially dysentery from dirty water, than from fighting.[31] But when soldiers complain in their letters about the food and conditions, they usually catch themselves, and add reassuringly (and perhaps a little confusingly) something like, "But I never felt better in my life."

The transience of some of the volunteers also meant that for some of them the war in South Africa was, partly, a chance to assess South Africa as a possible place to settle down. This is evident in Robinson's letters and comes across as well in the letters of the Rooke brothers, who had all been born in the United Kingdom. Charlie Rooke settled in South Africa, and Bert stayed for a couple of years before coming back to Canada.[32] Historians have recently become interested in this broader sense of imperial identity, evidenced by British subjects moving fairly easily between countries, reflecting a permeable sense of boundaries and identities. Canada's participation in the War in South Africa is usually seen as resulting in an increased sense of Canadian nationalism. The letters home discussing South Africa as a potential new home and opportunity, acceptable partly because of the colony's British connection, remind us that the British Empire was still a very tangible aspect of some Canadians' identity. The effort to pacify and anglicize South Africa by encouraging British and colonial soldiers to settle and raise families there is also interesting in its embodiment of the imperial mission through familial duties.

After the capture of the Boer capitals, it was widely understood that the war was all but over. But the Boer commandos refused to give up, fighting a mobile guerrilla war that frustrated the numerically superior British and colonial troops. Lord Roberts' response was the scorched earth campaign, burning the farms of those thought to be aiding the commandos and relocating civilians to concentration camps. Because of crowding, unhygienic conditions, and general maladministration, over twenty-eight thousand detainees, largely women and children, died in the camps. Another fifteen thousand died in separate camps for blacks.[33]

One way that Canadian soldiers' responses to the farm burnings and detentions are valuable is in terms of their sense of themselves as representatives of the Empire. The fit between what they were being asked to do and the war's stated aim of bringing British civilization to South Africa was, at best, awkward. Participation in the scorched earth campaign is not, however, part of our memory of the conflict; it's not something that Canada dealt with, at the time or later. Britain had a fairly strong, vociferous pro-Boer movement. Future prime minister Henry Campbell-Bannerman's denunciation of the "methods of barbarism" deployed by his country's army was perhaps the most famous example. In Canada, protest against the methods of the last two years of the war was comparatively weak.[34] Indeed, attention to the war generally faded in the Canadian press as time went on; stories about the war were less numerous and prominent in 1901 and 1902 than at its outbreak.

Reflecting the peaceable kingdom trope, Canadians historians have likewise been slow to criticize the war or our military.[35] A partial explanation for this absence of historiographical soul searching, at least in terms of the Boer War, seems to be a sense that Canada's responsibility was light. The policy was not our decision. Civilians went into concentration camps because the British commanders said that civilians would have to go into concentration camps.[36] However, although the policy might have been ordered by the British High Command, Canadian soldiers took part in it. Sometimes, they went beyond what was ordered, and they wrote about it, in fairly muted ways, in their letters and diaries.[37] There are frequent references to "foraging" food from farms, but local people often seem to be removed from the equation: "Almost every Dutch farm is deserted by the family, leaving all their stock, poultry, forage, furniture, and best of all, pigs, to take care of themselves. The army is allowed in written orders to commandeer all food or forage required from deserted farms, so that, just at present, we are well-off as far as grub is concerned."[38]

Where the people have gone and how the farms came to be deserted seems to be of little concern. Robert Rooke wrote his memoirs in 1918, and the space for reflection offered by the intervening years perhaps brought forward a sense that these actions might need to be justified:

> During this march the troops destroyed many fields of corn and kaffir corn or millet, the policy evidently being to compel surrender of the commandos by cutting off their food supplies. All the supply of meat for the troops was obtained by rounding up sheep and cattle, but I believe as careful a check as possible was kept of everything used and destroyed, and after the war was over, compensation was paid wherever valid claims were presented. The women and children on the farms in this territory were not disturbed and they were given vouchers for chickens, pigs and other produce commandeered."[39]

While soldiers "commandeering" food during a war in which their superiors had serious difficulties providing adequate provisions can be passed over as necessity, the line between commandeering and looting was not always a fine one. Charlie Twedell wrote in his diary about his brigade's arrival in the town of Jacobsdal:

> As soon as the brigade was dismissed all hands ran towards the little town & captured all the Cattle, Sheep, Pigs & Fowl they could lay hands on. It was a sight of a lifetime to see the Kilties & all the other regmts. capturing & butchering fresh meat for our dinners. Some made for the gardens & rooted up all they could find. Water cress, Water melons, Corn & fruit in small quantities ... The boys ransacked all the houses & took all sorts of things. Some got Jewelry, some got Albums full of pretty photos, some went in for clothes such as Pants, shirts, handkerchiefs, Shawls etc. etc. some got Parasols & Japanese fans, straw hats (ladies), Ostrich feathers Ribbons & all sorts of truck. One chap got a lovely Guitar. Treggett went Stamp hunting & got quite an assortment. I was looking for grub but got very little in that line. I got 3 bottles of herbs for flavouring meats or soups a lot of Ladies belts & some Photos & Statuts [statues]. As we are outward bound I might say every weight tells so I left or gave away nearly all I had commandeered.[40]

The soldiers' dual burdens of domestic and imperial responsibility would seem to have reached their closest intersection in the actions taken against the

Boer's homes. The home was often understood in late Victorian times as a feminine space. But the clash between imperial directives about "capturing" goods from farms and houses in towns and the men's gendered role as protectors of the home was often unremarked upon. Soldiers generally seem to have followed orders without much thought. Indeed, in their letters they mention being worried about potential retribution for being too zealous in their "foraging" and incurring the wrath of their superiors. They express little guilt over the destruction they caused.

Canadians had a reputation in some quarters for not only being particularly good at gathering food in this way but also of going beyond their orders in the severity of their response to farmers thought to be aiding the commandos. One English soldier wrote admiringly of one group of Canadians:

> There are some very good stories afloat about Strathcona's Horse. They are a long way superior to all the other mounted corps. One report is that they lynched six Boers near Standerton hanging them for the usual white-flag farmhouse game. Just as they had finished, a staff officer came up in a towering rage and called them murderers etc. One of the Yanks looked him up and down for some time and then said, 'I guess, Stranger, there is room for another one up there.' The staff officer quickly departed. They will go anywhere. If a patrol is sniped at, they don't stop but go for the sniper. The Boers really fear them. We are very sorry we haven't got them with us here now. They are very good at looting.[41]

There is a reference to what seems to be the same incident in Rooke's memoirs, which, he says, "Gave all the Canadian mounted troops a rather sinister name throughout the country afterwards." Rooke was with the Strathcona's but did not witness the event, which involved a combination of Canadians and members of the local South African Light Horse:

> I have no definite proof that this incident actually happened as related, although I was riding in the same line within a mile or two, but the troop of our fellows who were concerned in it were fully capable of it, being a B.C. troop, largely composed of miners, lumbermen etc. Moreover, the South Africans were naturally very bitter over their comrades being shot down from the cover of that white flag and I am pretty well convinced that it occurred. It certainly struck through the army, and it was one of the incidents used by the Boers to accuse our troops of violating the laws of war, although it was their men doing that very thing which caused it.[42]

The tension between varieties of manliness is evident here. The impromptu trial is exalted as an example of frontier masculinity, one for which these Canadians were well known, and Rooke saw the reports of crimes as credible because of who was committing them, "miners and lumbermen," themselves archetypes of frontier masculinity. At the same time, Rooke seems uncomfortable with the event. He does not mention the incident in his letters home.[43] And, when farm burnings and looting come up later in his memoir, he recasts them as being within the realm of British codes of civility – the destruction, he claims, was limited and overseen carefully, and the owners of property were properly compensated for their losses.

The Boer War provided an opportunity for Canadian men to participate personally in British imperialism and incorporated familial duties as part of the imperial mission. An examination of the various ways that constructions of colonial masculinity, including ideals of domestic and familial responsibility, were articulated and understood offers insight into how imperialism was understood on an individual level. Indeed, colonial troops embodied the imperial mission, not only through their soldiering but also through their perception of their familial duties. Letters home show that the Anglo-Boer War provided Canadian men with an opportunity to fulfill ideals of masculinity, bringing forward tensions between imperial codes of civility and Canada's frontier masculinity.

Notes

1 Donal Lowry, in his introduction to *The South African War Reappraised* (Manchester: Manchester University Press, 2000), asserts that this war shaped imperialism, affected religion, and made the self-governing colonies more assertive but that, in spite of this, "The war has been all but forgotten in the public memories of the former dominions, even in Canada, where the war had made such a crucial political impression" (14). "Understudied" does not, of course, mean unstudied; Carman Miller's *Painting the Map Red: Canada and the South African War, 1899–1902* (Montreal/Kingston: McGill-Queen's University Press, 1993) is an important and thorough examination of Canadian activities in the war.

2 The First Anglo-Boer War, or Transvaal War, was fought from December 16, 1880, to March 23, 1881. The British were defeated at several battles, and in the aftermath the Transvaal regained its independence. The memory of these losses helped shape British and colonial attitudes in the Second Boer War.

3 The first concentration camps were used by the Spanish in Cuba during the Spanish American War in 1898. These *reconcentrados* were intended to move Cuban civilians to central locations, where they would be under the control of the Spanish army until the Spanish were victorious. The camps were poorly administered, and thousands died as a result of poor conditions. The camps were highly criticized by both the Americans and the British, though both used them themselves shortly afterwards – the Americans in the Philippines and the British in South Africa. See Jonathan Hyslop, "The Invention of

the Concentration Camp: Cuba, Southern Africa and the Philippines, 1896–1907," *South African Historical Journal* 63, 2 (2011): 251–76.

4   For an overview of Canadian reactions to and participation in the war, see Miller, *Painting the Map Red*, and Robert Page, *The Boer War and Canadian Imperialism* (Ottawa: Canadian Historical Association, 1987). For a selection of contemporary British views, see *The Boer War: Why Was It Fought, Who Was Responsible?* (Boston: D.C. Heath, 1965). A good overview of the historiography of the war's outbreak, which concludes that it was primarily about British fears of losing paramountcy in South Africa rather than about control of the gold deposits there, is Iain R. Smith's "A Century of Controversy over Origins" in Lowry, *The South African War Reappraised*, 42.

5   "Canadian Outlanders," *Toronto Globe*, September 16, 1899, 1.

6   C.M., "The Children of the Blood," in *Poems and Songs on the South African War*, ed. J. Douglas Borthwick (Montreal: Gazette Publishing, 1901), 52–53.

7   Quoted in J. Castell Hopkins, *Canada in the Nineteenth Century* (Toronto: Progress of Canada Publishing, 1900), 574.

8   Annie Elizabeth Mellish, *Our Boys under Fire* (Charlottetown: n.p., 1900), 34, and Miller, *Painting the Map Red*, 109. The Battle of Paardeberg took place on the anniversary of a British loss in the First Anglo-Boer War.

9   Robert (Bert) Rooke to his mother, February 11, 1900, Canadian Letters and Images Project (hereafter CLIP), http://www.canadianletters.ca.

10   Bert Rooke to his mother, February 23, 1900, CLIP.

11   Charlie Rooke to his mother, February 12, 1900, CLIP.

12   Bert Rooke to his mother, March 26, 1900, CLIP.

13   For Canadian attitudes about the superiority of their volunteers to British professionals, see Chapter 3, "Don't Call Me Tommy," in James Wood, *Militia Myths: Ideas of the Canadian Citizen-Soldier, 1896–1921* (Vancouver: UBC Press, 2010), 80–114.

14   Interestingly, in his later memoirs, Bert Rooke describes his motivations for joining up more prosaically: "Charlie and I had no thought of making application until Wednesday night when a remark passed by our sister-in-law at whose house we were dining set us thinking of it, and on our way to the hotel at which we were staying, we decided on having a try to get into the regiment, as we had nothing particular in sight in the way of work" (1). Imperial fervour seems not to have stood the test of time or perhaps was more the language for the placating of worried mothers.

15   Thomas Bertrand Day to his father, January 7, 1902, CLIP.

16   "Civilization Advances," *Methodist Reporter*, October 18, 1899, cited in Miller, *Painting the Map Red*, 18.

17   Gordon L. Heath, *A War with a Silver Lining: Canadian Protestant Churches and the South African War, 1899–1902* (Montreal/Kingston: McGill-Queen's University Press, 2009), 23.

18   Charlie Rooke to Eva Rooke, February 21, 1900, CLIP.

19   Michael Dawson, "'That Nice Red Coat Goes to My Head Like Champagne': Gender, Antimodernism, and the Mountie Image, 1880–1960," *Journal of Canadian Studies* 32, 3 (1997): 119–39, and Bonnie Reilly Schmidt, "Contesting a Canadian Icon," Female Police Bodies and the Challenge to the Masculine Foundations of the Royal Canadian Mounted Police in the 1970s," in *Contesting Bodies and Nation in Canadian History*, ed. Patrizia Gentile and Jane Nicholas (Toronto: University of Toronto Press, 2013), 368–86.

20   Mary G. Chaktsiris discusses the contrast between the Canadian and British uniforms in "'Our Boys with the Maple Leaf on Their Shoulders and Straps': Masculinity, the

Toronto Press, and the Outbreak of the South African War, 1899," *War and Society* 32, 1 (2013): 23.

21 Charlie Rooke to Jim Rooke, February 21, 1902, CLIP.

22 George Rooke to his mother, January 21, 1902, CLIP.

23 Thomas Bertrand Day to his father, January 7, 1902, CLIP.

24 Noble Jones to Nellie, April 13, 1900, CLIP.

25 Noble Jones to his mother, April 8, 1900, CLIP.

26 Thomas Bertrand Day to his father, January 7, 1902, CLIP.

27 Robert S. Robinson to Art Galoska, September 14, 1900, CLIP.

28 Library and Archives Canada (hereafter LAC), RG 38, vol. 12,005, microfilm T-2084.

29 J.L. Granatstein and David Bercuson, *War and Peacekeeping: From South Africa to the Gulf – Canada's Limited Wars* (Toronto: Key Porter, 1991), 47.

30 Robert S. Robinson to Art Galoska, August 3, 1900, CLIP.

31 Three times as many of the British dead died of wounds or disease (16,168) than immediately by enemy action (5,774). Keith Jeffery, "Kruger's Farmers, Strathcona's Horse, Sir George Clark's Camels and the Kaiser's Battleships: The Impact of the South African War on Imperial Defence," in Lowry, *South African War Reappraised,* 197.

32 Robert Rooke, *Boer War Reminiscences of Trooper Robert Percy Rooke* (Winnipeg: n.p., 1994).

33 Elizabeth van Heyningen, *The Concentration Camps of the Anglo-Boer War: A Social History* (Johannesburg: Jacana Media, 2013).

34 See Amy Shaw, "Dissent in Canada against the Anglo-Boer War, 1899–1902," in *Worth Fighting For: Canada's Tradition of War Resistance from 1812 to the War on Terror,* ed. Lara Campbell, Michael Dawson, and Catherine Gidney (Toronto: Between the Lines, 2015), 37–50, and Carman Miller, "English-Canadian Opposition to the South African War as Seen through the Press," *Canadian Historical Review* 55, 4 (December 1974): 422–38.

35 Robert Teigrob compares Canadian historical attitudes here to American responses to their contemporaneous Spanish American War in "Empires and Cultures of Militarism in Canada and the United States," *American Review of Canadian Studies* 43, 1 (March 2013): 30–48.

36 For the interpretation that this was not Canada's responsibility, see O.D. Skelton, ed., *Life and Letters of Sir Wilfrid Laurier* (Toronto: McClelland and Stewart, 1965). For Canada's distinctive reluctance to appraise this conflict critically, see Robert Teigrob, "Glad Adventures, Tragedies, Silences: Remembering and Forgetting Wars for Empire in Canada and the United States," *International Journal of Canadian Studies* 45, 46 (2012): 441–65.

37 It is worth noting that neither this kind of frontier violence nor efforts to distance it from Canadian identity were new. James Daschuck shows the violence that was used to settle western Canada in the years just before the Anglo-Boer War in *Clearing the Plains: Disease, Politics of Starvation, and the Loss of Aboriginal Life* (Regina: University of Regina Press, 2013).

38 Robert Robinson to Art Galoska, April 3, 1900, CLIP.

39 Rooke, *Boer War,* 101.

40 C.H. Tweddell, *Charlie's First War: South Africa, 1899–1900,* ed. Carman Miller (Montreal/Kingston: McGill-Queen's University Press, 2014), 126–27.

41 Alfred Markham to his cousin Guy, November 23, 1900, in *Ladysmith and Lydenburg: The Anglo-Boer War Letters of Alfred Markham,* ed. Grant Christison (Pietermaritzburg: n.p., 1993), 14. It is interesting, and evidence of the success of the North American frontier persona, that the Canadians were referred to as "Yanks."

42 Rooke, *Boer War,* 25.
43 Though examples are sparse, Tim Cook demonstrates that Canadian soldiers wrote
more explicitly about killing prisoners in their letters home during the First World
War, suggesting that Canadians became more comfortable with less honourable aspects
of warfare and more accepting of their rough reputation. Tim Cook, "The Politics of
Surrender: Canadian Soldiers and the Killing of Prisoners in the Great War," *Journal
of Military History* 70, 3 (July 2006): 637–65. Rare examples of forthright Canadian
reports of looting are available in Chris Madsen, "Between Law and Inhumanity: Canadian Troops and British Responses to Guerilla Warfare in the South African War," in
Inventing Collateral Damage: Civilian Casualties, War and Empire, ed. Stephen J. Rockel
and Rick Halpern (Toronto: Behind the Lines, 2009), 152.

2

Daughter in My Mother's House, but Mistress in My Own
Questioning Canada's Imperial Relationship through Patriotic Work, 1914–18

Steve Marti

> *Daughter am I in my mother's house,*
> *But mistress in my own.*
>
> – RUDYARD KIPLING

RUDYARD KIPLING PENNED the words to his poem "Our Lady of the Snows" in 1897 in response to the passage of the Customs Tariff Act by Canada's Parliament. Kipling's poem celebrated Canadian imperial loyalty, as the act instituted preferential tariffs to make goods from Britain and the other colonies of the Empire more affordable than imports crossing the border from the United States. While praising its loyalty, Kipling acknowledged the Dominion's growing independence by describing Canada's relationship to Britain as the relationship between a mother and her mature daughter. Frequent references to Britain as the mother country reflected the popularity of using the mother-daughter relationship to symbolize the mature sovereignty of the senior Dominion and its relationship to the imperial capital.[1] The ambiguous constitutional status of Britain's self-governing colonies of settlement was commonly simplified through allegorical representations of Britain's relationship with its Dominions such as the matriarchal bond depicted in Kipling's poem.

The outbreak of war in 1914 provided an opportunity to turn imperial allegories into concrete demonstrations of national maturation and imperial loyalty, yet wartime patriotism also revealed contradictions between the two. In mobilizing members of the Imperial Order Daughters of the Empire (IODE) to contribute donations of time and money for the imperial war effort, the executives of the IODE inadvertently compelled them to question the society's symbols for Canada's imperial relationship. Members did more than question the use of matriarchal symbols to evoke Canada's relationship to Britain, however: wartime mobilization led them to challenge the society's definition of an imperial sisterhood. Prior to 1914, the IODE had modelled itself as a society that offered a platform for British women of the upper classes to take a leading role in the Empire's civic society. By 1918, the membership of the IODE had relaxed its exclusive membership rules to include women of lower classes as well as women who did not necessarily identify themselves as British. Rather than view themselves as links in an imperial chain that connected the women of Britain's settler colonies to the mother country, the membership of the IODE began to model itself as a national – though not entirely nationalist – organization.

The IODE was founded on the symbolic maternal bond between Britain and Canada, with members of the IODE embodying both daughters of Britain and mothers of Canada. The filial element of this relationship was maintained by restricting membership to women of British descent, while the matriarchal function of the IODE was reflected by the IODE's exclusive membership, which was restricted to women of the upper classes. The outbreak of war prompted Canadian patriotic societies, such as the IODE, to mobilize their members as a voluntary workforce that would support the imperial war effort by knitting socks for soldiers and collecting money for various patriotic funds. These patriotic efforts were initially steeped in rhetoric and symbolic performances that idealized Canada's dual status as both a burgeoning nation and loyal Dominion of the British Empire. As the war progressed, however, the expansion of the IODE's war effort necessitated a revision of the society's exclusive membership. In principle, Canadian contributions to the imperial war effort suited the Dominion's ambiguous status, but the products of patriotic work – pairs of knitted socks or funds collected – were not so easily shared between Canadian and British soldiers.

The task of allocating a finite quantity of patriotic work forced members of the IODE to reassess Canada's idyllic maternal relationship to Britain. While contributions by Amy Shaw and Will Pratt in this volume examine how soldiers reflected on their attachments to home, the nation, and the empire as they travelled to and from the front, the records of the IODE offer an opportunity to explore how women at home thought about their relationship to nation and empire as they sent comforts to soldiers overseas. The competing demands of the British and Canadian war efforts forced members of the IODE to confront and question the founding structures of their organization, which were meant to reflect Canada's idealized relationship to Britain.

The symbol of a matriarchal bond between Canada and Britain permeated the literature produced by voluntary and patriotic societies to promote Canada's imperial relationship to Britain. No organization took this rhetoric to heart more than the IODE. The IODE was conceived in 1900 by Margaret Clark Murray, a Montreal journalist who called for an empire-wide league of women to promote civic activism among British women. Clark Murray's call for action prompted a meeting in Fredericton, New Brunswick, where women formed a voluntary society to provide comforts to Canadian soldiers fighting in South

Africa. The IODE was incorporated as a nation-wide organization, with head-quarters established in Toronto in 1901, and grew to achieve the largest membership of any Canadian women's voluntary society.[2]

The organization and activities of the IODE reveal how British women in Canada constructed their identity as citizens of the wider nation and empire. As historian Katie Pickles demonstrates in her study of the IODE, *Female Imperialism and National Identity,* its members imagined themselves as both daughters of the Empire and mothers in their own right. They took on the work of travellers' aids societies to provide young British women arriving in the Dominion with a network of surrogate mothers who would protect the purity of young British women and promote the values of middle-class respectability, turning these young women into the mothers of a nation.[3] Examinations of the IODE's wartime work build on a broader scholarship on the relationship between women and the nation – either in the form of the Canadian state or the Canadian imagined community – during wartime. Historians of the First World War have highlighted that prescribed ideals of female citizenship linked women's voluntary participation in wartime to traditional constructions of motherhood, femininity, and class.[4] Wartime patriotism shaped, and was shaped by, prescribed ideals of a woman's role in the nation, and scholars such as Katie Pickles and Jessica Schagerl argue that the civic activism of the IODE shaped Canadian women's understanding of their role in both the nation and the Empire.[5]

The rhetoric of organizations such as the IODE reflected the ideals of the elite women who formed the IODE executive. These prescriptive views on women's citizenship were woven into the fabric of the organization. Studying the coordination of women's work within these societies, however, reveals how the members of these societies negotiated these prescriptions of citizenship, nation, and empire. The duality of IODE women as both daughters and mothers complicated the IODE's familial metaphor for the imperial connection, leaving an ambiguous model for understanding the relationship between nationalism and imperialism. Although the work of the IODE continued to reflect traditional constructions of femininity and motherhood, Pickles argues that after the First World War the organization's outlook shifted from imperial loyalism to national imperialism. The subtle shift between these two still-ambiguous categories moved the centre of the IODE's identity from the Empire to Canada while maintaining the organization's imperial roots. The transition from one brand of imperialism to another, however, did not happen overnight. A close examination of the IODE's wartime work reveals that the imagined relationship between nation and empire was debated and resolved over the course of the First World War. Most importantly, the IODE's transition to a national society was more than an ideological exercise inspired by Canada's evolving constitutional status.

The transition played out in the daily and weekly wartime activities of the IODE as members discussed, debated, and passed resolutions to produce a larger national contribution of voluntary work for the imperial war effort.

The mobilization of the IODE in support of the war effort initiated a gradual transformation of the society. Given the status of the IODE as the leading women's society in Canada, the society's membership strove to take a prominent role in mobilizing Canadian women to support the national and imperial war effort. IODE chapters and their growing membership were inducted into the society through patriotic rituals that punctuated meetings and included symbols that reminded members of the ties that bound nation and empire. These rituals of imperial citizenship moved well beyond the confines of the society's meetings. The executive of each chapter, for example, encouraged their members to alter their daily habits by exercising imperial preferences in their household purchases. Public displays, such as parades and assemblies, were organized to impress upon the remainder of Canadian society the good example set by the IODE. These performances of imperial citizenship, however, often raised questions among members. Women asked about the implied meaning behind these patriotic exercises as well as their accuracy in symbolizing the relationship between Canada and the Empire. Rather than blindly accepting the intended meaning behind the symbols and rituals, members questioned these performances of imperial pageantry and confronted the dichotomies between nation and empire.

Attitudes towards Canada's relationship to Britain shifted along with the wartime expansion of the IODE's membership. Before 1914, IODE chapters had exercised heavy restrictions on membership to maintain the society's exclusive status and to ensure that only the most respectable women participated. Class barriers to joining the IODE, however, were lowered during the war years to achieve a greater patriotic output. Women from less prestigious social strata were selectively brought into the fold to participate in patriotic performances. Non-British communities, particularly French Canadians, were encouraged to partake in the IODE's war effort, albeit on a limited scale; their presence challenged the generic "Britishness" of the imaginary imperial sisterhood. The wartime expansion of the IODE altered the activities of the society as well as its membership. As members confronted the meaning of their imperial rhetoric and ceremonies, the emotional labour that sustained patriotic work prompted members to focus on the communal connections to which they were most closely attached.

The desire among members to devote their resources in support of the war overseas turned the society's rhetorical relationship with the Empire from an abstract idea into a very real and emotional labour, one in which members produced tangible products such as knitted socks and care packages and raised funds to purchase military hardware such as motor ambulances and machine guns.[6] Coordinating this outpouring of voluntary action among the various primary chapters forced members and their executives to determine exactly whose efforts were to be mobilized and how their labours would be dispersed. Their discussions highlighted the choice to be made between supporting the imperial war effort (by contributing to a fund such as the British Red Cross), supporting the national war effort (by supporting an organization such as the Canadian Patriotic Fund), or supporting the local war effort (by sending socks to soldiers from their own community). Faced with a multitude of competing demands, all of which supported the overall war effort, members of the IODE reconstructed their idea of the imperial relationship as they prioritized the complementary but competing needs of the local, national, and imperial war efforts. The IODE was founded to celebrate the shared sisterhood of British women throughout the Empire, but the coordination of wartime patriotic work among the various primary chapters caused the members of the organization to grapple with the duality of their status as both daughters of the Empire and mistresses of their own homes.

The structure of the primary chapters – along with their weekly meetings, which were punctuated by performances that symbolized their imperial loyalty – reinforced the imperial rhetoric of the IODE. The organization's motto, "One flag, one throne, one empire," was reflected in the titles of each chapter's executives. Meetings were presided over by an elected or appointed regent, who represented the Empire's "one throne." Larger chapters located in provincial capitals enjoyed a more official personification of the throne by inviting the patronage and prestige of the wife of the province's vice-regal representative, often bestowed with the title "honorary regent." The Empire's "one flag" was carried by an official standard-bearer, who was elected by each chapter to carry in the Union Flag at the beginning of each meeting.[7] The imperial pageantry continued as chapters opened their meetings with the IODE prayer and often concluded by singing "God Save the King." This patriotic gesture was sometimes accented with a further embellishment. The Victoria and Albert Chapter, located in Prince Albert, Saskatchewan, passed a bylaw requiring its members to stand at attention when signing the anthem.[8] Not satisfied with making a patriotic display at their meetings, the regents of primary chapters in Quebec City instructed their members to implore their relatives to stand at attention during public performances of the national anthem, "thus setting a good example in respect to those who are careless in these matters."[9] Yet the rhetoric and ceremony attached to the singing of anthems raised questions about the meaning of "God Save the King." Two members of the Municipal Chapter of Edmonton raised a motion instructing the chapter's secretary to determine for certain whether Canada had its own national anthem, distinct from "God Save the King," and if so, whether members would be right to stand at attention for the Canadian anthem as well.[10]

The chapters of the IODE extended their patriotic performances beyond their meetings by celebrating patriotic holidays to promote their imperial mandate while also using these holidays as occasions to raise funds through public appeals. The IODE celebrated the Canadian victory at Paardeburg during the South African War as a significant contribution to the defence and maintenance of the Empire. In February 1916, however, the regent of the Beaver House Chapter in Edmonton raised a motion against the continued celebration of Paardeburg Day because it was "a most ungracious and ungenerous act," given the sacrifices that the Union of South Africa had made during the current war.[11] A prominent member of the Beaver House Chapter was born in South Africa, prompting a discussion among the membership regarding the holiday's potential contradiction to imperial unity. Chapters of the IODE in Edmonton ceased to observe Paardeburg Day, and the motion was forwarded to the national chapter for consideration at the next national convention.[12] The delegates to the IODE's 1917 convention decided that "national patriotic holidays" that framed an ambiguous (if not complementary) relationship between nation and empire – such as Empire Day, Dominion Day, Victoria Day, and the monarch's birthday – would remain mandatory observances. Celebrating Paardeburg Day, however, was optional.[13] Primary chapters were left to debate and determine for themselves whether commemorating the Canadian victory at Paardeburg was a nationalist affront to imperial unity.

Beyond ceremonies, members of the IODE found ways to turn their daily habits into acts of imperial citizenship. The purchasing power of women offered a way to complement the economic warfare waged through the Royal Navy's blockade of the Central powers. Following the example set by the Edith Cavell League, a member of the Baden Powell Chapter in Montreal asked her compatriots to sign a pledge promising not to buy German or Austrian goods for the duration of the war. This simple act of wartime consumer activism was met with skepticism by members who would not sign without "going into the matter more thoroughly."[14] In the end, the members of the Baden Powell Chapter committed to a pledge with a "less drastic tone" and promised to give preference to goods manufactured in Allied countries over those originating in the Central powers "whenever possible."[15]

The Jellicoe Chapter likewise circulated a proposal among the other primary chapters in Vancouver to urge members to show their support for the imperial war effort by only purchasing goods produced within the British Empire.[16]

Regents from chapters in Vancouver met to discuss the proposal. Speaking for the members of their chapters, most of the regents present agreed with the proposed boycott against goods originating from the German and Austro-Hungarian empires, yet a simple preference for imperial merchandise raised a heated debate. Everyone present supported a boycott of German and Austrian produce, but the "general opinion" at the meeting was to prioritize the purchase of local goods and then extend preferential buying outwards to goods produced in British Columbia, Canada, and then, finally, the rest of the Empire. Lady Tupper, wife of the former prime minister, quelled the debate between buying local and buying imperial by introducing a motion to require members of the IODE in Vancouver to boycott goods from the Central powers and to "confine" their purchases to goods produced in the British Empire and its allies.[17] The tone of this motion was evidently too strong for the wider membership of the IODE. At the following meeting of the Municipal Chapter, Lady Tupper's resolution was revised to instruct the women of the IODE to "give the strongest possible preference" to goods produced in the Empire.[18]

The women of the IODE did not participate passively in the organization's imperial pageantry, rhetoric, and civic activism, nor did the ideals represented by these actions seep unnoticed into women's subconscious to solidify their sense of an imperial community. The imagined relationship between nation and empire changed alongside the constitutional bonds between Britain and the Dominion of Canada. The debates held among the members of the primary chapter of the IODE reflected their evolving ideas of Canada's place within the Empire. The underlying ambiguity in the relationship between nation and empire, brought to the surface with the outbreak of war, heightened the need for patriotic action. The desire to make overt displays of loyalty during the war prompted obsession over the observance of Britain's imperial anthem, which in turn raised questions about a Canadian national anthem. The events of the war overseas, particularly South Africa's contribution to the war effort cast doubt on the IODE's traditions for celebrating Canada's participation in Britain's war in South Africa. The effort to contribute to Britain's blockade of the Central powers conflicted with the reality of members' purchasing habits and the availability of goods produced outside the Empire. The debates sparked by these displays of imperial loyalty reflect the importance and purpose behind the actions. These were not hollow gestures but manifestations of active citizenship that reflected members' ideas about Canada's place in the Empire. As the events of the war overseas changed the context in which the acts were performed, members began to question the meaning behind them and whether they accurately reflected their own changing ideas of citizenship.

The IODE's membership also changed significantly over the course of the war. Its social composition broadened somewhat during the war years. The wartime mobilization of women's voluntary work presented an ideal opportunity to advance the IODE's imperial mission by encouraging more women to participate actively in the imperial war effort. One member of the Municipal Chapter of Montreal articulated the relationship between patriotic work and imperial citizenship by stating, "In knitting a Balaclava cap we were knitting the Bond of Empire."[19] Leading Canadian women to knit the bonds of empire would surely contribute to the IODE's goal of fostering deeper imperial loyalty in Canada. Yet expanding the war work of the IODE meant expanding the membership of an organization that prided itself on its exclusivity.

Chapters maintained their elite status through exclusive rules that often capped membership and required the nomination of new members to be ratified by popular vote. The demands of the war effort led many chapters to relax these restrictions and allow more women to participate in patriotic work. In many cases, the changes were only incremental. The Royal Edward Chapter, in Charlottetown, voted to expand its membership to allow women on its waiting list to join because "it only seemed right, especially in wartime ... where there was so much work to be done."[20] The members postponed discussions to determine a new membership quota, but eight nominees were immediately voted in, raising the chapter's membership from fourteen to twenty-two.[21] The Valcartier Chapter, in St. John, New Brunswick, voted to raise its membership to twenty-five but also stipulated that any nominee whose membership was voted down twice would be removed permanently from the chapter's waiting list.[22] Three women were subsequently nominated for membership, but, at the following meeting, only two were voted in.[23] The Valcartier Chapter eventually raised its membership to forty women in 1917.[24] The members of the Columbia Chapter, in Vancouver, did not raise its membership quota but pushed out non-active members to allow women on their waiting list to take their place.[25]

While existing chapters maintained relatively closed membership, the overall membership of the IODE swelled with the formation of new primary chapters. In Winnipeg alone, fifteen new chapters were organized over the course of the war, bringing total membership in the city to well over one thousand women and girls.[26] Youth chapters were established to allow young women to partake in war work. The Valcartier Chapter was founded by Rosamond McAvity, daughter of the St. John steel magnate, to organize patriotic work among young women, while the St. Julien Chapter – later renamed the Flanders Chapter – was established in September 1917 to mobilize young women in Vancouver.[27] The creation of new chapters also allowed women from the working classes to join the IODE. In Quebec City, the Munitions Chapter was organized for women employed at the Ross Rifle factory, while nurses in Montreal banded together to form the Edith Cavell Chapter.[28] The decision to incorporate these women into the voluntary war effort reflected classist values regarding the virtues of paid work and voluntary labour. Nurses and workers at the Ross Rifle factory contributed to the war through their paid labour, but the members of the IODE felt it necessary to impart these women with the spirit of patriotism by encouraging them to offer further contributions of voluntary labour. These new chapters reflected the IODE's mission of social uplift and betrayed the values that drove this mission; at the same time, these new chapters broadened the social composition of the IODE in terms of age and class. New wartime chapters organized around a uniting quality, such as age or occupation, reflected specific identities at odds with the more exclusive membership of the pre-1914 IODE.

The formation of new chapters also stretched the generic Britishness of the IODE. While the literature of the IODE left the definition of *British sisterhood* somewhat vague, the organization's rituals revealed some of the defining characteristics of their society. As mentioned, members affirmed their loyalism through patriotic oaths and anthems, while the recitation of prayers hinted at the organization's Protestant leanings. Certainly, the majority of anglophone members belonged to one of the Protestant denominations, as evidenced by the wording of the IODE Prayer, but the expansion of the Canadian war effort required the accommodation of a more diverse membership. A group of Jewish women in Montreal founded the Grace Aguilar Chapter of the IODE in the spring of 1917 and earned the distinction of forming the first Hebrew chapter of the organization. The women of the Grace Aguilar Chapter devoted their efforts to providing for the needs of soldiers enlisted in the Jewish Infantry Reinforcement Draft.[29]

The newfound unity of the war effort also prompted members of the IODE to extend an invitation to French Canadian women. The Municipal Chapter in Quebec City resolved to "endeavour" to form a chapter among French Canadian women, but the details of this effort were carried over to the next meeting.[30] In 1918, six French Canadian women formed the Chapitre Courcelette in Quebec City and organized two tea concerts to raise a few hundred dollars. The chapter failed to attract more French Canadian members. In presenting their accomplishments for the IODE annual report, published in August 1919, the members of the Chapitre Courcelette reported their last meeting had taken place in late May of the previous year.[31]

This overture to French Canadian women walked a fine line between the British imperial mandate of the IODE and the spirit of the new Canadian nationalism. A rapprochement between French and English in the province of Quebec would advance Canadian unity, but how would the inclusion of French

Canadian women fit into the IODE's founding vision for an empire-wide league of British women? The Madeleine de Verchères Chapter, formed in Ottawa, cultivated a bicultural membership under the patronage of their honorary regent, Lady Laurier, wife of the former prime minister. Marie-Louise Casgrain, a Parisian elected as the chapter's regent, spearheaded the IODE's collection to provide humanitarian relief to wartorn France. The IODE French Relief Fund raised over $35,000 in donations from chapters across the country, but it represented a fraction of a percent of the IODE's total wartime collections – conservatively estimated at $5 million.[32] The cultural divide between French and English presented itself as more than a matter of how to allocate donations. The members of the Municipal Chapter of Edmonton received complaints from several chapters in the city over the Madeleine de Verchère Chapter's raffling of an ornate Cross of Lorraine to raise funds for a military hospital.[33] The use of such an overtly French and Catholic religious icon as part of an IODE fundraiser seemed uncomfortably foreign for some English Canadian members.

The growth of the IODE over the course of the war and the practice of creating new, specialized chapters to sustain that growth, led to the formation of chapters that reflected more limited identities. Many of these chapters challenged the ideal of a homogenous British sisterhood uniting the women of the Empire into a common, civilizing mission. Scottish women in Calgary organized a separate chapter and debated which Scottish regiment of the British army their chapter should be named after. They eventually dubbed themselves the Royal Scots Chapter, IODE.[34] A group of Welsh women in Vancouver likewise established their own chapter, naming it the Tywysog Cymru (Prince of Wales) Chapter.[35] While most primary chapters of the IODE represented local nodes in a transnational sisterhood of British women, the activities of Scottish and Welsh chapters demonstrated that their members were devoted to maintaining more limited identities within the Empire. To orchestrate a larger war effort, the IODE broadened its membership to include chapters with more diverse affiliations, but these unique chapters altered the outwardly British face of the IODE and reflected some of the diversity of Canada's diasporic communities.

As the members of the IODE orchestrated their wartime work, they were confronted with countless avenues to channel their efforts. Disparate voluntary societies – such as the Red Cross, the Victoria League, the Navy League, the Canadian Club, and patriotic and repatriation funds – mirrored the IODE in seeking to orchestrate voluntary contributions for the war effort. Primary chapters of the IODE could organize their own initiative or contribute to an existing effort coordinated by a different organization. The Royal Edward Chapter, in Charlottetown, clearly preferred to promote the contributions of its local community, as it chose to devote $400 of the $438 the chapter had raised in October 1915 to support the Prince Edward Island Ward of the Canadian Stationary Hospital in Le Touquet. It contributed only $25 to the national IODE's 1915 Trafalgar Day appeal to raise funds for the British Red Cross.[36] In March 1915, the Victoria and Albert Chapter in Prince Albert, Saskatchewan, voted to knit under the direction of the Red Cross, rather than sending their work to be collected and counted by the provincial IODE.[37] Two years later, the members of the Victoria and Albert Chapter again declined to respond to the appeal organized by the provincial IODE to purchase Christmas gifts for soldiers overseas because the Victoria and Albert Chapter had organized its own campaign to send parcels directly to local soldiers serving overseas.[38] The dispersal of monetary collections or knitted items allowed some chapters to allocate their work to either local or imperial efforts. Empire- or nation-wide appeals organized by the Red Cross or the IODE promised to distribute collections at the imperial or national level, but primary chapters often preferred to reserve their efforts to respond to appeals from the local community.

To a large extent, primary chapters of the IODE could decide whether credit for their wartime work counted as part of the provincial or national contributions of the IODE. Most primary chapters preferred to coordinate their work on a local scale, rather than contributing to provincial or national efforts. Cooperation with local efforts was often facilitated by the fact that executives of IODE chapters often exercised their prestige by taking the lead in more than one voluntary society. The regents of the Colonel Macleod Chapter and the Military Chapter of the IODE in Calgary, for example, both sat on the executive of the Provincial Red Cross Society.[39] Dual membership could facilitate co-operation between voluntary societies. At the outset of the war, the members of the Royal Edward Chapter eagerly contributed to the Canadian Patriotic Fund.[40] Two years later, however, the members voted to stop raisings funds for the Canadian Patriotic Fund because most were already making donations through their church.[41] The doctrine of the IODE impressed its members with a British imperial worldview, but the IODE did not hold a monopoly on their members' voluntary activities. The desire to contribute to local efforts often diverted members from the imperial aims of the national IODE to assist with local appeals.

Other chapters preferred to reserve their efforts for British rather than Canadian soldiers. The Royal Scots Chapter, in Calgary, raised $622 in January 1918 to send maple syrup to soldiers of the Royal Scots, the regiment of the British army that was their chapter's namesake. In June 1918, the chapter forwarded $625 to the City Chamberlain of Edinburgh in order to provide additional comforts to the Royal Scots.[42] The Tywysog Cymru Chapter sent whatever funds it raised to Margaret Lloyd George, for the benefit of Welsh soldiers of the British army.[43] Such restrictive efforts were not limited to chapters defined by their nationality. The Baden-Powell Chapter in Quebec City sewed children's clothing for Belgian relief and later contributed to the care of convalescing soldiers in Quebec, but the chapter always honoured its namesake with prompt answers to local and international appeals from the Boy Scouts. Sixty dollars was sent to purchase warm clothing for Boy Scouts on coast guard duty in England.[44] Efforts organized by these newly formed chapters represented something more specific than a simple devotion to the Empire. These appeals were directed to regiments that reflected the particular cultural identity of those chapters' membership. The prioritizing of patriotic work for Scottish or Welsh units of the British army, to the exclusion of others, suggests that the transnational connection maintained by these two chapters of the IODE did not necessarily extend to all corners of the British Empire. Their patriotic contributions followed the personal networks of the women who collected, packed, and shipped them to reflect the networks that formed their own imagined communities.

The outbreak of war prompted a groundswell of voluntary action, as women mobilized their knitting needles for the war effort. This rising tide lifted the overall membership of the IODE, which opened new chapters in the hopes of channelling Canadian women's enthusiasm for wartime voluntary action towards their brand of empire loyalism. The IODE's decision to take a leading role in directing the voluntary labour of Canadian women undoubtedly attracted new members to the organization. In 1914, Mrs. E.A. Cruikshank, wife of the 13th Military District's general officer commanding, formed the Military Chapter of the IODE. Cruikshank and her chapter fit nicely within the IODE template, where elite anglophone women led others in voluntary patriotic service. The Military Chapter outlasted the war and finally disbanded in 2002.

These new wartime chapters followed the mould of the IODE, but the wartime surge in membership, particularly the social and cultural composition of new members, warped that mould. Scottish and Welsh chapters celebrated their ties to an Anglo-Celtic sisterhood, but these chapters did not necessarily cherish their ties to the wider British imperial family promoted by the IODE's official rhetoric. Francophone chapters adopted the trappings of the IODE but raised questions about the IODE's goal to promote an international sisterhood of British women. Including French Canadian chapters in the IODE war effort promoted English Canadian nationalism in Quebec, but the inclusion of these new chapters stretched the IODE's definition of British imperial sisterhood. Wartime fundraising among French Canadian members could, meanwhile, upset the anglophone sensibilities of other chapters.

By the time of the Armistice in November 1918, the IODE had accomplished its mission of mobilizing Canadian women for the imperial war effort. While the IODE aligned its work with the national, imperial, and Allied war effort, the organization appealed to a wider demographic of women who felt compelled to participate in patriotic work. To mobilize more women, the IODE overlooked its strict social criteria, which would have kept these new members from the elite ranks of the prewar IODE. The working-class women of the Munitions Chapter or the Edith Cavell Chapter brought a new kind of member to the IODE, while francophone members, such as the members of the Chapitre Courcelette or the de Verchères Chapter, led initiatives that complemented the Allied war effort but worked outside of the IODE's traditional focus on Britain and the Empire. Whether working-class women would continue to perform unpaid labour under the banner of the IODE, whether French Canadian women would participate in the peacetime activities of the IODE, and whether the wealthy anglophone women who still dominated the IODE would continue to compromise on the founding principles of their society remained uncertain in November 1918.

IODE membership reached its high-water mark of fifty thousand members during the First World War. In the interwar years, membership shrank by one half as the society refocused on the work of assimilating European migrants into British culture while championing restrictive immigration laws in favour of British immigration.[45] Membership rebounded at the outbreak of the Second World War, but, even as the IODE mobilized Canadian women for another war, the Quebec provincial organizing secretary reported that membership in the province continued to decline.[46] Not until the sweeping decolonization of the 1960s would the chapters of the IODE relinquish their model of British femininity and accept the kind of open and inclusive membership that the organization practised during the First World War.[47] In peacetime, the IODE's membership reflected its founding principles. British upper-class women privileged enough to join the IODE cherished their status as both daughters of Britain and mothers of Canada and exercised this role through community outreach that promoted imperial patriotism in Canada and nurtured the maternal instincts of single female migrants arriving from Britain.

Wartime mobilization challenged members of the IODE to evaluate the duality of being both daughters of Britain and mothers of Canada. The executive hoped to take up their role as mothers of the nation to marshal Canadian women's voluntary labour in support of the war effort. The process of national mobilization, as part of an imperial war, raised questions about Canada's relationship to the Empire among members of the IODE. The meeting minutes of various chapters reveal a flurry of debates among members, who discussed the meaning and implications of their wartime patriotism. As other historians have demonstrated, women's voluntary action provides a valuable lens on the relationship between gender, citizenship, and imagined communities. The disparate voluntary efforts orchestrated by the IODE during wartime reflected a rich discourse on the nature of national and imperial citizenship. The onset of a world war led many chapters to show their support for the imperial war effort by intensifying imperialist rituals at their meetings and public assemblies. Motions to sing "God Save the King," to exclusively purchase British goods, or to celebrate Canada's victory at Paardeburg sparked inquisitive discussions about the meaning of these actions and how they reflected on the imagined relationship between Canada and the Empire. The coordination of patriotic work – such as knitting comforts, assembling care packages, or raising funds – likewise resulted in competing priorities among local, national, and imperial appeals.

Throughout the war, Canadian women sought avenues to participate in the voluntary war effort. National mobilization complemented the aims of the IODE's imperial sisterhood, and the society seized this wartime enthusiasm as an opportunity to take a leading role in Canada's voluntary mobilization. Over the war, the membership of the IODE expanded, and new chapters were founded, but the constitution of these new chapters compromised the British imperial sisterhood that defined the IODE. The society formed chapters to accommodate French Canadian, Jewish, Welsh, and Scottish women, and the members of these chapters organized efforts that reflected the smaller imagined communities of their own diasporic networks, rather than the sweeping British sisterhood idealized by the IODE. The IODE also formed chapters for younger women and working women such as nurses and factory workers to impart within these communities the IODE's brand of imperial patriotism. Together, these new chapters made substantial contributions to Canada's voluntary war effort, but their composition challenged the IODE's exclusive prewar membership. Drawing more women into Canada's voluntary war effort required the creation of chapters that accommodated Canada's cultural diversity.

The mobilization of Canadian women during the First World War pushed the IODE to temporarily expand its membership beyond the imaginary matrilineal network that defined its British patriotism. The IODE sought to play a leading role in coordinating women's work in defence of the Empire by allowing more women to join the organization, just as women who might not be inclined to join the IODE felt compelled to join the IODE in order to take part in patriotic work. The signing of the Armistice in November 1918 allowed the IODE to return to its peacetime work of uplifting rather than mobilizing working-class and immigrant women in Canada. Only with the decline of British immigration during the Great Depression and the threat of another European war looming on the horizon would the members of the IODE begin to promote an internationalist interpretation of Canada's membership in the British Empire.[48] Women's mobilization during the First World War revealed the inherent contradictions between the IODE's mission to promote an imperial sisterhood and the work of coordinating Canadian women's voluntary labour. So long as women's work contributed to the defence of Empire, these contradictions could be overlooked.

Notes

1 Martin Thornton, *Churchill, Borden and Anglo-Canadian Naval Relations, 1911–14* (London: Palgrave Macmillan, 2013), 1.
2 Katie Pickles, *Female Imperialism and National Identity: Imperial Order Daughters of the Empire* (Manchester: Manchester University Press, 2002), 16–17.
3 Ibid., 40–41.
4 A number of essays in the collection edited by Margaret Higonnet examine the relationship between political activism and women's wartime service. See Margaret R. Higonnet, Sonya Michel, Jane Jenson, and Margaret Collins Weitz, eds., *Behind the Lines: Gender and the Two World Wars* (New Haven: Yale University Press, 1987). The edited collection assembled by Amy Shaw and Sarah Glassford explores how these themes developed in Canada during the First World War. See *A Sisterhood of Suffering and Service: Women and Girls of Canada and Newfoundland during the First World War* (Vancouver: UBC Press, 2012). Susan R. Grayzel's study of women in Britain and France examines depictions of women and their wartime work in propaganda and the press to draw conclusions about the persistence of traditional gender norms, particularly those prescribing ideals of motherhood, despite the unprecedented entry of women into male-dominated spheres of work. See *Women's Identities at War: Gender, Motherhood, and Politics in Britain and France during the First World War* (Chapel Hill: University of North Carolina Press, 1999). Peter Grant argues that the nature and organization of patriotic work in Britain relied on existing structures of gender and class and that these structures were strengthened through the mobilization of women for war work. See *Philanthropy and Voluntary Action in the First World War: Mobilizing Charity* (New York: Routledge, Taylor and Francis, 2014). Melanie Oppenheimer has demonstrated that the importance of traditional conceptions of gender roles and class structures were equally important in guiding the coordination of wartime voluntary efforts. See *All Work No Pay: Australian Civilian Volunteers in War* (Walcha, N.S.W.: Ohio Productions, 2002).
5 Pickles, *Female Imperialism*, 4–5; Jessica Schagerl, "The Tensions of Global Imperial Community: Canada's Imperial Order Daughters of the Empire (IODE)," in *Renegotiating Community: Interdisciplinary Perspectives, Global Contexts*, ed. Diana Brydon and William D. Coleman (Vancouver: UBC Press, 2008), 201–15.
6 See, for example, Cameron Pulsifer, "The Great Canadian Machine Gun Mania of 1915: The Public, the Press, and Government Decision Making in Procuring Machine Guns for the Canadian Expeditionary Force," *Histoire sociale/Social History* 46, 1 (2013): 91–120.
7 Mrs. D. Tennant was identified as the standard-bearer for the Valcartier Chapter, and Mrs. C.H.B. Longworth was elected standard-bearer for the Royal Edward Chapter. Meeting minutes, September 11, 1914, S66–1, IODE Valcartier Chapter Minute Book, 1914–18, New Brunswick Museum (hereafter NBM); meeting minutes, February 27, 1915, Royal Edward Chapter, IODE fonds, acc. 2990, series 1, file 3; minute book, February

1913–January 1917, Public Archives and Records Office, Prince Edward Island (hereafter PARO-PEI).

8   Meeting minutes, September 25, 1917, GR 427, IODE fonds, series 6, Victoria and Albert Chapter, Prince Albert, Minute Book, 1909–20, Provincial Archives of Saskatchewan (hereafter PAS).

9   Minutes of executive meeting, November 13, 1916, P678, Fonds IODE, S3.SS4.D3, IODE Municipal Chapter of Quebec, 2/11, Procès verbaux, 1916–19, Bibliothèque et Archives nationales du Québec (hereafter BAnQ).

10   Meeting minutes, November 11, 1915, IODE fonds, acc. 77.137, box 1, item 1, Municipal Chapter of Edmonton, Minute Book, 1913–18, Provincial Archives of Alberta (hereafter PAA).

11   Meeting minutes, February 3, 1916, IODE fonds, acc. 65, 103/41, Beaver House Chapter, Minute Book, 1915–19, PAA.

12   Meeting minutes, February 10 and 28, 1916, IODE fonds, acc. 77.137, box 1, item 1, Municipal Chapter of Edmonton, Minute Book, 1913–18, PAA.

13   Resolutions, annual meeting, IODE, 1917, IODE fonds, P5513/1, National Chapter, Annual Reports, 1910–82, Archives of Manitoba (hereafter AM).

14   Meeting minutes, October 7, 1914, P678, Fonds IODE, S3.SS5.D2, Municipal Chapter of Quebec, Baden Powell Chapter, 4/25, Procès verbaux, 1910–16, BAnQ.

15   Ibid.

16   Meeting minutes, October 14, 1914, AM5, Daughters of the Empire fonds, box 515-B-4, file 6, Vancouver Municipal Chapter Minute Book, 1915–24, Vancouver City Archives (hereafter VCA).

17   Meeting minutes, October 22, 1914, ibid.

18   Meeting minutes, November 16, 1914, ibid.

19   Meeting minutes, September 24, 1914, P678, Fonds IODE, S3.SS1.D5, Municipal Chapter of Montreal, 2/28, Procès verbaux et rapports annuels, 1910–16, BAnQ.

20   Meeting minutes, December 1, 1915, IODE fonds, acc. 2990, Royal Edward Chapter, series 1, file 3, Minute Book, February 1913–January 1917, PARO-PEI.

21   Ibid.

22   Meeting minutes, September 28, 1915, S66-1, IODE Valcartier Chapter Minute Book, 1914–18, NBM.

23   Meeting minutes, October 8, 1915, ibid.

24   Meeting minutes, November 27, 1917, ibid.

25   Meeting minutes, February 17, 1916, AM255, Daughters of the Empire fonds, box 515-A-2, file 4, Coronation Chapter Minute Book, 1915–24, VCA.

26   Sixth annual report of the municipal chapter of the City of Winnipeg, March 27, 1918, P5504/5, IODE Municipal Chapter, Annual Reports, 1913–43, AM.

27   Meeting minutes, October 10, 1917, AM5, Daughters of the Empire fonds, box 515-A-5, file 7, Flanders Chapter Minute Book, 1917–28, VCA.

28   Meeting minutes, January 5, 1916, P678, Fonds IODE, S3.SS1.D5, Municipal Chapter of Montreal, 2/28, Procès verbaux et rapports annuels, 1910–16, BAnQ.

29   Seventh annual report for year ending April 26, 1917, P678, Fonds IODE, S3.SS1.D5, Municipal Chapter of Montreal, 1/28, Procès verbaux et rapports annuels, 1917, BAnQ.

30   Minutes of executive meeting, October 29, 1916, P678, Fonds IODE, S3.SS1.D5, Municipal Chapter of Montreal, 2/28, Procès verbaux et rapports annuels, 1910–16, BAnQ.

31   *Yearbook of the Imperial Order Daughters of the Empire and Children of the Empire* (Toronto: IODE, 1919), 1057–58.

32   Ibid., 822–23.

33 Meeting minutes, December 9, 1915, IODE fonds, acc. 77.137, box 1, item 1, Municipal Chapter of Edmonton, Minute Book, 1913–18, PAA.

34 Meeting minutes, August 17, 1917, IODE (Calgary) fonds, M-1690, Royal Scots Chapter, file 1, Minute Book, 1917–24, Glenbow Archives (hereafter GA).

35 Meeting minutes, May 28, 1918, AM5, Daughters of the Empire fonds, box 515-A-4, file 7, Tywysog Cymru Chapter Minute Book, May 1917–January 1923, VCA.

36 Meeting minutes, October 21, 1915, acc. 2990, Royal Edward Chapter, IODE fonds, series 1, file 3, Minute Book, February 1913–January 1917, PARO-PEI.

37 Meeting minutes, March 23, 1915, GR 427, IODE fonds, series 6, Victoria and Albert Chapter, Prince Albert, Minute Book, 1909–20, PAS.

38 Meeting minutes, September 25, 1917, ibid.

39 Meeting minutes, October 10, 1914, Red Cross fonds, M-8228.15, Minute Book, 1914–16, GA.

40 Meeting minutes, September 8 and October 21, 1914, acc. 2990, Royal Edward Chapter, IODE fonds, series 1, file 3, Minute Book, February 1913–January 1917, PARO-PEI.

41 Meeting minutes, February 28, 1916, ibid.

42 Meeting minutes, January 2, 1918; meeting minutes, June 6, 1918, IODE (Calgary) fonds, M-1690, file 1, IODE Royal Scots Chapter, Minute Book, 1917–24, GA.

43 Meeting minutes, May 24, 1918, Daughters of the Empire fonds, AM 515-A-4, file 7, Tywysog Chapter Minute Book, May 1918–January 1923, VCA.

44 Meeting minutes, May 3, 1916, P678, Fonds IODE, S3.SS5.D2, Municipal Chapter of Quebec, Baden Powell Chapter, 4/25, Procès verbaux, 1910–16, BAnQ.

45 Pickles, *Female Imperialism*, chap. 3.

46 "Report of the National Organizing Secretary," *Minutes of the Fortieth Annual Meeting Imperial Order Daughters of the Empire and Children of the Empire*, 37; MG28, Imperial Order Daughters of the Empire, series I17, vol. 12 (Part 2), Library and Archives Canada. I am grateful to Tyler Turek for sharing this information from his research on the IODE during the interwar years.

47 Pickles, "Conclusion," in *Female Imperialism*.

48 Tyler Turek, "Mobilizing Imperial Sentiment: Identities, Institutions, and Information in British Canada's Road to War, 1937–1940," *Études canadiennes/Canadian Studies* 73 (2013): 13–31.

3

Postal Censorship and Canadian Identity in the Second World War

William John Pratt

DURING THE SECOND WORLD WAR, some half a million Canadians sailed across the Atlantic to encounter a British culture that was both familiar and foreign. Once on campaign, soldiers sought respite from the dangers and hardships of soldiering and longed to return to their friends and loved ones both in Canada and Britain. The mail was the connection that maintained relationships during these long absences, and it provides a unique perspective on Canadian identity and preferences. Postal censors recorded a great deal about Canadians' attitudes towards their British hosts and about lingering conceptions of Britishness after their cultural encounter. Although the Canadian army monitored men's mail for security and morale purposes, the reports contain evidence of a complicated patchwork of identities, suggesting that soldiers found no contradiction between their Britishness and their Canadianess. Amy Shaw's chapter in this volume demonstrates that Canadian soldiers during the Boer War embodied the ideals of British imperial masculinity while displaying Canadian flair through their uniforms and attitudes. During the Second World War, postal censors' reports reveal a desire for food, drink, and entertainment, echoing the complicated interplay of nation and empire. In particular, varied reactions to the goods and services provided to keep morale up show that preferences could be both nationalistic and imperial and at times even American. These partialities provide a way to examine what Canadian soldiers found familiar or foreign, exposing their varied tastes as they travelled as tourist soldiers. The Britain they encountered was restricted to the limitations of wartime supply. After their encounter with the bland pantry of a rationed motherland, or the standard (or perhaps substandard) fare of imperial soldiering, the occasional Canadian food or drink obtained in canteens or through parcel post was all the sweeter. However, the period of training in Britain, where small groups of men bonded on their leave time in London and elsewhere, was not soon forgotten. Soldiers' preferences for Canadian comfort items and entertainment, and their huge demand for mail, reveal a powerful longing for home, one that was mitigated, however, by the British "holiday" they experienced during the long wait to invade the Continent.

Canadian citizen-soldiers made themselves at home in Britain during the First World War, and their return after 1939 shows that a sense of Britishness remained. Historian Jonathan Vance has argued that Canadians arriving in Britain "found themselves in a familiar land, even those who had never been there before."[1] They recognized the models of their value system in British Parliament, liberalism, and religious tolerance, and they toured well-known landmarks such as Canterbury Cathedral or the Tower of London.[2] Their behaviour was not always to their commanding officers' liking, and it took some time for Canadians to warm to their British hosts.[3] After 1942, many grew to appreciate Britain, some having lived there for years, all the while subject to military training and discipline. It is no surprise, then, that when Canadians finally invaded the Continent, they brought with them British mannerisms and memories and left behind them friends, lovers, and wives. While historians have studied the frictions and familiarities that Canadians experienced in Britain during the world wars, the study of how this interregnum moderated the experiences of those that served on active duty in Europe has yet to be explored.[4]

The vast majority of Canadian soldiers who crossed the Atlantic either remained overseas until the war was over or became casualties.[5] By late 1944, Canadian soldiers on campaign in Europe were complaining about their lack of leave. One gunner wrote home with wry hyperbole, not expecting leave any time soon: "Guess the papers have quite a write-up about the '39 boys coming home for Christmas leaves. At the rate they are going about it, I'll likely be home about 1960. We have sent two men out of about 500."[6] A noncommissioned officer in Italy wrote his wife to discourage her from assuming that he would be home shortly: "For Gawd sakes try and stop thinking about me coming home. The allotment they allow to go seems very small. Everyone is getting letters from their wives expecting them home for Xmas and there was a lousy 200 went from here. I'll try my damndest to be home soon dear, but please relax and try not to think of it. We are all about burnt up about the whole affair."[7]

Criticism of the small number of men allowed on leave increased in late December 1944. Men complained of the false optimism raised in families at home and of the lack of leave to the United Kingdom for men with wives there. Some in Italy resentfully compared their situation to that of soldiers in northwest Europe, who could embark on short leave to England and who were granted a larger percentage of home leave to Canada.[8] These complaints continued into 1945, and those who had lost points because of a revision of the leave formula were especially angry.[9] Some compared their lot to the Americans, who were sent home after eighteen or twenty-four months, and English soldiers, who received home leave after three-and-half to four-and-a-half years overseas.[10]

The logistic and manpower constraints that kept men in Europe strengthened their imperial bonds. That Britain became a home away from home is evident in soldiers' demands for enough leave time to get there. In the Northwest Europe campaign, the introduction of a forty-eight-hour leave period in late 1944 had a beneficial effect on morale, yet many considered this period too short.[11] In October, the announcement of the scheme produced widespread indignation at a mere forty-eight hours away from the front.[12] Men asked either for leave to England or an extended continental leave. From January 5, 1945, the men of 3rd Canadian Infantry Division who had served since D-Day were allotted seven days' privilege leave in the United Kingdom.[13] Evidence of frequent leave to England is observable in the medical record, with a notable increase in venereal disease contracted there.[14] Despite the demands for leave, the army needed to keep men in the line, and the combination of travel times and manpower needs limited the numbers of men sent home.

A unique form of military geography reveals that Canadians who served in the Italian campaign still remembered their time in Britain. When soldiers sought familiar names for the rebranding of Italian streets, they drew on both Canadian and English names. Streets in Campobasso were renamed "Piccadilly Circus" and "Pall Mall."[15] In early 1944, when men received time out of the line in Italian towns, they tacked up familiar names over their predecessors. In Ortona, men could visit the Beaver Club, the Red Shield Club (after the symbol of the Salvation Army), or the "Hole-in-the-Wall," named after a pub near Waterloo Station in London, where many Canadians had spent the last moments of their leave.[16] As a member of the Canadian Section at General Headquarters put it,

> Our years in England have I suppose made us more English than we realized. There is a pub (or should I say vino shop) up behind the front which the Canadians have taken over. They call it the "Sussex Inn" and have taught the Italian waiter to say "Time Gentlemen Please." You run into things like that quite often which illustrates our "Anglicised outlook."[17]

Curiously, instead of creating an homage to Canada, soldiers were simulating their temporary home in Britain, where they had bonded together during the lighter moments of military service. Their collective memory, as regiments and smaller social groups, replicated this shared intermediate place rather than the myriad private homes back in Canada. Perhaps imagined Britain was a nostalgic site that was less painful and more lighthearted to visit than distant home. For the majority of soldiers, letters from loved ones would have to suffice as a private connection to Canada.

Historians of the world wars have increasingly emphasized the connections between home fronts and theatres of combat.[18] The Canadian army fostered this association in recognition of the importance of mail to morale. Letters and packages were considered an essential bond to both Canada and Britain, and they showed soldiers that those back home supported their efforts and had not forgotten them. Men built up great anticipation for mail delivery, and there was real disappointment if no news from home or Britain arrived. Near the end of the war, a soldier wrote, "Did you ever see the look on a soldiers's [sic] face when there isn't any mail from home. Mail is the biggest morale builder and breaker they have found out so far in this war. Some of the boys said that they would sooner be under fire than get no mail."[19] Mail service was steadily expanded; photographic and aviation technology allowing the introduction of airgraphs and airletters in 1941.[20] Despite these new tools, delivery of large volumes of mail did not come without logistical friction, and troops in the Mediterranean frequently complained of slow delivery.

The mail service provided more than just letters. Parcels were another major morale booster, as they could contain cigarettes, chocolate, socks, and other personal comfort items.[21] The demand for Canadian goods in these packages shows that, despite the time spent in England, material connections to Canada remained strong. The flavour of imperial soldiering was at times bland, and Canadians were grateful for a taste of home when they could get it. The Canadian army recognized the importance of these linkages and aimed to maintain them through official supply. Although historians have studied selected topics on Canadian army morale in the Second World War, the opportunity to use soldiers' reactions and preferences for comfort items and entertainment as a lens to view their identity and connection to home and Britain is a new path worth treading.[22]

Food played a critical role in troop morale, and the main fare Canadians were served overseas was on British supply lines. Soldiers showed a clear preference for familiar Canadian comfort items over the goods of other nations. Officially, items considered on "continuing Canadian supply" were provided from Canadian stocks and shipped directly from Canada.[23] Food and beverages were to be supplied from imperial stocks. When the auxiliary services could get their hands on familiar Canadian goods, they were welcomed with enthusiasm. In the Second World War, a Canadian pamphlet for junior officers published in 1940 warned that, "The most important single factor affecting the health and morale of the soldier is the food he gets and yet it is often ignored ... The difference in the meals served out of the same rations by a good cook and a bad cook is unbelievable until experienced."[24] On campaign, so-called compo rations were served when fresh food was unavailable or impossible to supply. Cooks had a particularly hard time with tinned bacon, as "even the most adept cook can do little to make it appear – let alone – taste appetizing."[25]

Unit canteens were one means by which soldiers could supplement bland rations, and many soldiers wrote of their appreciation of the ability to purchase Canadian candy, chocolate, and cigarettes.[26] Typical rations included fifty cigarettes and a chocolate bar per week. Items for sale at the canteen were also rationed. The auxiliary services could occasionally supplement these quotas, likely contributing to their near-universal praise by troops. In Britain, the British Navy, Army and Air Force Institutes (NAAFI) ran entertainments and canteens for Canadians during their earliest days overseas, but they were never particularly popular with Canadian troops. Establishments run by the Canadian auxiliary services were much preferred. In Italy, complaints were raised when British cigarettes and chocolate were found in the canteens, when it was known that Canadian stocks had been shipped to the theatre.[27] In fall 1944, the lack of Canadian goods in canteens was a consistent feature of letters. One gunner in the 5th Canadian Light Anti-Aircraft Regiment wrote, "We get a canteen issue every week and here is a list of the things [that] were offered – Palestine chocolate, Rangoon orange drink, English cigarettes, Australian shoe polish, and Indian matches, and most of the beer we get is either English or Italian. Last winter we had the liberty to visit a South African canteen and found their supplies were all Canadian."[28]

Cigarettes were another comforting product in great demand, and complaints about tobacco supply and quality were a frequent grievance for Canadians. It was the familiar flavour of Canadian cigarettes that men preferred. In December 1944, in Italy, the chief complaint concerning welfare was the shortage of cigarettes, especially Canadian cigarettes, as the "V" cigarettes (an imperial brand manufactured in India) were particularly unpopular.[29] A member of the Royal Canadian Artillery wrote home, explaining that soldiers received a free weekly issue of fifty cigarettes and that they could buy another fifty per week, but lamented that they were the army "V" cigarettes. Another member expressed his disapproval in no uncertain terms. Complaining of the lack of cigarettes since landing in Sicily, he griped, "We are issued Indian cigarettes called V's – just so much camel dung."[30] The "V" cigarettes were useless to barter; as a member of 2nd Canadian Armoured Regiment put it, "You [can't] trade them or give them away for love nor money."[31] The complaints continued into August 1944, when rumours of new shipments of large stocks of Canadian cigarettes and chocolate bars made receiving British items from canteens sting all the more.[32]

Liquids are difficult to transport because of their bulk and weight, so tea was one way to provide a comfort beverage that would not tax the logistic system. Supply dictated what was available to the men, and it appears that Canadians adapted well to British customs. A member of the 48th Highlanders wrote in

December 1943: "We still survive on our dose of bully-beef and hard tack which at times becomes painful but are OK when one is hungry. Thank God that tea is plentiful. We've all become firm tea-drinkers and just can't do without our morning cup except when we don't get it."[33]

Alcohol in armies has long been considered an important morale booster, yet it was also a potential disciplinary problem when abused. Canadians in England found English society much more permissive when it came to drink, and there was a period of adjustment to these new freedoms.[34] As historian Terry Copp writes, "British beer, especially in its weak wartime guise, compared poorly with the real Canadian stuff, but it was still possible to consume it in large quantities."[35] Canadian beer was always more welcome than imperial varieties. As one member of the 11th Field Regiment in Italy wrote, "We had our weekly bottle of beer last night and much to my delight it was the same as I used to drink back home, "Frontenac White Cap" and did it ever taste good – hope we get the same next week."[36] During the Christmas celebrations of 1943, Canadian beer was highly appreciated.[37] A few months later, however, a soldier noted that he had had his first sip of Canadian beer in nearly three years.[38] In late October 1944, the censors observed that the short supply of beer was a constant grievance.[39] One soldier wrote they were supposed to receive two bottles per month. In early November 1944, the increase of the beer supply received instant gratitude in letters. Soldiers welcomed both the greater quantity of beer and that Canadian suds were available.[40] It was often a yearning for the familiarities of home life that men turned to when expressing their troubles with soldiering in their letters. Preference for the familiar tastes of Canada survived the encounter with British wartime cuisine.

Requests for Canadian content in reading material and entertainment were more explicitly linked to a sense of continued Canadian culture. Men needed something to occupy their minds during rest time, and reading material was always in demand. In December 1943, in Italy, the lack of current news was considered a chief complaint in some units. The *Eighth Army News* was popular among those who could find a copy, especially as it had a small corner dedicated to Canadians. Postal censors noted that the scarcity of reading material was mentioned frequently in letters home, and men hoped for Canadian content to be sent by mail.[41] In January 1944, the introduction of the *Maple Leaf,* an army-run newspaper that covered news of Canadian people and events, was welcomed and added to the supply of scarce reading material.[42] It was considered important enough an item that it was flown to the front on press day.[43] Along with *Canadian Press News* (a short summary of news about Canada distributed to overseas troops since late 1939), the *Maple Leaf* was said to "fill a very real need."[44] In May 1944, however, the censors described the demand for reading material in

Italy as persistent in all units: men were asking for small books and magazines from home instead of foodstuffs.[45] In the fall, the number of requests for reading material increased yet again.[46] One private wrote, "I thought I would get something to read by this time from you – some Western Stories, for it is hard on us and if we had something to read we would not think so much, and it is not so good to think for we start to think of home and it makes us feel terrible."[47] Reading material was in demand late in the war in northwestern Europe as well. One private from the Toronto Scottish Regiment spoke of the value of print material, "I started to read a pocket edition magazine. I got half way through it and someone beat me for it. Reading material is at a premium and so you have to watch it."[48]

Radio was a readily available form of entertainment and, once again, it was national content, which provided a connection to Canada, that was in demand. The BBC had services aimed at the Dominions before 1939, but it expanded their content to particular audiences across the Empire during the war.[49] The Canadian high commissioner to Britain, Vincent Massey, attempted to improve early content, which was described as "fumbling and dull."[50] BBC broadcasts from England featured messages home from Canadians and attempted to add national content.[51] Starting with the 1940 broadcast of the final period of a National Hockey League game, programming expanded to just over two hours of Canadian content.[52] Of the programs, the most popular was the *Johnny Canuck Review*, a Canadian variety show featuring soldiers' concert parties. Censorship reports for January 1944 in Italy noted that rebroadcasts of Hockey Night in Canada, featuring announcer Foster Hewitt, were enjoyed.[53] On campaign, the BBC was unpopular, aside from its news service, and American programs were much preferred. As a member of the 3rd Infantry Brigade Workshops put it, "That Goldarn BBC hasnt had a good program all evening. They like too many talks and too much high f'lutin music."[54] In contrast, the music played in German propaganda broadcasts was appreciated, and the efforts of Axis Sally, the English-language propaganda radio personality who tried to lower Allied morale, were considered highly amusing.[55]

Canadian entertainments were preferred on the stage. The *Canadian Army Show* was popular and much preferred to the British ENSA shows.[56] In Italy, the *Canadian Army Show* played to twenty-five thousands soldiers from May to August 1944.[57] Both Canadians and Britons felt that ENSA shows were crude, "too low-brow and suggestive in tone."[58] As historian C.P. Stacey records, "Vulgar, alas, was ENSA's middle name."[59] In 2nd Canadian Corps' lines in northwestern Europe, during the first half of 1945, two to five welfare shows performed at all times, aided by a few bands.[60] The Tin Hats, formed under the Canadian Legion, were the first official Canadian army concert party.[61] They started performing in London in September 1941. The *Canadian Army Show* was one of the most popular official troupes later in the war. It had originally been a project of the Directorate of Recruiting but went overseas to entertain troops in October 1943. Live music was also popular with the troops, and in late December 1944 the First Canadian Army had at least thirteen concert parties rotating through the divisions.[62] Bands included the Haversacks, Forage Caps (a *Canadian Army Show* unit), and Belgian Variety Party. ENSA bands included the Josephine Baker Party and 4 Smart Girls.

Although there was a great demand for Canadian content on the page, stage, and airwaves, when it came to film, soldiers wanted Hollywood. Although the Canadian National Film Board came to be known as a leader in documentary film during the war, the men preferred escapist American films. Most favoured feature films about nonmilitary topics over those about the war. Speaking of the British documentary *Desert Victory* (1943), a member of No. 24 Canadian Field Ambulance wrote, "Most of the men felt that movie entertainment should be about pretty girls and song and dance etc – as these war pictures are just the thing one wants to get away from."[63] The writer expressed a preference for Hollywood's romantic romp *Sun Valley Serenade* (1941), featuring the Glen Miller Orchestra. A soldier from the 4th Canadian Armoured Division echoed these remarks, noting, "Who want's to see a blood and thunder picture, What we want is music, songs and gals."[64] Films were the only form of entertainment mentioned in some regiments.[65] A private wrote that he had seen the film *Holiday Inn* (1942), an Irving Berlin musical featuring Bing Crosby and Fred Astaire, at least five times.[66] The film *Road to Morocco* (1942), featuring Bob Hope and Bing Crosby competing for the love of an Arabian princess, was another that received heavy rotation in some units the following month.[67] American jazz and film seemed to hit the middle notes between the crass comedy of ENSA shows and the stifled, high-brow BBC.

An examination of postal censorship during the Second World War reveals that Canadian soldiers longed for many familiar forms of Canadian culture. Sights, sounds, and tastes of home were welcome to those who spent years overseas in the oftentimes uncomfortable, boring, and sometimes deadly environment of the active armed forces. Many men longed for connections to their friends and family in Canada, but mail also travelled to and from Britain, where bonds had been formed during years of preparation for battle. Leave in Britain was coveted and in high demand. Many men hoped to travel to this home away from home, where both fleeting companions and lifelong friends were visited. When men came to name local streets and shops in Italy, they drew on their shared experience in Britain. The customs adopted during their pilgrimage back to the imperial motherland remained as they campaigned across

Europe. Yet, when it came to the primal comforts of soldiering – food, beer, and cigarettes – they preferred familiar Canadian tastes to bland imperial flavours. Watered-down beer and acrid Indian cigarettes were wartime stand-ins for Britain; they only amplified soldiers' yearning for a Canadian home. The continued demand for news articles, radio shows and, above all, mail from Canada also suggests that the soldiers' connection to national events and identities was strong. For Canadian soldiers in the Second World War, there were two home fronts that mattered. They certainly longed for Canada, but their encounter with Britain, and the period spent bonding in that home away from home, would not soon be forgotten.

Notes

1 Jonathan F. Vance, *Maple Leaf Empire: Canada, Britain, and Two World Wars* (Don Mills, ON: Oxford University Press, 2012), 221.
2 John Burwell Hillsman, *Eleven Men and a Scalpel* (Winnipeg: Columbia Press, 1948), 20.
3 C.P. Stacey and B.M. Wilson, *The Half-Million: The Canadians in Britain, 1939–1946* (Toronto: University of Toronto Press, 1987).
4 For Canadian soldiers in the First World War identifying as both Canadian and British, see Luke Flanagan, "Canadians in Bexhill-on-Sea during the First World War: A Reflection of Canadian Nationhood?," *British Journal of Canadian Studies* 27 (October 2014): 131–49. Flanagan argues that divisions between French Canadians and English Canadians over conceptions of the state complicate the idea that Canadian identity was enhanced during the conflict. For Canadian encounters with British institutions as fostering a sense of Canadian nationalism, which modified but did not reject ties to colonial Britain, see C.P. Champion, "Mike Pearson at Oxford: War, Varsity, and Canadianism," *Canadian Historical Review* 88, 2 (June 2007): 263–90.
5 In November 1944, a home leave system was adopted because of the pressing demand by troops. It was hoped that additional conscripts would reduce manpower constraints and allow overseas soldiers to leave active theatres for a break. The initial scheme for granting leave to 250 men per month was quickly expanded to 450 men per month. Of the approximately 370,000 Canadian soldiers sent to Europe by June 21, 1945, only 626 officers and 9,603 other ranks had been able to return to Canada. See C.P. Stacey, *Six Years of War: The Army in Canada, Britain, and the Pacific* (Ottawa: Edmond Cloutier, 1955), 427–30.
6 Major C.C.B. Rice, Chief Base Censor, Central Mediterranean Force (hereafter CMF), entry for December 21, 1944, Appreciation and Censorship Report No. 58, for period December 1–15, 1944, Inclusive, RG 24, vol. 12–323, Library and Archives Canada (hereafter LAC).
7 Ibid.
8 Major C.C.B. Rice, Chief Base Censor, CMF, entry for January 7, 1945, Appreciation and Censorship Report No. 59, for period December 16–31, 1944, Inclusive, RG 24, vol. 12–323, LAC.
9 Major C.C.B. Rice, Chief Base Censor, entry for February 6, 1945, Appreciation and Censorship Report No. 61, for period January 16–31, 1945, Inclusive, RG 24, vol. 12–323, LAC.
10 Major C.C.B. Rice, Chief Base Censor, CMF, entry for November 21, 1944, Appreciation and Censorship Report No. 56, for period November 1–15, 1944, Inclusive, RG 24, vol. 12–323; Major C.C.B. Rice, Chief Base Censor, CMF, entry for March 5, 1945,

Appreciation and Censorship Report no. 63, for period February 15–28, 1945, Inclusive, RG 24, vol. 12–323, LAC.

11 Deputy Chief Censor, entry for November 19, 1944, censorship report for period November 1–15, 1944, Canadian Army Overseas, 21 Army Group, RG 24, vol. 10–706, LAC.

12 Major C.V. Thompson, Deputy Chief Censor, entry for November 2, 1914, Censorship Report, for period October 15–31, 1944, Canadian Army Overseas, 21 Army Group, British Liberation Army (BLA), RG 24, vol. 10–706, LAC.

13 Leave priority was drawn by ballot. Diary entry for January 6, 1945, War Diary, 3rd Canadian Infantry Division (3CID), Assistant-Deputy Medical Services (ADMS), RG 24, vol. 15–661, LAC.

14 From No. 7 Canadian Field Hygiene Section to ADMS, 3CID, April 1, 1945, "Monthly Hygiene Report Sanitary Epidemiological State–3 Cdn Infantry Division–Mar 1945," War Diary, 3CID, ADMS, March 1945, Appendix 39, RG 24, vol. 15–661, LAC.

15 Vance, *Maple Leaf Empire*, 119, 199.

16 The Beaver Club was a Canadian establishment organized by the Massey family in London. Its name alluded to the Beaver Hut, operated in the Strand during First World War by the YMCA. Stacey and Wilson, *The Half-Million*, 102; see also Kent Fedorowich, "Directing the War from Trafalgar Square? Vincent Massey and the Canadian High Commission, 1939–42," *Journal of Imperial and Commonwealth History* 40, 1 (March 2012): 95, 105.

17 "Appreciation and Censorship Report No. 40 for period 1–15 March 1944 Inclusive," Department of National Defence (DND), Folder 46-3-5/INT, Censorship Reports, CMF, November 1943 to April 1945, 215C1.98(D334), Censorship Reports, RG 24, vol. 10–705, LAC.

18 For the British Eighth Army in North Africa, see Jonathan Fennell, "The Front Was Not an Island but a Living, Breathing Extension of the Homeland," in *Combat and Morale in the North African Campaign: The Eighth Army and the Path to El Alamein* (Cambridge: Cambridge University Press, 2011), 153. The opposite view of an isolated trench culture is found in Modris Eksteins, *Rites of Spring: The Great War and the Birth of the Modern Age* (New York: Anchor, 1989), 227–32. The French front in the First World War was "more of a peninsula than an island, its defenders were literally still part of French society as a whole": Stéphan Audoin-Rouzeau, *Men at War, 1914–1918: National Sentiment and Trench Journalism in France during the First World War* (Providence: Berg, 1992), 143. Historian Jessica Meyer suggests that for the British in the First World War, the idea of a heroic defence of the homeland and the idea of soldiers as fathers, brothers, and sons were central to conceptions of soldierly masculinity. See Jessica Meyer, *Men of War: Masculinity and the First World War in Britain*, Genders and Sexualities in History (Basingstoke: Palgrave Macmillan, 2012), 2, 4.

19 Major, Commanding 21 Army Group Base Censorship, "Censorship Report for the Period 16–31 March 1945–Canadian Army Overseas–21 Army Group," DND File "Censorship Reports: 21 Army Group February–April 1945," 215C1.98(D335), Censorship Reports, 21st Army Group, vol. 3, 46-3-6/INT, vol. 3, April 1, 1945.

20 Stacey, *Six Years of War*, 119; Peter Boyden, *Tommy Atkins' Letters* (London: National Army Museum, 1990), 36. In 1942, Canadian soldiers received an average of ten letters per month, resulting in 35 million individual pieces of mail sent overseas. See L. Dawson, "A History of the Canadian Forces Postal Services" (1992), http://members.shaw.ca/jemery26/Canadian%20Postal%20Corp%20-%20A%20History.pdf (accessed January 1, 2015), 32–33. The volume of mail sent overseas increased steadily. In 1940, 954,275 parcels were sent, and by 1942 that number had more than tripled. See D'Arcy Jenish,

"The Morale Department," *Legion Magazine*, July 15, 2012, https://legionmagazine.com/en/2012/07/the-morale-department/.

21 C.C.B. Rice, Chief Base Censor, CMF report for June 17, 1944, Appreciation and Censorship Report No. 46, for period June 1–15, 1944, Inclusive, CMHQ File 4/Censor Reports/3, Censorship Reports from AAI, RG 24, vol. 12–323, LAC; From Major E.L. Davey, CO, 7 Canadian Field Hygiene Section, to ADMS, 3CID, Monthly Hygiene Report (Sanitary and Epidemiological State), 3 Canadian Infantry Division, November 1944, War Diary, ADMS, 3CID, Appendix 13.

22 For a work that covers soldiers' morale alongside psychiatric issues, see Terry Copp and Bill McAndrew, *Battle Exhaustion: Soldiers and Psychiatrists in the Canadian Army, 1939–1945* (Montreal/Kingston: McGill-Queen's University Press, 1990); Reginald H. Roy, "Morale in the Canadian Army in Canada during the Second World War," *Canadian Defence Quarterly* 16, 2 (Autumn 1986): 40–45; Laurel Halladay, "'It Made Them Forget about the War for a Minute': Canadian Army, Navy and Air Force Entertainment Units during the Second World War," *Canadian Military History* 11, 4 (October 2002): 20–35; B.D. Rowland and J.D. MacFarlane, *The Maple Leaf Forever: The Story of Canada's Foremost Armed Forces Newspaper* (Toronto: Natural Heritage/Natural History, 1987); and S. Young, *Red Shield in Action: A Record of Canadian Salvation Army War Services in the Second Great War* (F.F. Clarke: n.p., 1949). For a paper that does touch on Canadian identity and morale, see Alex Souchen, "The Culture of Morale: Battalion Newspapers in the 3rd Canadian Infantry Division, June–August 1944," *Journal of Military History* 77, 2 (April 2013): 543–67.

23 C.P. Stacey, *Arms, Men and Governments: The War Polices of Canada, 1939–1945* (Ottawa: Queen's Printer, 1970), 173.

24 Brooke Claxton, "Notes on Military Law and Discipline for Canadian Soldiers," (Montreal: McGill University Contingent, 1940), 35.

25 Quarterly Report (October to December), Medicals, 2CID, Folder "HQ 2nd Cdn Inf Div A.D.M.S. Jan 45 to Oct 45," 152/(ADMS)-1-1-Jan 45, RG 24, vol. 15660, LAC.

26 L.B. Goodyer, Chief Base Censor, CMF, report for March 2, 1944, Appreciation and Censorship Report No. 39, for period February 16–29, 1944, Inclusive, DND Folder 46–3-5/INT, Censorship Reports, CMF November 1943–April 1945, 215C1.98(D334), Censorship Reports, RG 24, vol. 10705, LAC.

27 Appreciation and Censorship Report No. 50, for period August 1–15, 1944, Inclusive, CMHQ, File 4/Censor Reports/3, Censorship Reports from AAI; Major C.C.B. Rice, Chief Base Censor, CMF, Appreciation and Censorship Report No. 53, for period September 16–30, 1944, Inclusive. In October, these comments were considered a consistent feature of the mail. Major C.C.B. Rice, Chief Base Censor, CMF, Appreciation and Censorship Report No. 54, for period October 1–15, 1944, Inclusive, CMHQ, File 4/Censor Reports/3, Censorship Reports from AAI, RG 24, vol. 12–323, LAC.

28 Major C.C.B. Rice, Chief Base Censor, CMF, report for October 19, 1944, Appreciation and Censorship Report No. 54, for period October 1–15, 1944, Inclusive, RG 24, vol. 12–323, LAC.

29 Chief Base Censor, CMF, CMF-BNAF, report for January 4, 1944, Appreciation and Censorship Report No. 35, for period December 16–31, 1943, Inclusive, Part B, Canadian Expeditionary Force, DND Folder 46–3-5/INT, Censorship Reports, CMF, November 1943–April 1945, 215C1.98(D334), Censorship Reports 24, vol. 10–705, LAC.

30 Ibid.

31 Chief Base Censor, CMF, CMF-BNAF, Appreciations and Censorship Report No. 36, for period January 1–15, 1944, Inclusive, DND Folder 46–3-5/INT, Censorship Reports, CMF, November 1943–April 1945, 215C1.98(D334), Censorship Reports, RG 24, vol. 10–705, LAC.

32 Appreciation and Censorship Report No. 50, for period August 1–15, 1944, Inclusive, CMHQ File 4/Censor Reports/3, Censorship Reports from AAI, RG 24, vol. 12–323, LAC.

33 Chief Base Censor, CMF, CMF-BNAF, report for December 3, 1943, Appreciation and Censorship Report No. 34, for period November 16–December 15, 1943, Inclusive, Part B, Canadian Expeditionary Force, DND Folder 46-3-5/INT, Censorship Reports, CMF, November 1943–April 1945, 215C1.98(D334), Censorship Reports, RG 24, vol. 10–705, LAC.

34 Stacey and Wilson, *The Half-Million*, 34.

35 Terry Copp, *Fields of Fire: The Canadians in Normandy* (Toronto: University of Toronto Press, 2004), 17.

36 Chief Base Censor, CMF, CMF-BNAF, report for December 19, 1943, Appreciation and Censorship Report No. 34, for period November 16–December 15, 1943, Inclusive–Part B– Canadian Expeditionary Force," DND Folder 46-3-5/INT, Censorship Reports– CMF November 1943–April 1945, 215C1.98(D334), Censorship Reports, RG 24, vol. 10–705, LAC.

37 Ibid.

38 L.B. Goodyer, Chief Base Censor, CMF, "Appreciation and Censorship Report No 39 for Period 16–29 Feb 44 Inclusive," DND Folder 46-3-5/INT, Censorship Reports, CMF, November 1943–April 1945, 215C1.98(D334), Censorship Reports, RG 24, vol. 10705, March 2, 1944, LAC.

39 Major C.C.B. Rice, Chief Base Censor, CMF, report for November 4, 1944, Appreciation and Censorship Report No. 55, for period October 16–31, 1944, Inclusive, RG 24, vol. 12323, LAC.

40 Major C.C.B. Rice, Chief Base Censor, CMF, report for November 21, 1944, Appreciation and Censorship Report No. 56, for period November 1–15, 1944, Inclusive, RG 24, vol. 12–323; Major C.C.B. Rice, Chief Base Censor, CMF, report for December 6, 1944, Appreciation and Censorship Report No. 57, for period November 16–30, 1944, Inclusive, RG 24, vol. 12–323, LAC.

41 Chief Base Censor, CMF, CMF-BNAF, report for December 19, 1943, Appreciation and Censorship Report No. 34, for period November 16–December 15, 1943, Inclusive, Part B, Canadian Expeditionary Force, Censorship Reports, RG 24, vol. 10–705, LAC; L.B. Goodyer, Chief Base Censor, CMF, report for February 17, 1944, Appreciation and Censorship Report No. 38, for period February 1–15, 1944, Inclusive, DND Folder 46-3-5/INT, Censorship Reports–CMF, November 1943–April 1945, 215C1.98(D334), Censorship Reports, RG 24, vol. 10–705, LAC.

42 Chief Base Censor, CMF, Appreciation and Censorship Report No. 40, for period March 1–15, 1944, Inclusive, DND Folder 46-3-5/INT, Censorship Reports–CMF November 1943–April 1945, 215C1.98(D334), Censorship Reports, RG 24, vol. 10–705, LAC.

43 G.W.L. Nicholson, *The Canadians in Italy, 1943–1945*, vol. II, Official History of the Canadian Army in the Second World War (Ottawa: E. Cloutier, 1957), 384.

44 Major C.C.B. Rice, Chief Base Censor, CMF, report for September 16, 1944, Appreciation and Censorship Report No. 52, for period September 1–15, 1944, Inclusive, CMHQ File 4/Censor Reports/3, Censorship Reports from AAI, RG 24, vol. 12–323, LAC. Later, *Canadian Affairs* and *Canada Digest* offered more in-depth stories in magazine and *Reader's Digest* format, respectively. Jeff Keshen, *Saints, Sinners, and Soldiers: Canada's Second World War*, Studies in Canadian Military History (Vancouver: UBC Press, 2004), 228.

45 L.B. Goodyer, Chief Base Censor, report for May 17, 1944, Appreciation and Censorship Report No. 44, for period May 1–15, 1944, Inclusive, CMHQ File 4/Censor Reports/3, Censorship Reports from AAI, RG 24, vol. 12–323, LAC.

46   Appreciation and Censorship Report No. 50, for period August 1–15, 1944, Inclusive, CMHQ File 4/Censor Reports/3, Censorship Reports from AAI, RG 24, vol. 12–323, LAC.

47   Major C.C.B. Rice, Chief Base Censor, CMF, September 5, 1944, Appreciation and Censorship Report No. 51, for period August 16–31, 1944, Inclusive, RG 24, vol. 12–323, LAC.

48   Major, Commanding 21st Army Group Base Censorship, report for April 1, 1945, Censorship Report for the period March 16–31, 1945, Canadian Army Overseas, 21 Army Group, DND File Censorship Reports: 21 Army Group, February–April 1945, 215C1.98(D335), Censorship Reports, 21st Army Group, 46–3-6/INT, vol. 3, LAC.

49   Wendy Webster, "The Empire Answers: Imperial Identity on Radio and Film, 1939–1945," in *Rediscovering the British World,* ed. Phillip A. Buckner and R.D. Francis (Calgary: University of Calgary Press, 2005), 325.

50   Fedorowich, "Directing the War from Trafalgar Square?," 108.

51   Diary entry, October 1, 1941, 3CID, ADMS, War Diary, RG 24, vol. 15660, LAC.

52   Stacey and Wilson, *The Half-Million,* 108.

53   Chief Base Censor, CMF, Appreciations and Censorship Report No. 36, for period January 1–15, 1944, Inclusive, DND Folder 46–3-5/INT, Censorship Reports, CMF, November 1943–April 1945, 215C1.98(D334), Censorship Reports, RG 24, vol. 10–705, LAC.

54   Troops mention listening to the Fifth US Army's Mobile Station: L.B. Goodyer report for June 2, 1944, Appreciations and Censorship Report No. 45, for period May 16–31, 1944, Inclusive, CMHQ File 4/Censor Reports/3, Censorship Reports from AAI, RG 24, vol. 12–323, LAC.

55   C.C.B. Rice, report for August 4, 1944, Appreciation and Censorship Report No. 49, for period July 16–31, 1944, Inclusive, CMHQ File 4/Censor Reports/3, Censorship Reports from AAI, RG 24, vol. 12–323, LAC.

56   Major C.C.B. Rice, Chief Base Censor, CMF, report for September 5, 1944, Appreciation and Censorship Report No. 51, for period August 16–31, 1944, Inclusive, CMHQ File 4/Censor Reports/3, Censorship Reports from AAI, RG 24, vol. 12–323, LAC.

57   Keshen, *Saints, Sinners, and Soldiers,* 248.

58   J.A. Crang, "The British Soldier on the Home Front: Army Morale Reports, 1940–45," in *Time to Kill: The Soldier's Experience of War in the West, 1939–1945,* ed. Paul Addison and A. Calder (London: Pimlico, 1997), 63.

59   Stacey and Wilson, *The Half-Million,* 107.

60   First Canadian Army Administrative Reports, RG 24, vol. 10–667, LAC.

61   Stacey and Wilson, *The Half-Million,* 108.

62   Welfare, First Canadian Army, forecast for period December 3–9, 1944, RG 24, vol. 10–667, LAC.

63   Chief Base Censor, CMF, report for January 4, 1944, Appreciation and Censorship Report No. 35, for period December 16–31, 1943, Inclusive, Part B, Canadian Expeditionary Force, DND Folder 46–3-5/INT, Censorship Reports, CMF, November 1943–April 1945, 215C1.98(D334), Censorship Reports, RG 24, vol. 10–705, LAC.

64   Deputy Chief Censor report for November 19, 1944, censorship report for period November 1–15, 1944, Canadian Army Overseas, 21 Army Group, RG 24, vol. 10–706, LAC.

65   Chief Base Censor, CMF, CMF-BNAF, Appreciations and Censorship Report No. 36, for period January 1–15, 1944, Inclusive, DND Folder 46–3-5/INT, Censorship Reports, CMF, November 1943–April 1945, 215C1.98(D334), Censorship Reports, RG 24, vol. 10–705, LAC.

66 Major C.C.B. Rice, Chief Base Censor, CMF, report for January 22, 1945, Appreciation and Censorship Report No. 60, for period January 1–15, 1945, Inclusive, RG 24, vol. 12–323, LAC.

67 Major C.C.B. Rice, Chief Base Censor, CMF, report for March 5, 1945, Appreciation and Censorship Report no. 63, for period February 15–28, 1945, Inclusive, RG 24, vol. 12–323, LAC.

Part 2

Persons and Power

4

Guardians of Empire?
British Imperial Officers in Canada, 1874–1914

Eirik Brazier

> *I think it will not be out of place if I tell you the view I take of my position here in this country. I look upon myself as an officer lent to you by the Imperial Government, to give you the benefit of any experience and advice I may be able to give. Gentlemen, I look upon myself as the servant of Canada.*
>
> – MAJOR-GENERAL GASCOIGNE, 1895[1]

BRITISH IMPERIAL OFFICERS occupied an uncomfortable position when they assumed command of the Canadian militia. The imperial officer was charged with upholding the professional standards of the Canadian militia but, in the decades prior to 1914, many of them were drawn into disputes with Canadian politicians over the execution of their duties. Historians have interpreted these clashes as being integral to the emergence of a Canadian military identity and the development of separate and mature military institutions in Canada.[2] While civil-military relations remained a significant point of contention for imperial officers, their role reflected contemporary debates over the relationship between nation and empire. The early Canadian militia remained steeped in the trappings of British military culture while the Canadian public continued to celebrate its British heritage and pledge its loyalty to the monarch. Imperial officers arrived in Canada to find a familiar sight: Canadian militiamen dressed in scarlet tunics and British-styled accoutrements, drilling with British weapons and equipment, and being disciplined in accordance with the *Queen's Regulations and Orders for the Army*. Such uniformity reinforced ideals of a unified empire with armed forces at the ready and able to defend its territories. This worldview resonated with the contemporary idea of a "Greater Britain," which emerged during the late nineteenth century and which informed the thoughts and actions of the imperial officers.[3] In addition to exercising his authority as commandant of the Canadian militia, the imperial officer reinforced sentimental bonds between Canada and the Empire by maintaining a visible British military presence in the country.

Aspirations for imperial unity, however, remained fraught with contradictions. In particular, British imperial officers provided an important focal point as Canadians worked to define their military attachments to Britain and the Empire.

Imperial officers often relied on their authority to propose programs of reform, but the Canadian militia remained embroiled in local networks of political patronage, and such reforms threatened to upset the Dominion's political landscape. Military reform raised heated debate over the relationship between civil and military authority in Canada, while Canadian politicians remained suspicious that extensive military reforms would result in imperial military integration and would drag Canada into imperial conflicts.[4] The threat of dismissal by the colonial government, however, weighed against imperial officers' authority or ambition and acted as a break on many of the proposed reforms.

Beyond civil-military relations, the imperial officer became the centre of deeper conversations regarding the character of the Canadian soldier and the structure of the Canadian militia. While Britain embraced the professional attributes of a standing army, the citizen-soldier remained a powerful archetype in the Canadian imagination. Amy Shaw's chapter in this volume demonstrates how Canada's frontier past led Canadians to imagine themselves as free-spirited citizens who possessed the skill and strength necessary to settle the frontier. Canadians viewed themselves as natural soldiers who could rely on attributes inherited from their pioneering heritage to defend their families, friends, and country. In contrast, the British soldier was viewed as a downtrodden automaton who lived isolated from society. Yet Canadians also revelled in the splendour of British imperial and military spectacles. Thousands of Canadians gathered every year to watch military parades, training camps, and mock battles. The imperial officer attended these exercises as an honoured guest, and so his presence became an important centrepiece in military pageants. The appearance of imperial officers in the public eye emphasized the tension between Canadians' frontier identity and their lingering attachment to British military tradition.

The appointment of a British officer to command Canada's militia reflected practices that had emerged in other British settler colonies between the 1870s and 1914. British imperial expansion in Asia and Africa stretched the resources of the British army, which precipitated the appointment of imperial officers to command colonial militias. With garrison troops scattered throughout the Empire, British forces struggled to meet their defensive obligations.[5] The emergence of rival imperial powers, which threatened British possessions, highlighted the need for a comprehensive approach to imperial defence.[6] The rising expense of imperial defence pushed British decision makers to approach imperial defence in a manner that distributed costs throughout the Empire. Encouraging settler colonies to assume responsible government constituted an important component of imperial defence schemes, because self-government handed the responsibilities of planning and paying for local defence to the colonies. The increased reliance on independent colonial militias, however, worked to delegate the War

Office's authority over imperial defence to colonial governments. In an effort to maintain imperial unity and impose professional norms, the War Office offered the services of imperial officers to advise and command colonial forces, such as the Canadian militia. In Canada, South Africa, New Zealand, and the Australian colonies, imperial officers and local authorities crossed swords over how to reform and organize local defence forces.

The imperial officer's role was to provide practical military assistance and improve the defensive capabilities of whatever corner of the Empire they were appointed. One of the earliest examples of such an effort came in 1864, when Lieutenant-Colonel William Francis Drummond Jervois was appointed as an adviser to Canada in response to an official request for the services of an experienced imperial officer. Jervois authored a detailed report to offer a comprehensive review of the colony's defences and to provide local authorities with "every information in my power as to the measures which it is desirable to adopt for the defence of that colony."[7] His plans, however, were made with an eye for British – indeed imperial – defence and paid no heed to domestic considerations and political realities. Jervois's proposal to abandon large parts of western Canada in the event of an invasion and concentrate military forces in defence of the colony's urban centres in central Canada were received with dismay by Canadian politicians.[8] Such disagreement became a familiar narrative as imperial officers negotiated the differing priorities of Britain and its colony.[9]

The policy of appointing imperial officers to advise Canadian authorities became a regular practice in the 1870s and 1880s. Major-General Selby Smyth became the first British officer to command the Canadian militia in 1874 and was succeeded by Richard G. Luard in 1880. Meanwhile, Lieutenant-Colonel Jervois continued to spearhead the War Office's efforts to dispatch imperial officers to coordinate defences in other settler colonies. Jervois inspected military forces in the Australian colonies throughout the 1870s, until their governments appointed imperial officers to command local militias.[10] Imperial officers took up postings in South Australia (1877), Victoria (1883), Queensland (1883), and New Zealand (1892).[11]

While imperial officers served the designs of the War Office, their expertise was often welcomed in the colonies. The appointment of Major-General Edward Selby Smyth, a seasoned veteran of imperial service, in 1874 came at the request of Canada.[12] It was made with the support of the prime minister, John A. Macdonald, who remained convinced that only a British officer possessed the necessary expertise to bring order to the militia.[13] A decade later, the minister of militia, Adolphe Caron, also approved of "getting an experienced officer from the old country, until we in Canada can have men sufficiently experienced to take command of the Militia Force."[14] These officers provided more than military advice: they exercised formal command over the Canadian militia. Major-General Fredrick D. Middleton commanded the militia during the North-West Resistance of 1885, which confirmed the Dominion's dependence on British expertise in military affairs. From the outset, Britain was prepared to provide Canada and other colonies with military advisers, although the principles of colonial self-government dictated that control of internal military affairs rested firmly with local authorities.[15] Before his arrival, Selby Smyth received strict instructions from Whitehall that he was only to advise the Dominion government.[16]

Imperial officers such as Luard and Middleton often stepped outside of their role as advisers and provided the first incidents of open conflict between imperial officers and local authorities. Both officers were recalled to Britain after disagreements broke out with their hosts. In 1895, Major-General Ivor Herbert's appointment to Canada also came to a premature end as his rapport with both ministers and militia officers deteriorated beyond repair.[17] Major-General William J. Gascoigne fared little better, and his tenure in Canada was cut short in 1898 after his relationship with both the militia and political leaders also broke down in mutual distrust.[18] At the end of the decade, Major-General Edward Hutton was also dismissed for offering Canadian troops to reinforce British forces in South Africa, without notifying the Canadian government.[19] After the Boer War, the position of the colonial commander came under scrutiny, and Canadian statesmen continued to lobby for a Canadian-born officer to command the militia.[20] These efforts were realized in 1908 with the appointment of General William Otter. In the meantime, the position was filled by imperial officers Major-General Douglas Cochrane, Lord Dundonald, and Lieutenant-General Sir Percy Lake, whose tenures were also marred by conflict with local authorities.

These conflicts reflected what Wilfrid Laurier described as a contest between "the military power and civilian power," but they were also symptomatic of deeper tensions over the character and composition of the Canadian militia.[21] Upon his arrival in the Dominion, an imperial officer assumed responsibility for a local defence force that looked and felt British but lacked the professional standards and quality of the British armed forces. In reviewing the Canadian militia on his first official inspection tour in 1875, Major-General Selby Smyth was "struck with some disappointment" in his assessment of Canadian troops.[22] His response was a number of proposals to improve the militia and bring it in line with familiar British standards. In five annual reports from 1875 to 1879, he outlined plans and ideas to create a small and highly efficient military force that would retain a mixture of both regulars and volunteers.[23] His proposals, however, met only with limited success.[24] Selby Smyth's successors continued the struggle to raise professional standards and consolidate the large and underfunded Canadian militia into a smaller but more efficient military force.[25] Prior to his departure from Canada, however, Selby Smyth reluctantly admitted, as would other imperial officers, that his plans had made little progress. His annual report stated that "it is difficult to keep the necessity for military preparation before the eyes of a free and peaceful population, bent on energetically developing the vast resources that surround them, as it is to preserve from rust and from deterioration of prolonged peace the military institutions themselves."[26] Despite public and political declarations of support for "a gentleman of very great ability, one from whom they expected a good deal," Canada's devotion to the improvement of its defence force during the 1870s remained lackadaisical.[27] Indeed, Selby Smyth had found Canadians' lack of interest in military matters so discouraging that he was reduced to using his annual reports as a pulpit from which to preach the virtues of maintaining a national defence force.

In order to achieve their aims, Selby Smyth and his successors played up the ideal of a united empire to cultivate an atmosphere of professional culture. They viewed the deportment of Canadian militia soldiers as too laissez-faire for a military force and recommended a stronger emphasis on obedience, discipline, and sacrifice.[28] More than two decades after Selby Smyth's tenure, Major-General Dundonald was intent on improving what he considered to be the "many weaknesses" of the militia through introduction of regular training programs in "modern tactics and drills" and stricter discipline.[29] The rhetoric of professionalism often reflected imperial sentiment. Selby Smyth worked to convince Canadians that military service was not intended to satisfy the pleasure of personal or national rewards. Military service represented an expression of devotion "to the defence of their Sovereign and her Empire."[30] The defence of Canada was a defence of the Empire, and he bemoaned the withdrawal of imperial units from the Dominion, as British soldiers could have acted as role models for their younger cousins in the militia.[31]

Imperial officers in Canada looked to the British army as a yardstick to measure military professionalism and believed that the militia's purpose was to contribute to imperial defence, but the image of the British regular army conflicted with Canadian ideals of frontier masculinity. The imperial officers who advocated for professionalization in the Canadian militia often acted as a foil for the archetype of the Canadian citizen-soldier. Canadian parliamentarians led the opposition to reform, but many of them also held commissions in the Canadian militia and mounted a passionate defence of the institution's traditions. Early criticisms of military reform came from William Mckay Wright, member of Parliament and veteran of the Fenian raids. In Parliament, Wright argued that Selby Smyth's proposed reforms would not work because Canadians "were no mere machines, as were soldiers of the Old Country."[32] To Wright, the commandant's proposed reforms were un-Canadian. Selby Smyth was portrayed as a misguided outsider, a stranger to Canada. Casting imperial officers as outsiders and playing on contrasting British and Canadian stereotypes were prominent tactics in conflicts over militia reform. Canada and its militia was not Britain and the regular army, Wright argued, and Selby Smyth would have to realize that "he was placed in entirely different circumstances."[33] An imperial officer to Canada would have to "unlearn everything he had learnt before" if he was to be successful; he needed to understand that Canada was different from Britain, and so, too, was its militia.[34]

Opposition to imperial officers and their proposed reforms provided fertile soil in which ideas about the superiority of Canadian volunteers blossomed. In 1880, an editorial in the *Globe* accused Major-General Luard of attempting to turn the militia into a standing army and claimed that Luard had forgotten "the importance of the citizen-soldier."[35] It was "the volunteer's mission to teach British officers that Canada can safely depend on the patriotic spirit of her sons and the only military force she requires."[36] The imperial officer might represent "the military grandeur of the great British Empire," as another newspaper observed, but it did not qualify him for a Canadian appointment.[37]

The need to defend the Empire continued to provide an important rhetorical touchstone for imperial officers in Canada. Mindful of his predecessors' faith, Lord Dundonald, a hero of the Boer War, chose his words carefully when he attempted to rally the "true citizen of Canada," who should consider it a duty to train himself to a new standard in order "to defend the flag which flies over him."[38] This more ambiguous wording still carried the rhetoric of empire. Dundonald's flag was obviously the Union Flag, and Canadians were of "the same blood" as the British.[39]

Canadian statesmen received these appeals for imperial unity with suspicion. Loyalism was one thing; tightening imperial bonds through military reform seemed un-Canadian and risked entangling the Dominion in future imperial conflicts. The rigid discipline and obedience of professional soldiers was no way to draw the Dominion into closer ties with Britain. Only "silken ties" would keep the Dominion bound to the Empire: "He [Dundonald] seems to think the people of Canada are concerned about being in readiness for war, or that if they are not they are to blame and should be stirred up. Any man who thinks that way – and all European soldiers do – fails to grasp the essential distinction between Europe and North America. With Europe war is a condition. With us it is a theory."[40] Even Sam Hughes, a vocal supporter of many imperial officers, opposed a British system that converted "freemen into serfs or slaves, or men whose liberty is oppressed by so-called discipline. The discipline of these gentlemen belongs to the days when tyrants and divine right rulers held sway."[41] Canadians feared that the imperial officers had "lost sight of the teachings of history" and threatened to convert their country and the entire British Empire "into a military camp."[42] This logic warned that Dundonald's proposal to form a "national citizen army" would place Canada on a permanent "war footing" that would eventually drag Canada into "European and other international complications."[43] Through successive attempts to introduce reforms intended to raise the efficiency of the Canadian militia, the intentions of imperial officers were often distorted by alarmists who warned against creeping "European militarism" in the Dominion.[44]

The inflammatory rhetoric vilifying imperial officers resonated in Parliament and the press and concealed deeper anxieties about the prospect of military reform. Military professionalism threatened to upset Canadian political networks, which relied on patronage appointments in the militia. Officers commanding regiments in the Canadian militia often gained their appointments as a political quid pro quo. More than a few members of Parliament and cabinet ministers served as militia officers on the weekends. Political officers and officer politicians feared that a professional defence force, as defined by British standards, would end the practice of exercising political influence by awarding military promotion. One of Selby Smyth's initial reports warned against "local or other influence" on staff officers and proposed shorter terms of service and a system of rotating officers between different posts.[45] While his efforts eventually paid dividends, Selby Smyth faced energetic opposition in Parliament from both sides of the aisle.[46] He was not the only imperial officer to face such resistance, for staff and regimental appointments continued to be filled by men who owed their allegiance largely to political friends rather than the commandant.[47] Political patronage in the militia continued to be a source of frustration for consecutive imperial officers.[48]

From the outset, Britain and Canada agreed that the purpose of placing imperial officers in command of the militia was to coordinate defence plans, lend military expertise to Canadian officers, and elevate the professional standards of the defence force. In other words: reform. Military reform, however, often proved to be the downfall of an imperial officer. While later imperial officers such as Hutton and Dundonald succeeded in raising the professionalism of the permanent force, attempts to bring the militia into line with British military standards were met with resistance from Canadian politicians, who were offended by the cultural impact of transplanting British military ideas to Canadian soil or alarmed by the prospect of imperial entanglements. The difficulty of measuring military efficiency in peacetime contributed to the debates, as neither side could prove conclusively that their approach to reform worked best. There existed an uncertainty "in the public mind, and ... in the minds of those who are ... called upon to perform this duty," as one Canadian politician concluded.[49] Some historians have interpreted imperial officers' proposals as an attempt to amalgamate the Canadian militia with those of other settler colonies to form an imperial army under British control.[50] There is little or no evidence that imperial officers in Canada or other settler colonies pursued such integration. Most concentrated on improving local defence organizations within the boundaries of their assigned colony. Whether out of genuine concern for the character of the Canadian soldier, or as a measure to protect the practice of patronage in the militia, imperial officers and the reforms they proposed were presented as a threat to the Canadian ideal of the citizen-soldier.

Although some Canadians fought acrimoniously over proposals for military reform, defence policy did not always take priority in the peaceable kingdom. On his second day in Canada, Major-General Dundonald received a rude awaking during a meeting with Prime Minister Laurier, when the prime minister told a stunned Dundonald that he did not need to take the militia seriously. Laurier believed the United States' Monroe Doctrine provided Canada with sufficient protection from European aggression.[51]

While the work of drafting defence policy proved frustrating and unrewarding, British commandants continued their work to promote imperial unity in colonial militias by participating in military pageants that celebrated the shared heritage of British military forces. British imperial officers' ceremonial duties helped to maintain the symbolic ties between Britain and Canada. Like other representatives of the Crown, imperial officers played an important role in the spectacle that celebrated imperial glory and military power. These pageants became the focus of public interest, anticipation, and curiosity. News of an imperial officer's imminent arrival, the negotiations related to his appointment, and his military merits were the subject of newspaper articles long before he departed from Britain. His arrival in Canada was a significant event in the public calendar, and he was treated to receptions, reviews, banquets, and speeches. This pomp and ceremony helped to emphasize that the imperial officer was something more than a mere civil servant. He was a person of importance in Dominion society, and his status was reflected by the number of cabinet ministers who greeted him on his arrival in the Dominion.[52]

The official duties assigned to the post of general officer commanding the Canadian militia underlined the imperial officer's standing in Canadian political structure and society.[53] In the public eye, he became the personification of the Crown. His presence at training camps, military parades, and other militia events helped him gain some influence with members of the elite and impressed ordinary Canadians with the power of his appointment. While attending the militia's church parades, overseeing rifle competitions, or commanding training manoeuvres, the colonial commander received a place of honour. The events themselves were often of little military value but were crammed with elaborate ceremonies and rituals intended to unite Canadian and British or imperial identities. Few of these military spectacles were as popular in Canada as the celebration of the monarch's birthday.[54] This extravagant public holiday was meticulously planned to include militia parades and other military demonstrations. On the day itself, the imperial officer and other representatives of the Crown became the focal points for regal splendour. In 1891, for example, Major-General Herbert led the local militia through Quebec as more than ten thousand people lined the streets of the city.[55] Riding at the head of the procession, the imperial officer served to remind everyone about Canada's relationship to Britain as militia forces marched dutifully behind their imperial representative. For a brief moment, the physical distance between Canada and Britain disappeared, and the imperial officer became a tangible manifestation of the "silken ties" of the imperial relationship.[56] These military ceremonies were intended to both project and reinforce the existence of an imperial society.

Beyond their ceremonial duties, imperial officers used public occasions to emphasize the Dominion's symbolic, rather than legal, membership in a Greater Britain. In public and private, they spoke passionately about the many shared values that bound Canada to Britain. The warm greeting imperial officers received from Canadian crowds, his observations of public institutions, his participation in public celebrations, and even the geography of Canada presented an opportunity to comment on Canada's social and cultural similarity to Britain. In one of his first public speeches in Canada, Major-General Dundonald highlighted the existence of "certain bonds" or "links of iron" that tied the settler colonies closer to Britain than other imperial possessions.[57] Echoing the writings of Charles Dilke, Dundonald soon found a host of recognizable features in the landscape, as there were "very little difference between [Canada] and the Old Country."[58] In another speech, he spoke with passion of the many similarities in geography, the weather, the people, and, not least, the uniforms worn by the soldiers.[59] Dundonald concluded that, despite a separation of thousands of miles, this new realm and its people made him feel at home. This perception of homeliness and familiarity demonstrated that the imperial officer considered settler colonies, such as Canada, not foreign lands but physical and cultural extensions of Britain.

The continuity between British and Canadian military cultures presented itself in the reproduction of British military structures and codes of discipline in the Canadian militia. Titles, instructions, and commands were given in accordance with the British military system and anchored to the transcending power of the monarch. Consequently, British imperial officers arrived in Canada with a belief that their command rivalled that of the British army. Indeed, Major-General Dundonald observed in 1901 that the "powers" associated with an appointment to command the Canadian militia force were "exactly the same as those of the Commander-in-Chief in Great Britain."[60] In fact, Canadian politicians complained that the law itself did not "make it plain ... whether this officer is to be considered as being under the immediate orders of Her Majesty" or an officer dependent on the Department of Militia.[61] Thus, in appointing imperial officers, Canadians had added an element of uncertainty regarding the question of authority to their own military affairs. At the War Office, Joseph Chamberlain had also noted this underlying disharmony with regard to the appointment of imperial officers to Canada: "[They have] almost invariably come into conflict with the local authorities. It is not, in my opinion, a matter of blame to them, but arises from the difference of appreciation between British officers accustomed to our system and Colonial politicians proceeding on the other lines."[62] An imperial officer accustomed to "our system," as Chamberlain noted, would certainly view most aspects of the local militia force as a mirror image of home. It gave him a confirmation that he and Canada had one common cause and strengthened his resolve to carry out his task as guardian of empire.

In parades and speeches, the imperial officer easily reconciled the diverging interests of British imperialism and Canadian nationalism, but this fragile duality became fraught with contradictions as he tested the limits of his authority in Canada. As a serving British officer on temporary loan to the colony, his loyalty was to the governor general – the monarch's personal representative. On the other hand, as a serving member of the local administration, his duty was to provide advice to the prime minister and cabinet in Ottawa. Who did he serve? Unlike official British policy, which steadily evolved along a line of non-interference, the military laws, ordinances, and organizations that governed the Canadian militia did not offer the same degree of clarity.[63] The Canadian militia was governed by texts derived from British legal conventions. Consequently, the militia organization was clad in a military language that was comprehensively imperial in its vocabulary; definitions and concepts were copied from British codices that were intended to be used by a military force operating across the Empire.[64]

The power structures of the Canadian militia likewise followed the conventions of the British army and further muddied the authority of imperial officers. Imperial officers were given ranks and titles that were identical to those used in the British army. As previously noted, bestowing the title of "general officer commanding" generated certain expectations among imperial officers with regard to authority and influence. The equivalent position in Britain would be that of commander-in-chief, as specified in articles 155 and 156 of *The Queen's Regulations and Orders for the Army*.[65] The duties listed included, in addition to defence preparations and planning, keeping "the discipline and the efficiency for service of the troops," "the professional training of the officers and soldiers," and "the establishment of a proper system of regimental instruction."[66] On paper, there was little or no difference between the duties of a commanding officer on service in the British army and that of a Canadian commandant. British army regulations governed both forces.

The wholesale appropriation of British rules and regulations into Canadian military legislation allowed the imperial officer to preside over a military regime that was almost identical to the one he had left in Britain. Any member of the militia or volunteer forces was "subject to the *Army Act* passed by the Parliament of the United Kingdom," just as a regular soldier in the British army.[67] Such regulations governed every aspect of the militia's organization. Canadian military legislation contained some provisions that allowed for local variations, however, and several efforts were made to clarify these discrepancies.[68] Even so, militia legislation throughout the nineteenth and early twentieth century remained decidedly British in both its origin and appearance.[69] Despite regulating Canadian soldiers, local military legislation reproduced a legal system intended for British soldiers on active duty in an imperial army.

The representation of the Crown provided another complication to the question of imperial authority. As with other state institutions throughout the Empire, the Crown remained a ubiquitous symbol in the Canadian militia and impressed all aspects of local military culture.[70] The presence of royal symbols in the militia force were substantial: military laws were published as the "Queen's" regulations and orders, and militia officers received their commissions from the monarch and were bound to the sovereign by a personal oath. These rituals strengthened the imperial officer's assurance in his own authority, as a representative of the Crown, over the militia. To a British officer, who presupposed the existence of a personal bond between himself and the sovereign, the authority of the Crown was more than a symbol.[71]

The reproduction of British traditions in the Canadian militia raised questions about the nature of the imperial officer's authority in Canada. Did an imperial officer have the authority to enforce discipline on Canadians: to dismiss, reprimand, appoint, and promote individuals? How much authority could he exercise in carrying out reforms or reorganizing the militia? To which government did the imperial officer answer in times of military crisis? Such questions proved deeply contentious and remained unresolved during the decades that imperial officers served in Canada.[72] In the subsequent struggle to define the responsibilities of imperial commandants, senior officers in the militia, and the Dominion's civilian government, each party interpreted this relationship to suit its own interests. Whether the imperial officer served the Crown or the prime minister, whether he answered to the imperial or the Dominion government, whether his duty was to train a national or an imperial force remained open to interpretation.

Historians of Canada's military have traditionally approached the conflict between imperial officers and Canadian statesmen through a national framework. This interpretation considers the imperial officer's role in the context of the long professionalization of Canada's military forces. This process was mired by repeated clashes over the balance of civil-military relations. But these conflicts also reveal how ideas of nation and empire were constructed and contested in the Canadian militia and British military institutions. Studying the Canadian case through the lens of imperial relations and situating debates over defence policy in their broader social and cultural context reveal how questions of military efficiency and professionalism reflected wider ideas about the relationship between Canada and the Empire.

While most imperial officers offered measured proposals intended to raise professional standards in the militia, these policies proved controversial for many Canadians. Alarmists warned that such proposals threatened to corrupt the virtues of Canadian militiamen and replace them with "European militarism." In public, Canadians charged the imperial officer with conspiring to bring the Canadian militia under imperial control. These fierce attacks and public debates portrayed imperial officers as outsiders, as foreign interlopers who were meddling with an innately Canadian institution: the militia. In these critiques, the imperial officer became a straw man against which nationalists could rally to defend the archetype of the Canadian citizen-soldier.

The imperial officer exercised his influence outside of the chambers of power through his role as a leading dignitary at public events. As a representative of the Crown, the imperial officer received salutes and reviewed guards of honour. In receiving these public compliments, the imperial officer participated in a series of symbolic pageants that reminded Canadians of their place in Britain's imperial hierarchy. The speeches offered by imperial officers at these events softened this sometimes contentious relationship by drawing attention to the social and cultural similarities that bound Canada to Britain. These bonds also existed in the shared military traditions that blurred the lines between the regulations that governed the Canadian militia and those of the British army. As a British officer and a representative of the Crown, the imperial officer could not help but advance the interests of imperial defence.

Looking beyond imperial officers' efforts to reform the Canadian militia offers a new perspective on the role of the imperial officer, Canadian military identity, and British Canadian relations during the late nineteenth century. Focusing on the cultural and social duties of imperial officers reveals that Canadian society was enthralled with British military identity, culture, and policy. The Canadian militia remained British in its appearance, and it continued to imitate British military dress, traditions, and symbols. Canadian society was equally eager to embrace this Britishness and considered the imperial officer as both the embodiment and guarantor of a common Canadian-British military tradition, identity and history. This relationship resonated with imperial officers who saw themselves as champions of British military knowledge and experience and the exemplars of service to the imperial monarchy.

Canadians advocated for their own amateur military traditions even as they remained fascinated with British military pageantry. Their imaginary ties to Britain became strained as they struggled to make sense of the ambiguous relationship between their nation and their empire. As Claire Halstead's chapter in this volume shows, Canadians' interpretations of their relationship to the Crown became clearer through narratives they attached to the 1939 royal tour. But in the early decades of Confederation, imperial officers found themselves confounded by their ambiguous role as imperial officers appointed to command a colonial army. While imperial officers often negotiated this ambiguity with skill to advance their programs of military reform, those who pushed too aggressively found themselves at odds with Canadian statesmen who played on fears that British-styled military reforms would fundamentally alter the nature of civil-military relations in the Dominion. In the halls of the legislature, the imperial officer was a menacing outsider, but in public he was hailed as a guardian of empire.

Notes

1 Major-General William J. Gascoigne's speech was given at a dinner honouring James Patterson, who had recently retired as minister of the militia. Among the guests were Mackenzie Bowell, the prime minister; Charles Tupper, the man who would soon succeed him as prime minister; and Adolphe Caron, who had twice served as minister of the militia. *Daily Mail and Empire*, October 8, 1895.
2 See, for example, Norman Penlington, "General Hutton and the Problem of Military Imperialism in Canada, 1898–1900," *Canadian Historical Review* 24, 2 (1943): 156–71; Richard Preston, "The Military Structure of the Old Commonwealth," *International Journal* 17, 2 (1962): 98–121; Richard Preston, *Canada and "Imperial Defense": A Study of the Origins of the British Commonwealth's Defense Organization, 1867–1919* (Durham: Duke University Press, 1967); Desmond Morton, *Ministers and Generals: Politics and the Canadian Militia, 1868–1904* (Toronto: University of Toronto Press, 1970); and Stephen

Harris, *Canadian Brass: The Making of a Professional Army, 1860–1939* (Toronto: University of Toronto Press, 1988).

3 Duncan Bell, *The Idea of Greater Britain: Empire and the Future of World Order, 1860–1900* (Princeton: Princeton University Press, 2007); Duncan Bell, "Victorian Visions of Global Order: An Introduction," in *Victorian Visions of Global Order: Empire and International Relations in Nineteenth-Century Political Thought,* ed. Duncan Bell (Cambridge: Cambridge University Press, 2012), 1–25; and Eirik Brazier, "Strangers in a Strange Land: British and Imperial Officers in Canada and the Australian Colonies, ca 1870–1914" (PhD diss., European University Institute, 2013).

4 Byron Farwell, *Queen Victoria's Little Wars* (New York: Harper and Row, 1972), 187, and Hew Strachan, *The Politics of the British Army* (Oxford: Oxford University Press, 1997), 95.

5 Donald Gordon, *The Dominion Partnership in Imperial Defense, 1870–1914* (Baltimore: Johns Hopkins University Press, 1965), 2–3.

6 David Killingray, "Imperial Defence," in *The Oxford History of the British Empire,* vol. 5, *Historiography,* ed. William R. Louis and Robin Winks (Oxford: Oxford University Press, 1999), 342–48, and John Seeley, *The Expansion of England: Two Courses of Lectures* (Cambridge: Cambridge University Press, 2010), 205.

7 "Memorandum by Defence Committee on Report by Lieut.-Col. Jervois on Defence of Canada," WO 33/15, War Office Records, National Archives, London (hereafter NAUK), 5.

8 "Report on the Defence of Canada (Made to the Provincial Government with Reference to Letter from the Council Dated 18th October 1864)," WO 33/15, War Office Records, NAUK; Kenneth Bourne, *Britain and the Balance of Power in North America, 1815–1908* (Berkeley: University of California Press, 1967), 268–69; Preston, *Canada and "Imperial Defense,"* 40–44; Bryan Farrell, "Coalition of the Usually Willing: The Dominions and Imperial Defence, 1856–1919," in *Imperial Defence: The Old World Order, 1856–1956,* ed. Greg Kennedy (London: Routledge, 2008), 255–56; and Harris, *Canadian Brass,* 16.

9 Jervois was already experienced in assessing defence plans, having worked as secretary to the defence committee since 1857, prepared the plans for a committee studying the defences of London, and served as secretary to the royal commission inquiring into the defences of the United Kingdom. Jervois had already been mapping American defence installations close to the Canadian border during the early 1860s, in preparation for a possible US invasion, when he was appointed to the colony in the summer of 1864. Donald Schurman and John Beeler, *Imperial Defence, 1868–1887* (London: Frank Cass, 2000), 32.

10 Brazier, "Strangers in a Strange Land."

11 Jeffrey Grey, *A Military History of Australia* (Cambridge: Cambridge University Press, 1990), 45–46.

12 *Canadian Gazette,* October 17, 1874, 3; Harris, *Canadian Brass,* 31.

13 Smyth had entered the British army as an ensign in 1841 before seeing service in India, South Africa, Ireland, and Mauritius prior to Canada: Andrew B. Godefroy, "Army Biography: The First 'Chief of Land Staff'–Lieutenant-General Sir Edward Selby Smyth, KCMG," *Canadian Army Journal* 12, 1 (Spring 2009): 116–19; *The Canadian Biographical Dictionary and Portrait Gallery of Eminent and Self-Made Men: Ontario Volume* (Toronto: American Biographical Publishing Company, 1880), 19; and Harris, *Canadian Brass,* 28.

14 Canada, House of Commons, *Debates,* 5th Parl., 2nd Sess., 10 March, 1884, 754.

15 Arthur B. Keith, "Colonial Self-Government in the Nineteenth Century," *Journal of the Royal Society of Arts* 56 (1907–08): 339; Arthur B. Keith, *Responsible Government in*

the Dominions (Oxford: Clarendon Press, 1909), 138; and "The Department of Militia and Defence and the Military Force of Canada," art. 37, 625, CAB 18/2, Cabinet Papers, NAUK.

16 Britain was especially cautious in the case of Canada, as large segments of the colony were hostile to allowing their own military forces to be involved in military operations overseas. Brian P. Farrell, "Coalition of the Usually Willing: The Dominions and Imperial Defence, 1856–1919," in Kennedy, *Imperial Defence*, 260.

17 Morton, *Ministers and Generals*, 91–93.

18 Ibid., 126–32.

19 Ibid., 156–62.

20 Ibid., 193–200, and Harris, *Canadian Brass*, 70–81.

21 Canada, House of Commons, *Debates*, 9th Parl., 4th Sess., June 24, 1904, 5533; Brazier, "Strangers in a Strange Land."

22 "Annual Report of the State of the Militia 1877," CAB 18/1, Cabinet Papers, NAUK; "Report on the State of the Militia of the Dominion of Canada for the Year 1875," CAB 18/1, Cabinet Papers, NAUK.

23 "Report on the State of the Militia of the Dominion of Canada for the Year 1878," CAB 18/1, Cabinet Papers, NAUK.

24 Harris, *Canadian Brass*, 19–20.

25 "Annual Report of the State of the Militia 1875," CAB 18/1, Cabinet Papers, NAUK.

26 Ibid.

27 Canada, House of Commons, *Debates*, 3rd Parl., 2nd Sess., February 15, 1875, 150.

28 "Annual Report of the State of the Militia 1875," CAB 18/1, Cabinet Papers, NAUK.

29 *Morning Telegram*, December 20, 1902. Another imperial officer serving in Canada at the time, Colonel Gerald Kitson, publicly supported Dundonald in his endeavours, commenting that the militia did not lack bravery but was found "wanting in organization." See, for example, *Morning Telegram*, March 6, 1903. Dundonald's idea was to create a skeleton construction that "on the alarm sounding [would] be clothed with 'flesh and blood.'" *Morning Telegram*, February 8, 1903; *Morning Telegram*, November 20, 1903.

30 "Annual Report of the State of the Militia 1875," CAB 18/1, Cabinet Papers, NAUK.

31 "Annual Report of the State of the Militia 1879," CAB 18/1, Cabinet Papers, NAUK.

32 Canada, House of Commons, *Debates*, 3rd Parl., 2nd Sess., February 25, 1875, 327.

33 Ibid.

34 Ibid.

35 *The Globe*, September 8, 1880.

36 Ibid.

37 Quoted in *Marquette Review*, September 26, 1882.

38 *Morning Telegram*, October 27, 1903.

39 *Morning Telegram*, November 19, 1903.

40 John Hopkins, *The Canadian Annual Review of Public Affairs: 1903* (Toronto: Annual Review Publication Co., 1903), 271.

41 Canada, House of Commons, *Debates*, 9th Parl.,2nd Sess., April 14, 1902, 2696.

42 Hopkins, *Canadian Annual Review ... 1903*, 19.

43 Ibid.

44 John Hopkins, *The Canadian Annual Review of Public Affairs: 1904* (Toronto: Annual Review Publication Co., 1904), 148.

45 Both William McKay Wright and George Brown, who had been critical of Selby Smyth's proposals, were members of the militia. Quoted in Desmond Morton's review of the Canadian militia, Morton, *The Canadian Militia 1867–1900: A Political and Social Institution* (n.p.: n.p., 1964), 66.

46 Canada, House of Commons, *Debates,* 3rd Parl., 4th Sess., April 10, 1877, 1346–360; Harris, *Canadian Brass,* 19–20.
47 "Annual Report on the State of the Militia 1875," CAB 18/1, Cabinet Papers, NAUK; Morton, *The Canadian Militia,* 67–68.
48 Harris, *Canadian Brass,* 24–25.
49 Canada, House of Commons, *Debates,* 4th Parl., 3rd Sess., December 20, 1881, 170.
50 Norman Penlington, *Canada and Imperialism, 1896–1899* (Toronto: University of Toronto Press, 1965), 165.
51 Douglas Cochrane, *My Army Life* (London: E. Arnold, 1926), 191.
52 "My Command in Canada: A Narrative," C-1219, Sir Edward Thomas Henry Hutton fonds, Library and Archives Canada.
53 Department of Militia and Defence and the Military Force of Canada, art. 37, CAB 18/2, Cabinet Papers, NAUK.
54 The powerful image of May 24 had such an impact on colonial societies that even after Victoria's death in 1901 it remained a significant public day of celebration. David Cannadine, *Ornamentalism: How the British Saw Their Empire* (Oxford: Oxford University Press, 2001), 101–20.
55 *Quebec Daily Telegraph,* May 26, 1891; *Toronto Daily Mail,* May 26, 1891.
56 Hopkins, *Canadian Annual Review ... 1903,* 271.
57 *The Times,* August 8, 1902.
58 *Morning Telegram,* September 2, 1902.
59 Ibid.
60 Cochrane, *My Army Life,* 195.
61 Canada, House of Commons, *Debates,* 4th Parl., 3rd Sess., December 20, 1881, 170.
62 One of those officers had been Major-General Edward Hutton, who was forced to resign in 1900 from his position as general officer commanding (GOC) in Canada. A note of caution on the source of this quote should be added, as there are no direct references to the original source. But Dundonald referred to the statement in his own biography, and it was used again in his obituary in 1926: *Times,* November 19, 1926; Cochrane, *My Army Life,* 188; and George Stanley, *Canada's Soldiers: The Military History of an Unmilitary People* (Toronto: Macmillan of Canada, 1974), 294.
63 Chris Madsen describes the development of Canadian military law as "reactive, haphazard, and at times [confusing]." See Chris Madsen, *Another Kind of Justice: Canadian Military Law from Confederation to Somalia* (Vancouver: UBC Press, 2008), 6.
64 In 1887, Major-General Owen, who was the imperial officer in charge of the South Australian militia, commented on the consequences of the new regulations in South Australia's Defence Forces Act. He remarked that the principle difference was that the force would now be "liable to serve in any other colony" that might find itself in danger and that the force would be brought under the "discipline of the Imperial Army Act." *South Australian Register,* February 24, 1887.
65 In addition to Ireland, there were four districts of Britain in which the commanding officer was designated a general officer commanding: "Commanders to Be Designated 'General Officers Commanding in Chief,'" WO 32/6490, War Office Records, NAUK; War Office, *The Queen's Regulations and Orders for the Army* (London: Harrison and Sons, 1899), 47; and "The Department of Militia and Defence and the Military Force of Canada," art. 37, CAB 18/2, Cabinet Papers, NAUK. This inconsistency has been pointed out by Norman Penlington. See Penlington, *Canada and Imperialism,* 132.
66 War Office, *The Queen's Regulations and Orders for the Army,* 47–48, 50–53.
67 Defences and Discipline Act, 1870, art. 11.

68 Albert Palazzo, *The Australian Army: A History of Its Organization from 1901 to 2001* (Melbourne: Oxford University Press, 2001), 62; Stanley, *Canada's Soldiers,* 279.

69 For example, Canadian and Australian militia legislation limited the use of militia forces to inside the colony. Madsen, *Another Kind of Justice,* 6–7.

70 Cannadine, *Ornamentalism,* 101, 225.

71 Ibid., 225; Edward Spiers, "The Late Victorian Army, 1868–1914," in *The Oxford History of the British Army,* ed. David Chandler (Oxford: Oxford University Press, 1994), 194.

72 In his seminal work on the Canadian commandants, Desmond Morton concludes that the imperial officers' command was afflicted by ongoing conflicts over the question of authority. See Morton, *Ministers and Generals,* 68.

5

Francophone-Anglophone Accommodation in Practice
Liberal Foreign Policy and National Unity between the Wars

Robert J. Talbot

CANADA'S POST–FIRST WORLD WAR assertion of autonomy was the product of compromise between the country's French- and English-speaking populations. As Geoff Keelan demonstrates in his chapter in this volume, francophone and anglophone Canadians had felt very differently about the nature of Canada's participation in the war, and the conflict left the country more bitterly divided along cultural-linguistic lines than ever before in its history. The divisions wrought by the war served to convince postwar prime minister William Lyon Mackenzie King in particular, along with his closest French Canadian ally, the minister of justice, Ernest Lapointe, of the need for a foreign policy that would not pander needlessly to British interests and drag Canada into another foreign war.[1] Still, a complete break from Britain was out of the question. King and Lapointe remained strong supporters of Canada's membership in the Commonwealth – they knew as well as anyone that the Empire was important to many British Canadians. Given the party's political base among French Canadians, however, the Liberals' foreign policy would have to reflect the pro-clivities of both of Canada's two major cultural-linguistic groups.[2]

Once in power, the Liberals wasted little time in charting a new path for the country's international relations. In December 1921, mere days after the election that ousted Arthur Meighen's unabashedly pro-imperialist Conservatives, King rejected British prime minister David Lloyd George's call for imperial uniformity in foreign affairs. The following September, King refused to send Canadian troops to support Britain during the Chanak Crisis in Turkey, much to the embarrassment of the British Foreign Office.[3]

Despite having won a seat at the Treaty of Versailles negotiations and in the League of Nations, Canada's postwar international status remained uncertain. Was it an independent state, a colony, or something in between? In 1922, King sent Lapointe and Minister of Finance W.S. Fielding to the League of Nations conference in Geneva. Fielding, the most prominent of the old pro-conscription Union Government Liberals, told the conference that he was content with Canada's subservience to Britain in foreign affairs. Lapointe, however, asserted Canada's full and separate membership in the league by calling for an extremely limited interpretation of Article X, the league's collective security clause. Lapointe believed that disarmament, and not military commitments, provided the best means to ensure peace. "Great policies must be thought out rather than fought out," he proclaimed. His approach reflected opinion back home – Canadians were tired of war.[4]

French Canadians were reassured in the knowledge that much of Canada's foreign policy was being set by one of their own: Lapointe. The Conservative Opposition and older Liberals like Fielding objected to undue assertions of Canadian independence, but younger Liberals like Lapointe and Anglo-Quebec MP Andrew McMaster pushed for an even greater assertion of Canadian autonomy. Indeed, the Liberals' growing reputation as the party of Canadian independence would attract a coterie of new and energetic MPs, especially from Quebec.[5] King's sympathies were clearly with the new wave. By 1923, Fielding's influence within cabinet had declined significantly – like most of the other old Union Liberals, he was "heard but not heeded" when it came to international affairs.[6] Moreover, many Anglo-Canadians were pleased with the role being played by Lapointe. As the frequent head of Canadian delegations abroad, Lapointe's very name had become associated with Canada's new international status.[7] For French Canadians and at least some Anglo-Canadians, Canada's assertion of autonomy became a shared source of liberal civic nationalism.

English- and French-language histories acknowledge that Canadian identity changed significantly after the Great War. The similarity between the two historiographical approaches ends there. Anglophone historians have tended to emphasize how Canada's impressive wartime participation created a sense of pride and a desire to assert greater autonomy from Britain.[8] In contrast, some francophone historians have emphasized how Canada's conscription crisis created a sense of pessimism and helped transform French Canadian nationalism into Québécois nationalism.[9]

The Great War affected both cultural-linguistic communities in a singular way that has not been fully explored. For moderates from both groups, the war laid bare the fragility of a national unity that had been undermined for decades by the conflict between British Canadian imperialism (which espoused British cultural superiority and advocated for imperial unity) and French Canadian ultramontanism (which espoused French Canadian cultural homogeneity and advocated for a central role for the Catholic Church in the state and in society). The fallout of the war created a sense of urgency for rapprochement between French and English in domestic politics, which, in turn, shaped Canada's approach to foreign affairs – an approach that prioritized national unity over imperial unity. This was apparent in two things: (1) the government's consistent reluctance to commit to the principle of collective imperial security being promoted by Britain and (2) King and Lapointe's concurrent refusal to abandon the Commonwealth altogether.[10] Despite the presence of a loud minority of

British Canadians who continued to oppose any lessening of the imperial connection, and despite a resurgence of ethnic nationalism among some French Canadian intellectuals in the mid-1930s, the Liberals managed to craft an independent foreign policy of the "mushy middle" that more or less accommodated both cultural-linguistic groups. In 1919, the country exited a war deeply divided. By 1939, it was preparing to enter another one, relatively, and surprisingly, united.

From the outset, the League of Nations acted as a symbolic counterweight to Canada's imperial connection. King's choice of delegates to the league reflected French Canada's influence in the new approach to imperial and international relations, as well as the growing influence of the postwar moderate Anglo-Canadian intelligentsia. In addition to Lapointe, one of the most important figures in establishing the new Canadian foreign policy was O.D. Skelton, under-secretary of state for external affairs from 1925 to 1941. Skelton was born into a conservative Presbyterian family in Orangeville, Ontario, but his academic career introduced him to a more liberal Canadian identity that went beyond the constraints of Anglo-Saxon conservatism and the British Empire. Skelton developed a great affinity for Wilfrid Laurier, completing his *Life and Letters of Sir Wilfrid Laurier* in 1921 and joining the Bonne Entente, a civil society movement of francophones and anglophones keen on improving national unity. Skelton opposed Chamberlainian imperialism on the grounds that it was a centralizing, anti-democratic obstacle to national unity. He also saw former Prime Minister Robert Borden's policy of conscription for overseas service as having been designed to whip up British Canadian sentiment and win re-election rather than help win the war.[11] In Skelton's view, asserting Canadian independence in foreign policy was central to an anglophone-francophone rapprochement.

"No one," King recalled, "could have been more strongly for everything being done for Canada, as against Britain, than Skelton."[12] King was in the audience when Skelton gave a series of addresses on Canadian foreign policy to the Canadian Clubs in Toronto and Ottawa in 1922.[13] Speaking of the country's newfound de facto autonomy and of the need for Canada to safeguard its interests, Skelton "rejected the idea that it was possible to formulate a common imperial policy."[14] Impressed, King asked him to join the Canadian delegation to the 1923 Imperial Conference in London. Skelton accepted the assignment enthusiastically. In 1925, his role was made official with his appointment as under-secretary of state for external affairs. Skelton was little known to the public, but behind the scenes he was arguably the most influential bureaucrat in Ottawa, constantly encouraging King and Lapointe to strive for greater independence from Britain. Skelton saw in Lapointe, especially, an ally who could help "keep King on track" whenever the prime minister's British sentimentalism crept up.[15] At Skelton's urging, King joined the prime ministers of the Commonwealth's other two bilingual Dominions – South Africa and Ireland – in refusing British prime minister Lloyd George's call for a single imperial policy in foreign affairs. "Canada," declared King, "claimed [the] right of self-government in external affairs."[16] He insisted that the Canadian Parliament alone could commit Canada to war and announced that new treaties signed by Britain would no longer have any bearing on Canada without its signature.

Throughout all this, prominent French Canadian officials played a highly visible role. For his first new hire to the External Affairs bureaucracy, Skelton insisted on an officer with "a good knowledge of both English and French."[17] Jean Désy, a Université de Montréal law professor, got the job. He was followed not long after by Paul-Émile Renaud and Georges Vanier. By 1930, nearly a third of Skelton's officers were francophones. In addition to Skelton, King had brought then federal justice minister and former Quebec premier Lomer Gouin to the 1923 Imperial Conference. Gouin remained in Europe that year to act as Canada's chief representative at the League of Nations Assembly, where he upheld Lapointe's 1922 position on Article X to great effect, securing the support of every single member except Persia.[18] Gouin was succeeded by another prominent French Canadian, Liberal senator Raoul Dandurand, who served as Canada's representative to the league from 1924 to 1930. Dandurand was an eloquent speaker in French and in English – the languages of diplomacy at the league – and he gained in popularity as an advocate of minority rights. Dandurand brought Canada's stature to new heights when he became president of the League Assembly (1925–26) – a particular point of pride for French Canadian observers.[19] French Canadian moderates Thomas Chapais and Édouard Montpetit would also represent Canada in the assembly, in 1930 and 1935, respectively.[20] Dandurand made clear Canada's aversion to foreign security commitments when he pointed out to British officials that "le Canada [est] sur un pied d'égalité dans la Société des Nations avec toutes les autres nations membres de cette Société."[21] In the meantime, Lapointe was busy asserting Canadian autonomy abroad, leading trade discussions with Italy, Spain, and France. Francophone Canadians were especially proud to see one of their own negotiating directly with the old mère patrie. Lapointe set a precedent by concluding Canada's first international treaty without British involvement, a fisheries treaty with the United States, in 1923.[22]

The year 1926 proved to be the real watershed for Canadian autonomy from Britain. When the governor general, Julien Byng, refused King's request for a dissolution, King resigned anyways, and his opponent, Arthur Meighen, failed to retain the confidence of the house, precipitating the very election that King had wanted in the first place. During the campaign, King portrayed Byng as an arrogant British lord who had meddled in internal Canadian affairs. The pro-autonomy platform helped win King the election, and barely a month later, in October, he headed to the Imperial Conference in London with the experience fresh in his mind. Having just been re-elected on the autonomy question, King knew that he could push the issue with the support of most Canadians.[23] The delegation included several civil servants and officials sympathetic to the autonomist position and to anglophone-francophone crosscultural accommodation: Lapointe and Skelton; the Canadian high commissioner to London, Peter Larkin; the soon-to-be minister plenipotentiary to Washington, Vincent Massey; Skelton's recent recruit to External Affairs, Jean Désy; the national archivist, Arthur Doughty; the young Quebec City lawyer and Lapointe's personal assistant, Philippe Picard; and the chief of staff general, James MacBrien.[24] The independent MP Henri Bourassa, a leader in the promotion of bicultural, pan-Canadian nationalism, also played an unofficial role. When they arrived in London, King and Lapointe met with Bourassa at the Ritz Hotel to discuss the upcoming conference. Bourassa commended King and Lapointe for their ongoing assertion of Canadian autonomy, and all three agreed that they should continue to make common cause with the Irish Free State and South Africa.[25]

At the conference, Lapointe hammered out terms to recognize the equal status of the self-governing states of the Commonwealth, including the United Kingdom. Britain's chief negotiator, Lord Balfour, attempted to retain some control over foreign policy through the creation of a central imperial foreign policy committee, whereby Britain would sign international agreements on behalf of the Empire. Skelton rejected this completely, asserting that such an arrangement would diminish "equal status, either in the League or elsewhere."[26] Lapointe agreed, and was joined by Prime Minister Hertzog of South Africa, who threatened to declare outright independence. The British chancellor, George Cave, "stamped out of the conference," declaring that "he was not going to be a party to the breaking up of the British Empire," and a deal was signed.[27]

The terms were announced in the 1926 Balfour Declaration. The declaration made clear that the Commonwealth was a free association of equal nations, none subordinate to any other, and each free to develop its external relations as it saw fit. The declaration also stipulated that governors general were representatives of the Crown and not of the British Government. This symbolically significant measure flowed directly from the Canadian constitutional crisis of that year.[28] Canadian governors general would from now on take their direction from Ottawa, not London, and inform the Crown directly. Relations would henceforth be handled by diplomats appointed by each government. As French Canadian historian Gustave Lanctôt asserted at the time, the declaration had effectively changed the role of the governor general from British representative to "souverain du Canada."[29] The terms of the declaration would be constitutionally formalized with Parliament's passage of the 1931 Statute of Westminster.

The Balfour Declaration emboldened both Anglo- and French Canadian officials in External Affairs. Lapointe proudly pointed out that the declaration was not merely the product of British benevolence but rather a formal recognition of established fact, "une reconnaissance par des égaux."[30] As Canada's representative to the League of Nations, Senator Raoul Dandurand, explained in 1926, "Je ne consens pas à être le sujet des sujets du roi. J'entends être le sujet direct du roi, tout comme les citoyens de Londres."[31] In one heated exchange, when Canada's vote on several League Council items had not been officially recorded owing to its being part of the British Empire, Dandurand banged his fist on his desk and shouted that Canada was not "under anybody's wing and Canada should appear like any other member."[32] In 1917, French Canadians had virtually no say in the conduct of Canada's international affairs, resulting in the full-scale imposition of conscription for overseas service in the name of imperial solidarity and collective security. Less than a decade later, Canadian foreign policy was being shaped with French Canadian and moderate Anglo-Canadian priorities in mind.[33]

The reception of the Balfour Declaration in the newspapers reflected the ongoing divisions within Anglo-Canadian opinion over the country's role in the British Empire. The staunchly conservative Toronto *Mail and Empire* and the Orangist *Telegram* bemoaned the undermining of the imperial connection.[34] The *Manitoba Free Press*, however, commended Lapointe in particular for having "played a large part" in negotiating and drafting the document.[35] It dubbed the declaration "the Charter of Dominion Independence" and dismissed naysayers as simple reactionaries who were out of touch with the times:

> This achievement of status ... has been bitterly resisted by a considerable body of opinion ... in Canada on the ground that it would break the British connection and put an end to the British Empire. If the people holding this view were right these disasters are now upon us; but, of course, they were wrong and we shall hear little more from them. They will accept the change, as people of like reactionary bias have accepted other changes in the past.[36]

The French-language press, meanwhile, welcomed the Balfour Declaration and the efforts of Canada's representatives. *Le Devoir* called it "la 'grande charte' des Dominions" and emphasized "l'égalité absolue ... pour les questions étrangères et domestiques."[37] It reprinted the entire declaration in French, pointing out that Canada could no longer be committed to a war against its will.[38] While by no means an Anglo-Canadian "defeat," then, the Balfour Declaration was undoubtedly a French Canadian victory.

Crosscultural compromise in foreign affairs required an awareness and acknowledgment of the sensibilities of both sides, francophone and anglophone. As Dandurand later explained in his memoires, "Je n'avais jamais cessé d'être un Canadien intégral, anti-impérialiste, sans oublier toutefois le respect que je devais aux sentiments très naturels de mes compatriotes envers leur mère patrie."[39] In February 1927, King and Lapointe hosted a huge banquet in Toronto at which they reassured some fourteen hundred members of the British Canadian elite of Canada's ongoing commitment to the Commonwealth. Lapointe shone in his address to the audience. Through autonomy, Lapointe asserted, Canada would not drift towards republicanism but, rather, it would become a true constitutional monarchy. Those who feared freedom and equal status within the Commonwealth, he argued, were "timid souls" who harboured an "inferiority complex, the subordinate state of mind." Lapointe was proud of the role played by French Canadians in furthering Canadian autonomy, but he reassured the crowd that autonomy was the best means to preserve both national unity and the British connection:

> Let me tell you the men of my race have been in the very forefront of the battle for responsible government in this country; that they believe in self-government, freedom and national status within the British empire and under the British throne, and they do not believe that a condition of subordination and colonial inferiority is essential to the preservation of their sacred rights.[40]

The speech was a success, captivating Lapointe's audience and receiving acclaim in the local press.[41]

The Conservative Opposition leader, R.B. Bennett, initially protested that these developments would speed along the end of the British Empire, but, like most Canadians, he eventually accepted the new reality of de facto independence and moved on.[42] Bennett, although outwardly an imperialist, still placed Canada's interests above those of Britain and the Empire. Moreover, he recognized that the anti-autonomy position had become more of a political liability than anything else – it simply no longer reflected popular opinion among Anglo-Canadians and had all the appeal of a poison pill among French Canadians.[43] His government promptly ratified the Statute of Westminster in 1931, putting an end once and for all to the old British Canadian dream of Imperial federation. The following year, at the Commonwealth Conference in Ottawa, Bennett's hard-nosed negotiating with Britain eliminated the prospect of establishing a common Imperial tariff zone. Instead, Bennett wrestled concessions from Britain that favoured Quebec and Ontario manufacturers. As a disgruntled Neville Chamberlain confided in his diary, Bennett espoused a devotion "in body and soul to the Empire, [but] he did little to put his sentiments into practice. Instead of directing the conference in his role as chair, he conducted himself simply as the leader of the Canadian delegation."[44]

French Canadian observers were noticeably proud of Canada's gradual achievement of independence.[45] "Dans l'histoire immédiate du Canada," wrote Gustave Lanctôt in 1934, "le fait qui domine, c'est son ascension au statut international."[46] Even clerico-nationalists such as Lionel Groulx celebrated the Statute of Westminster.[47] After all, this process towards independence had been led by one of French Canada's own, Ernest Lapointe.[48] But it had also been supported by most English-speaking Canadians. The apparent shift in Anglo-Canadian identity gave French Canadians hope in the possibility of a shared allegiance to a Canada that was no longer beholden to Britain. Perhaps Confederation could, after all, meet the aspirations of both peoples.[49] The genius of the statute, according to Lanctôt, was its ability to reconcile the views of both English- and French-speaking Canadians; it provided French Canadians with the independence in foreign policy that they so desired, while at the same time maintaining an imperial link for British Canadians by creating "le dominion impérial et indépendant."[50] The last, formal step to cement this independence, Lanctôt concluded, would be for Canada to exercise its right to declare war or peace independently from Britain.[51]

Returned to power in October 1935, the Liberals continued to avoid commitments to collective security out of a concern for national unity. Later that year, and with the support of O.D. Skelton, King reversed an initiative under the Conservative government that would have implemented League of Nations economic sanctions against Italy for its illegal invasion of Abyssinia.[52] This was a clear concession to French Canadian opinion. "In the minds of the people of Quebec," explained Anglo-Quebec MP Chubby Power, "it became the first test of the government's seriousness with respect to Canadianism and to a strongly Canadian policy."[53] Within cabinet, Lapointe, Power, and Cardin, who feared that the league was becoming a platform for imperial rivalries, sought to limit Canada's commitment to a minimum. Above all, they dreaded the possibility of drawing Canada into a war against Catholic Italy. More ardent interventionists, such as the minister of revenue, J.L. Isley, called for sanctions in the face of fascist aggression. The division in opinion was also reflected in the English- and French-language papers. Lapointe privately advised King that he would resign if the government endorsed the sanctions, and King relented. National unity, the prime minister confessed in his journal, was more important than any perceived international obligations. King went on vacation, and Lapointe, acting as interim prime minister, announced Canada's withdrawal of its support for the sanctions against Rome.[54]

As tensions grew in Europe, many Anglo-Canadian moderates, both in and out of the Liberal government, spoke in favour of Canadian neutrality. They included politicians, academics, and public servants such as Escott Reid, O.D. Skelton, Percy Corbett, Lester Pearson, Jack Pickersgill, Hugh Keenleyside, Frank Underhill, J.S. Woodsworth, and F.R. Scott.[55] Many of the Anglo-Canadian foreign policy isolationists like Scott were driven by a desire to accommodate French Canada. They feared that without full independence, the country would be vulnerable to another major division, which would then enflame territorial-based Québécois nationalism.[56] Quebec-centred French Canadian nationalism had undergone a resurgence during the mid-1930s. This was partly a result of the Great Depression. Where the 1920s had witnessed relative prosperity and improved conditions for most Quebecers, including French Canadians, the 1930s certainly had not. French Canadians were more likely to be working-class wage-earners instead of salaried employees, and French Canadian entrepreneurs were more likely to operate small businesses than to head larger companies. Consequently, they felt the full effects of the Great Depression. Moreover, the Depression laid bare the ongoing socioeconomic inequality that separated English- and French-speaking Quebecers, creating fodder for nationalistes such as Lionel Groulx who advocated cultural and spiritual separation from Anglo-Canadians. Discontent with the provincial Liberals brought the new Union Nationale party of Maurice Duplessis to power in Quebec in August 1936, much to the consternation of observers in and outside of Quebec for whom Canadian unity was a chief concern.

The spectre of Québécois secessionism influenced many Anglo-Canadian moderates to cast off the imperial connection.[57] In the fall of 1938, Alan Plaunt and Norman Lambert, head of the National Liberal Federation, created the nonpartisan Neutrality League. The league's *Canadian Unity in War and Peace: An Issue of Responsible Government,* published in March 1939 and co-authored with Scott, emphasized Canada's autonomy in foreign policy matters.[58] Initiatives like the Neutrality League were important because the discourse they promoted served to head off some of the jingoistic rhetoric that had been characteristic at the outset of the Great War and had led to so much animosity against French Canadians. The French-English dynamic of fall 1939, then, would be far different from the French-English dynamic of fall 1914.

The call for Canadian independence in foreign affairs also led to collaboration with moderate French Canadian nationalistes who were equally keen on delineating a noninterventionist foreign policy for the country. The young nationaliste politician and Action Nationale director, André Laurendeau, was a leading figure.

As part of the Groulx-inspired nationaliste Jeune-Canada movement of the 1930s, Laurendeau had at one point seriously flirted with Quebec secessionism.[59] As a student in France, however, Laurendeau's exposure to the French Catholic Left had led him to question the corporatism and conservative social teachings promoted by Groulx. Moreover, during his studies under the renowned French Protestant sociologist and historian André Siegfried at the Collège de France, Laurendeau began learning more about Canada outside "Laurentie." Anglo-Canadians, he discovered, were not all belligerent imperialists.[60] Returning to Canada as editor of *l'Action Nationale* in 1937, Laurendeau remained a nationaliste and an admirer of Groulx, but he was determined to establish a less ethnocentric and conservative tone for the journal, and to focus instead on the need for social and economic reforms. Moreover, Laurendeau wanted to meet Anglo-Canadians of his own age and political leanings, as Siegfried had counselled him to do. He came to suspect that the perceived Anglo-Canadian threat had been exaggerated owing to "la survivance des attitudes historiques."[61] In 1938, Laurendeau enrolled in a sociology class at McGill and discovered a group of left-wing, anti-imperialist, Anglo-Canadian students and professors, including Scott, who shared many of his views. By early 1939, they had become close acquaintances.[62]

Scott, whose pacifism and neutrality appealed greatly to Laurendeau, saw an opportunity to work against "a replay of the conscription crisis of 1918," which he feared would destroy the country.[63] In spring 1939, the two spearheaded a group of "Quebec nationalists and left-of-centre English and French Canadians on Canadian foreign policy."[64] It included such diverse figures as François-Albert Angers, professor at the École des hautes études commerciales, contributor to *L'Action nationale,* and head of the St. Jean-Baptiste Society; Gérard Filion of the Union des cultavateurs catholiques; Georges E. Cartier, McGill student and eventual Bloc populaire supporter; Madeleine Parent, Marxist trade unionist and secretary of the League for Social Reconstruction; Neil Morrison and Alec Grant of the Student Christian Movement; and George Laxton from the Fellowship for a Christian Social Order.[65] Despite its idealist membership, the group attempted a certain pragmatism. The members reluctantly accepted that Canada could not avoid the coming conflict but insisted that French- and English-speaking Canadians must agree beforehand as to what exactly Canada's role would be.

The group produced a policy piece aimed at the federal government titled "Toward a Canadian Foreign Policy in the Event of War/Pour une politique canadienne en cas de guerre prochaine." Setting out a foreign policy tailored to Canada's bicultural dynamic was the document's central purpose. French- and English-speaking Canadians, the authors explained, were "striving to create together one Canadian nation based on a mutual respect for each other's ideals." That Scott had been able to forge a common position in which an unabashed nationaliste such as Angers and a former secessionist such as Laurendeau endorsed the idea of "une nation canadienne" was no small achievement.[66] The authors argued that Canadian foreign policy must not jeopardize national unity – it must at all costs be a compromise between both national groups. Canadian interests must be supreme in the formation of any foreign policy. The policy paper advocated for neutrality, as favoured by many French Canadians and by some Anglo-Canadians, and it acknowledged the understandable desire of some English-speaking Canadians to come to the aid of Britain, the Empire, and other democratic allies in their hour of need by encouraging those Canadians who felt duty-bound to enlist in the militaries of Britain and her allies. Still, the policy asserted that Canada could favour Britain by placing an embargo on exports to Germany and its allies while allowing Britain to buy whatever it required.[67] Consciously or unconsciously, the policy echoed the compromise approach adopted by another great French Canadian statesman, Sir Wilfrid Laurier, during the Boer War forty years earlier.

While French- and Anglo-Canadian intellectuals were busy pre-empting a crosscultural schism in 1939, Canada's political leaders had not been idle. Hitler's annexation of the Sudetenland the year before had made war imminent. In anticipation of the intensification of Anglo-Canadian pro-war and French Canadian anti-war sentiment, King and Lapointe skilfully manoeuvred to placate both as best they could. In Parliament, King promised Anglo-Canadians that Canada would not sit idly by in a war between Britain and Germany. He reassured French Canadians by insisting that the country would not resort to conscription for a foreign war.[68] Lapointe attempted to persuade francophones to support entry into the war for the sake of national unity. Strict neutrality would hardly be fair to Anglo-Canadian sentiments: "La politique du Canada doit rallier l'adhésion aussi générale que possible de sa population," he explained. "L'orientation de notre politique étrangère est une phase du problème de l'unité nationale."[69] In the same vein, Lapointe appealed to Anglo-Canadian MPs to understand that conscription had to be avoided for the sake of national unity. He implored them to try to appreciate "les sentiments, la mentalité" of French Canada. French Canadians, he explained, had "seulement un pays, une patrie."[70] They would fight for Canada but could never acquiesce to being forced to fight on the other side of the Atlantic. Lapointe's speech was widely hailed in the Anglo-Canadian press. *Saturday Night* called Lapointe "Canada's number one statesman" for having delivered "the most courageous utterance ever made by a French Canadian."[71] Politically, Lapointe had stuck his neck out when he told his fellow French Canadians that neutrality was impossible because of the risk to national unity, and English-speaking Canada knew it.[72]

When the royal couple visited as King and Queen of Canada in May 1939, the reception in Quebec and across the country was overwhelmingly positive, as Claire Halstead shows in her chapter on the royal visit in this volume. Lapointe and Fernand Rinfret, the secretary of state, convinced Cardinal Villeneuve – a prince of the Church and thus French Canada's closest equivalent to a royal – to provide visible support for the visit. Villeneuve issued a directive to parishioners to welcome the royals upon their arrival at Quebec City. For King and Lapointe, however, the event marked an opportunity to once again underscore Canadian autonomy and reinforce national unity. The royals opened the new Supreme Court building, without the presence of the governor general, while the prime minister accompanied the royal couple throughout their tour. Lapointe and Rinfret insisted on this symbolic assertion of Canadian sovereignty.[73] Lapointe took particular pleasure in the Queen's bilingual parting remark: "'Que Dieu bénisse le Canada, God bless Canada.'"[74]

The relative national unity with which Canada confronted the Second World War was the result of a twenty-year process to construct a more dynamic and unifying relationship between anglophones and francophones on sensitive issues such as foreign policy and Canada's place within the British Empire. The emergence of an alternative identity for moderate Anglo-Canadians after the Great War was especially important in making a rapprochement possible. By war's end, a great many (but by no means all) Anglo-Canadians had lost their zeal for the aggressive, exclusive, and ethnocentric British Canadian nationalism of the prewar period. Moreover, Anglo-Canadians' desire for autonomy from Britain after 1918 would prove more compatible with French Canadians' conceptions of the country's place in the world.[75] By the end of the interwar period, most Anglo-Canadians appeared to perceive Canada as a nation independent from Great Britain.[76] Moderate intellectuals played a crucial role in effecting this change – as authors, teachers, journalists, and bureaucrats.

In French-speaking Canada as in English-speaking Canada, the debate over identity raged among intellectuals. With the disillusionment that followed the Great War and the conscription crisis, many French Canadians had appeared ready to abandon the pan-Canadian bicultural nationalism once advocated by Henri Bourassa in favour of Canon Lionel Groulx's brand of clericonationalism and his deep skepticism of Anglo-Canada.[77] Moderate intellectuals both in and outside the church, however, insisted that French Canadians throughout Canada could and should claim a more meaningful and rewarding role in the federation by engaging with Anglo-Canadians.[78]

The Liberal Parties of Quebec and Canada, meanwhile, were especially import-ant in implementing real policies that helped restore national unity. Moreover, they were increasingly confident that public opinion had grown more understand-ing of the principle of cultural federalism, whereby major decisions affecting the future of the nation required the acquiescence of both major cultural-linguistic groups.[79] The deft handling of Canadian foreign policy by Prime Minister King and Justice Minister Lapointe, in particular, helped restore French Canadians' confidence that they, too, had a meaningful say in the direction of the country.

When it comes to the Second World War, the return of the conscription debate, and its implications for crosscultural relations, there is a temptation to read his-tory backwards; to assert that any desire for rapprochement on the part of anglophones before 1939 had been meaningless. Yet, the country was far more united entering the Second World War than it had been exiting the Great War, and this unity would not have been possible without the meaningful crosscultural compromise of the interwar years. King and Lapointe steadfastly refused to make any formal commitment to collective security with Britain. When Britain and France finally declared war on September 3, 1939, King and Lapointe insisted that the country remain neutral until having made its own sovereign declaration. This formal assertion of neutrality was unprecedented in Canadian history. Even the nationaliste press had to concede that the Canadian government had done everything in its power to avoid a blind commitment to war.[80] It was only after Anglo- and French Canadian MPs had voted overwhelmingly to declare war that Canada entered the conflict, on September 10, 1939, announced in a nation-wide bilingual radio address by King and Lapointe.[81]

Over five years later, the state of national unity at the end of the Second World War, although strained, was far better than it had been a generation earlier. The Liberals had placated early calls for conscription with a system of obligatory national registration for home service. In terms of maintaining national unity, the compromise was, initially, a success. Nationaliste petitions against the measure "found few signers," and Quebecers complied with few exceptions – even André Laurendeau registered, albeit unenthusiastically.[82] By and large, most Anglo-Canadians had also hoped to avoid imposing conscription early on for the sake of national unity.[83]

Significantly, Quebecers demonstrated more support for the war effort than they had twenty years earlier – not out of some newfound enthusiasm for British imperialism but precisely because of Anglo-Canadians' relative turn away from it. Enlistment rates in Quebec were more than double what they had been in 1914–18, and Quebecers bought war bonds at the same rate as other Canadians.[84] Whereas in 1914 the minister of defence, Sam Hughes, had opposed accommodating the French language in the military, in 1939 the top brass were anxious to demonstrate a greater openness to French Canadians for the sake of national unity. By 1941, one French-language and two bilingual training centres had been established.[85] During the Great War, only one field unit (the 22nd battalion) had operated in French. During the Second World War, the military employed six French-speaking units at the front.[86] From early on, the generals placed the French-speaking units in brigades alongside English-speaking units in the hope that it "would give French and English speaking Canadians wider contacts. Men from the prairie would be working daily with French speaking Canadians from Quebec. The result would be a contribution of great national value to the future life of the Dominion."[87]

To suggest that the sum effect of the Second World War was to unite Anglo- and French Canadians in common cause would be delusional. But it did not divide them to nearly the same extent as the previous war. With pressure mounting for conscription for overseas service after the disastrous fall of France, and German and Japanese advances in the East, Prime Minister King called and won a plebiscite in 1942 to release his government from its initial promise, although Quebec voted overwhelmingly against doing so. Under intense pressure, King held out as long as he could. Instead of imposing across-the-board conscription for overseas service (as Borden had done in April 1917), in November 1944 he acceded to a one-time instalment of men who had already been conscripted and trained for home service to be sent overseas. Only 2,500 conscripts served at the front, one tenth the number that served at the front in 1917–18.[88] The measure sparked protest in Quebec and elsewhere in Canada. Soft nationalists such as André Laurendeau were deeply disillusioned.[89] But there were no violent riots like those in Quebec City on Easter Monday 1918.[90] Quebecers expressed their growing dismay over the renewed call for conscription at the ballot box, ousting Adélard Godbout's Liberals in August 1944 and electing Duplessis's Union Nationale. Still, the provincial Liberals managed to win the popular vote, and many Quebecers proved more upset over wartime economic controls than by the change in policy over conscription.[91] Laurendeau's vigorously anti-conscription Bloc populaire, meanwhile, captured only four seats. In the federal election of June 1945, the results were even less impressive for the Bloc, and Quebecers helped re-elect the Mackenzie King Liberals. After the war, working- and middle-class anglophones and francophones moved on to embrace the new Canadian social welfare state of King and Louis St. Laurent and Canada's position as an independent middle power – an American (more so than British) ally against the communist Eastern Bloc in a New World Order that would leave less and less room for the European empires of old.[92]

Notes

Robert J. Talbot is manager of research at the Office of the Commissioner of Official Languages of Canada. The views expressed in his chapter are the author's alone and do not represent those of the organization.

1 Lapointe was fisheries minister from 1921 until 1924, when he assumed the far more prominent justice portfolio.
2 As John MacFarlane has explained, "Both King and Lapointe were more followers than leaders of public opinion" when it came to foreign affairs. See John MacFarlane, *Ernest Lapointe and Quebec's Influence on Canadian Foreign Policy* (Toronto: University of Toronto Press, 1999), 4. Although MacFarlane emphasizes "francophone Quebec's influence on Canadian foreign policy," the autonomist position of the interwar period was also the product of moderate Anglo-Canadian public opinion.
3 See Lester B. Pearson, *Mike: The Memoirs of the Right Honourable Lester B. Pearson* (New York: Quandrangle Books, 1972), 65, and Bernard Saint-Aubin, *King et son époque* (Montreal: La Press, 1982), 271.
4 The suppression of Article X and Lapointe's role in it were well received in much of the English-language press and especially in the French-language papers. Lita-Rose Betcherman, *Ernest Lapointe: Mackenzie King's Great Quebec Lieutenant* (Toronto: University of Toronto Press, 2002), 50, 59. See also C.P. Stacey, *Canada and the Age of Conflict,* vol. 2, *1921–1948: The Mackenzie King Era* (Toronto: University of Toronto Press, 1981), 56.
5 By 1939, the attractiveness of the federal Liberals for young energetic Quebec pan-Canadians had left the provincial party somewhat weak. See Charles Gavan Power, *A Party Politician: The Memoirs of Chubby Power* (Toronto: MacMillan, 1966), 127.
6 Carman Miller, "William Stevens Fielding," *Dictionary of Canadian Biography,* vol. 15 (Toronto/Montreal: University of Toronto/Université Laval, 2000), www.biographi.ca. See also Saint-Aubin, *King et son époque,* 268, and Ernest Lapointe, *La situation internationale du Canada* (Montreal: n.p., 1928), 12.
7 By 1923, Lapointe had become popular with the influential *Maclean's* columnist J.K. Munro for asserting Canadian autonomy abroad. See Betcherman, *Ernest Lapointe,* 62.
8 See Desmond Morton, "Was the Great War Canada's War of Independence?," National Film Board, *Images of a Forgotten War,* 2011 (accessed September 15, 2013), http://www3.nfb.ca/ww1/independence.php.
9 See, for instance, Denis Monière, *Le développement des idéologies au Québec: Des origines à nos jours* (Montreal: Québec/Amérique, 1977), 361.
10 See Zara Stein, *The Lights That Failed: European International History, 1919–1933* (Oxford: Oxford University Press, 2005), 349.
11 See O.D. Skelton, *Life and Letters of Sir Wilfrid Laurier,* vol. 2, *1896–1919* (Toronto: McClelland and Stewart, 1965 [1921]), 35, 123.
12 Norman Hillmer, "O.D. Skelton: Innovating for Independence," in *Architects and Innovators: Building the Department of External Affairs and International Trade, 1909–2009,* ed. Greg Donaghy and Kim Richard Nossal (Montreal/Kingston: McGill-Queen's University Press, 2009), 70.
13 The Diaries of William Lyon Mackenzie King, January 21, 1922, Library and Archives Canada, MG26-J13, http://www.bac-lac.gc.ca/eng/discover/politics-government/prime-ministers/william-lyon-mackenzie-king/Pages/search.aspx.
14 Carl Berger, *The Writing of Canadian History: Aspects of English-Canadian Historical Writing, 1900–1970* (Toronto: Oxford University Press, 1976), 51.
15 This would be the case, for instance, during the crucial Balfour Conference of 1926. See MacFarlane, *Ernest Lapointe and Quebec's Influence,* 57.

16 John W. Dafoe diary, October 14, 1923, in Ramsay Cook, "J.W. Dafoe at the Imperial Conference, 1923," *Canadian Historical Review* 41, 1 (March 1960): 26.

17 Norman Hillmer, "National Independence and the National Interest: O.D. Skelton's Department of External Affairs in the 1920s," in *In the National Interest: Canadian Foreign Policy and the Department of Foreign Affairs and International Trade, 1909–2009,* ed. Greg Donaghy and Michael Kiernan Carroll (Calgary: University of Calgary Press, 2011), 15.

18 Stacey, *Canada and the Age of Conflict,* 2:66, and Betcherman, *Ernest Lapointe,* 65.

19 Gustave Lanctôt, *Le Canada et la révolution américaine* (Montreal: Librairie Beauchemin Limitée, 1965), 8–9.

20 Université de Montréal, division des archives, "Délégué," Fonds Édouard-Montpetit, http://www.archiv.umontreal.ca/exposition/montpetit/delegue/delegue1.htm.

21 "Canada [is] on an equal footing in the League of Nations with all other member countries of that organization." All translations provided by the author. In Stéphane Paquin, "Raoul Dandurand: Porte-parole de la conscience universelle," in *Architects and Innovators,* ed. Donaghy and Nossal, 46.

22 See MacFarlane, *Ernest Lapointe and Quebec's Influence,* 51–54, and Stacey, *Canada and the Age of Conflict,* 2:49.

23 Power, *A Party Politician,* 115.

24 See D.B. Macrae to J.W. Dafoe, October 29, 1926, in Ramsay Cook and D.B. Macrae, "A Canadian Account of the 1926 Imperial Conference," *Journal of Commonwealth Political Studies* 3, 1 (1965): 54–56. MacBrien was "a neighbour of [civic nationalist C.A.] Bowman in Rockliffe." He was "commissioned to prepare the draft on Canada's position as it related to Imperial defence. Bowman and Skelton were close colleagues." See Michael Nolan, *Foundations: Alan Plaunt and the Early Days of CBC Radio* (Montreal: CBC Enterprises, 1986), 51.

25 Bourassa wrote to Lapointe: "'En faisant bloc avec les Irlandais et Afrikanders [sic] vous pouvez faire ce que vous voulez à la conférence.'" In MacFarlane, *Ernest Lapointe and Quebec's Influence,* 57.

26 In Betcherman, *Ernest Lapointe,* 125. See also D.B. Macrae's letters to J.W. Dafoe during the conference, in Cook and Macrae, "A Canadian Account of the 1926 Imperial Conference," 50–63.

27 D.B. Macrae to J.W. Dafoe, November 21, 1926, in ibid., 61.

28 As D.B. Macrae reported at the beginning of the conference, "The Canadian plan is to have him [the governor general] made a viceroy. He would be appointed by cooperation between the British and Canadian governments but once appointed would be responsible directly to the Crown and no longer an official of the British government." D.B. Macrae to J.W. Dafoe, October 29, 1926, in ibid., 55.

29 "Sovereign of Canada." See Lanctôt, *Le Canada,* 164, 205.

30 "'A recognition by equals.'" In Saint-Aubin, *King et son époque,* 277.

31 "'I do not consent to being the subject of subjects of the king. I mean to be a direct subject of the king, in the same way as the citizens of London.'" In ibid., 278.

32 In Betcherman, *Ernest Lapointe,* 164.

33 See MacFarlane, *Ernest Lapointe and Quebec's Influence,* 197–98.

34 See ibid., 127–28.

35 "Play Large Part in Drafting Report," *Manitoba Free Press,* November 22, 1926, 1.

36 "The Charter of Dominion Independence," *Manitoba Free Press,* November 23, 1926, 13. Liberal editor Charles A. Bowman's *Ottawa Citizen* struck a similar tone. See *Ottawa Citizen,* November 20–24, 1926.

37 "The 'great charter' of the Dominions," it emphasized "absolute equality ... in foreign and domestic questions." In "La 'rande charte' des Dominions," *Le Devoir,* November

20, 1926, 3. *Le Droit* also welcomed the motion but called for greater clarity as to what Canada's obligations remained to the new "Commonwealth." See Charles Gauthier, "Les relations interimpériales," *Le Droit*, November 24, 1926, 3.

38 "Texte français du rapport de la conférence," *Le Devoir*, November 22, 1926, 1.

39 "I have never ceased to be a wholehearted Canadian, an anti-imperialist, without forgetting the respect that I owe to the natural sentiments of my compatriots towards their mother country." Dandurand, *Le sénateur-diplomate: Mémoires, 1861–1942* (Québec: Presses de l'Université Laval, 2000), 135.

40 In Betcherman, *Ernest Lapointe*, 129.

41 *Toronto Daily Star*, February 4, 1927, 1.

42 See Power, *A Party Politician*, 115, and Saint-Aubin, *King et son époque*, 278.

43 Indeed, his campaign in 1930 was relatively silent on foreign affairs questions and focused instead on "the remedies he thought would cure unemployment." See Power, *A Party Politician*, 115. He was also influenced in these views by Skelton, who managed to keep his job despite the change in government. See Hillmer, "O.D. Skelton: Innovating for Independence," 66.

44 In Saint-Aubin, *King et son époque*, 239.

45 Achievements like the Balfour Declaration had "attracted considerable attention from the intellectuals in Quebec." See Power, *A Party Politician*, 115.

46 "In the recent history of Canada, the fact that stands out is its ascension to international status." Lanctôt, *Le Canada*, 163–64.

47 Groulx was a keynote speaker at a particularly large rally in Montreal organized by nationalists to celebrate the anniversary of the statute, on November 27, 1938. See Betcherman, *Ernest Lapointe*, 255.

48 Canada's constitutional evolution and the role of French Canadians also garnered some attention in France. See, for example, André Siegfried, *Le Canada: Puissance internationale*, 2nd ed. (Paris: Librairie Armand Colin, 1937).

49 For Lapointe, especially, it was "important ... for francophone Quebecers to know that their views were not ignored by the majority." MacFarlane, *Ernest Lapointe and Quebec's Influence*, 199.

50 "The imperial and independent Dominion." Lanctôt, *Le Canada*, 204.

51 Ibid., 167.

52 See Norman Hillmer, *O.D. Skelton: A Portrait of Canadian Ambition* (Toronto: University of Toronto Press, 2015), 240.

53 Power, *A Party Politician*, 120–21.

54 See MacFarlane, *Ernest Lapointe and Quebec's Influence*, 94, and Saint-Aubin, *King et son époque*, 283–84.

55 See Sandra Djwa, *The Politics of the Imagination: A Life of F.R. Scott* (Toronto: McClelland and Stewart, 1987), 160–61, 165, 177–78, and Michael Oliver and Sandra Djwa, "F.R. Scott: Quebecer," in *On F.R. Scott: Essays on His Contributions to Law, Literature, and Politics*, ed. Sandra Djwa and R. St. J. Macdonald (Montreal/Kingston: McGill-Queen's University Press, 1983), 167.

56 During 1937–38, Escott Reid and Percy Corbett encouraged Scott to write "Canada Today," a position paper that asserted that Canada had a right to neutrality in part because of its cultural-linguistic division over wartime participation. Djwa, *Politics of the Imagination*, 177.

57 José Igartua has emphasized the post–Second World War period in understanding this phenomenon. José E. Igartua, *The Other Quiet Revolution: National Identities in English Canada, 1945–1971* (Vancouver: UBC Press, 2006).

58 Nolan, *Foundations*, 156–57.
59 André Laurendeau, *Notre nationalisme*, Tract 5, Jeune-Canada, October 1935 (Montreal: Le Devoir) (accessed March 12, 2012), faculty.marianopolis.edu.
60 Ramsay Cook and Michael Derek Behiels, *The Essential Laurendeau* (Toronto: Copp Clark, 1976), 8.
61 "The survival of old attitudes." He argued that the United States posed a much greater threat. See André Laurendeau, "Menaces de l'américisme," *L'Action nationale* 10, 4 (December 1937): 312–23. He had learned from Siegried that Anglo-Canadians retained their Britishness out of a desire to prevent assimilation into the materialist American model. It was on this basis that Anglo- and French Canadians could make common cause. See André Siegried, *Le Canada: Puissance internationale*, 2nd ed. (Paris: Librairie Armand Colin, 1937), 69–71.
62 See Guy LaForest, *Trudeau and the End of a Canadian Dream* (Montreal/Kingston: McGill-Queen's University Press, 1995), 63, and Ramsay Cook, *Canada and the French-Canadian Question* (Toronto: MacMillan, 1966), 111.
63 LaForest, *Trudeau and the End of a Canadian Dream*, 63.
64 Oliver and Djwa, "F.R. Scott: Quebecer," 167.
65 Djwa, *Politics of the Imagination*, 183.
66 Quoted in Oliver and Djwa, "F.R. Scott: Quebecer," 168.
67 See André Laurendeau, "La guerre," *L'Action nationale* 14, 1 (1939): 3–6.
68 "Pas de conscription," *La Presse*, March 31, 1939, 1.
69 "The policy of Canada must have the general support of the population in as far as possible," he explained. "The orientation of our foreign policy is but one phase of the problem of national unity." "Le très hon. M. Lapointe prend parti à son tour," *La Presse*, April 1, 1939, 24.
70 "One country, one homeland." Ibid.
71 Betcherman, *Ernest Lapointe*, 267.
72 Ibid., 267.
73 J. William Galbraith, "Fiftieth Anniversary of the 1939 Royal Visit," *Canadian Parliamentary Review*, Autumn 1989, 7–11; Stacey, *Canada and the Age of Conflict*, 2:243–48.
74 In Betcherman, *Ernest Lapointe*, 281.
75 David E. Smith, *Federalism and the Constitution of Canada* (Toronto: University of Toronto Press, 2010), 158.
76 In a survey published in the Toronto *Daily Star* in August 1942, when asked, "Do you think of Canada as an independent country or still dependent on Great Britain?," 52 percent of Anglo-Canadian respondents answered yes, 6 percent were undecided, and 42 percent answered no. See Stanley B. Ryerson, *French Canada: A Study in Canadian Democracy* (Toronto: Progress Books, 1943), 234.
77 See, for instance, Susan Mann Trofimenkoff, *Action Française: French Canadian Nationalism in the Twenties* (Toronto: University of Toronto Press, 1975), 6.
78 MacFarlane, *Ernest Lapointe and Quebec's Influence*, 14–15. Claude Couture makes a similar argument in *Le mythe de la modernisation du Québec: Des années 1930 à la révolution tranquille* (Montreal: Méridien, 1991), 10–11, 49–110.
79 See David E. Smith, *Federalism and the Constitution of Canada* (Toronto: University of Toronto Press, 2010), 5, 155.
80 See MacFarlane, *Ernest Lapointe and Quebec's Influence*, 151, and Betcherman, *Ernest Lapointe*, 273–74.
81 Betcherman, *Ernest Lapointe*, 281, and Saint-Aubin, *King et son époque*, 308.

82 Betcherman, *Ernest Lapointe*, 318, and Saint-Aubin, *King et son époque*, 321. See also MacFarlane, *Ernest Lapointe and Quebec's Influence*, 175.

83 The *Globe* reminded readers that "the French Canadians, equally concerned for the freedom assured by British institutions but without the same background [as us] ... lack the urge to go back to Europe to fight for a cause sponsored by a nation to which allegiance has no direct appeal." "The Conscription Issue," *The Globe*, September 19, 1939.

84 The rate of enlistment among men of military age in Quebec was 10 percent during the First World War and 26 percent during the Second World War. See Robert Brown and Donald Loveridge, "Unrequited Faith: Recruiting the CEF, 1914–1918," *Canadian Military History* 24, 1 (Spring 2015): 58; Veterans Affairs Canada, "Military–Historical Background," n.d. (accessed July 10, 2013), http://www.veterans.gc.ca/eng/remembrance/history/second-world-war/la-force-francophone/military; and MacFarlane, *Ernest Lapointe and Quebec's Influence*, 177.

85 MacFarlane, *Ernest Lapointe and Quebec's Influence*, 177.

86 See Jean-Pierre Gagnon, "Les historiens canadiens français et la participation canadienne française à la Deuxième Guerre mondiale," *Bulletin d'histoire politique* 3, 3 (1995): 25–44, and Jean-Yves Gravel, *Le Québec et la guerre* (Montreal: Boréal, 1974), 108.

87 General Odium to General McNaughton, in C.P. Stacey, *Official History of the Canadian Army in the Second World War*, vol. 1, *Six Years of War: The Army in Canada, Britain and the Pacific* (Ottawa: National Defence, 1955), 45. See also Jean Pariseau and Serge Bernier, *Les Canadiens français et le bilinguisme dans les forces armées canadiennes*, vol. 1, *1763–1969: Le spectre d'une armée bicéphale* (Ottawa: National Defence, 1987), chap. 5.

88 Twenty-four thousand Canadian conscripts served at the front in the last months of the Great War. See Desmond Morton, *A Military History of Canada*, 4th ed. (Toronto: McClelland & Stewart, 1999), 221.

89 Laurendeau wrote a memoire of the event. See André Laurendeau, *La crise de la conscription: 1942* (Montreal: Les Éditions du Jour, 1962).

90 The greatest threat of violence occurred not in Quebec but in British Columbia, when a group of conscripts from Saskatchewan threatened to turn their guns on their superiors. See "Armed Violence Threat Holds Unit in Camp," *The Globe*, November 28, 1944.

91 See Power, *A Party Politician*, 146–47, 176–77. Duplessis established his razor-thin majority of forty-eight seats with 38.0 percent of the popular vote to the Liberals' 39.4 percent of the popular vote. "History of Quebec Elections," *CBC News*, last modified February 18, 2014, http://www.cbc.ca/elections/quebecvotes2014/features/view/election-history-timeline.

92 See Dominique Marshall, *The Social Origins of the Welfare State: Quebec Families, Compulsory Education, and Family Allowances, 1940–1955* (Waterloo: Wilfrid Laurier University Press, 2006), 161.

6

Claiming Canada's King and Queen
Canadians and the 1939 Royal Tour

Claire L. Halstead

> *Every phase of their activities has been covered with dignity and you have given us a permanent record of all the endearing acts of the King and the Queen which have gone straight to the hearts of Canadians.*
>
> – O.T.G. WILLIAMSON, TORONTO, ONTARIO,
> LETTER TO THE EDITOR OF THE *GLOBE AND MAIL*[1]

THE 1939 ROYAL tour put Canada's monarchy on display for the whole nation. For the first time, Canadians would see *their* King and Queen. The month-long train tour stopped in major cities and small towns across the country, allowing many Canadians unprecedented access to their monarchs. As Canadians enjoyed the brightly coloured spectacle, full of pomp and circumstance, media coverage of the event was flooded with descriptions of large, enthusiastic, and loyal flag-waving crowds. Yet, rather than exploring how Canadians chose to engage with their monarchs through the royal tour, historians have instead taken a top-down approach and view the tour as a strategy for drumming up support for the monarchy in the hope that, in the event of war, Canada would stand by Britain. Historians have also argued that Canadian organizers used the tour as an opportunity to project Canada's national and democratic identity to the monarchs. How Canadians experienced and perceived the royal tour has garnered less attention, even though the royal tour was crafted as an event for public consumption, and its "success" depended largely on the enthusiastic reception that Canadians were willing to display.

How did Canadians engage with the royal tour? If it is true that individuals claim agency through their actions, then sources reveal that Canadians exhibited agency by choosing how to engage with the tour, spectate the parade, and create their own representations of the event. Although the sheer vastness of Canada's geography and the country's anglophone-francophone divisions make it admittedly difficult to put forward broad claims, it is clear that Canadians perceived the royal tour as a unique and unprecedented spectacle, and they did so even if, in some instances, they lacked physical access to a royal parade. Canadians "consumed" the royal tour and crafted personal narratives of it through commemorative items, radio broadcasts, mail, parades, films, and scrapbooks. Through these personalized mementos, Canadians routinely centred their narratives of the tour on themselves and their local communities, thereby writing themselves into the royal tour and bringing themselves closer to their monarchy. The result was that Canadians consumed the royal tour in such a way that they claimed King George VI and Queen Elizabeth as their own monarchs.

As social and cultural historians know, accessing the people's perspective, rather than the political motivations behind the tour, depends on searching for material created for, and left behind by, the people. While documents that detail the decisions of statesmen or broadcasters have made it possible for historians to reveal the intentions behind the choreography of the tour, gauging the popular response to the visit remains a challenge. The keepsakes through which individual Canadians recorded their response to the royal tour remain hidden in personal collections (and attics) across the country. As the generation that engaged with the tour ages, some of these artifacts are passing into public archives, but many remain in private holdings. However, as personal mementos turn into collectibles, we can get a glimpse of these items as they are listed in online exchanges such as eBay. The richness of these sources and their reflection of the public's engagement with the royal tour have yet to be uncovered in the historiography.

The literature on the 1939 royal visit is surprisingly sparse.[2] Historians have tended to either portray the tour as a precursor to the outbreak of the Second World War or focus on one particular aspect of the tour, such as radio broadcasting. Heather Metcalfe, for instance, opens her dissertation on prewar Canadian public opinion towards international relations with the royal tour. She argues that the tour demonstrated "Canada's connection to the Empire, and the nature of the international system" that necessitated Canada's involvement in international issues.[3] Alternatively, Simon Potter and Mary Vipond have looked to the tour as an important media event. Examining radio broadcasts, Potter argues that the BBC and the CBC, although working towards their own agendas, were able to collaborate and produce coverage that portrayed the Empire as united in loyalty to the Crown, despite race or class divisions.[4] In a similar vein, Mary Vipond posits that radio broadcasts of the royal tour enabled the then newly formed CBC to legitimize itself and gain authority as Canada's public broadcaster.[5] Molly Pulver Ungar focuses on reports and representations of three significant banquets held for the monarchs during the tour and suggests that they offered Canadians a form of culinary tourism and escape from Depression-era hardships. The dinners, she argues, maintained the country's democratic identity while simultaneously expressing enthusiasm for the Empire, and they represented Canada's national pride in preparing high-quality food.[6] Similarly, J. William Galbraith argues that the tour had significant constitutional importance and even acted as a catalyst in the growth of Canada into a sovereign nation.[7] Thus, historians have argued that the tour enabled Canada to display itself as a mature, senior Dominion, simultaneously sovereign and loyal to the monarchy.

It has been widely stated that the purpose of the tour was to garner support in Canada for the monarchy in the event that Britain went to war. Even Library and Archives Canada's brief description of the tour suggests "one of the main reasons for the royal tour was to stimulate Canadian affection and support for Britain in the coming conflict."[8] Indeed, the King and Queen would not have made such a lengthy and momentous journey, particularly as the situation in Europe worsened, had it not been of benefit. But this interpretation overshadows Canada's role in initiating the royal visit. Both Canada's governor general and the prime minister harboured the idea of a royal tour as early as 1937. According to the tour's official historian, Gustave Lanctôt, Lord Tweedsmuir proposed the idea in 1937 after the abdication of Edward VIII. Prime Minister King then presented the official invitation when he travelled to London for the coronation of King George VI. Although the visit was confirmed in 1938, the unstable European situation meant that the tour was subject to change. Tweedsmuir was inspired by Canada's sovereign status stemming from the Imperial Conference in 1926 and the Statute of Westminster in 1931. For the first time, King George VI would act not as King of the United Kingdom but as King of Canada, and a royal visit would allow Canadians to "see *their* king performing royal functions, supported by his Canadian ministers."[9] King viewed the tour as an opportunity to unite the country.[10] He saw the royal tour as the pinnacle of pomp and circumstance (of which he was always a promoter), and he took on the role of chief organizer and made most of the major decisions.[11] For those organizing the tour, it was an opportunity to secure national unity, to display Canada's hospitality and, most importantly, its sovereignty.

The 1939 royal tour offered Canadians an unprecedented spectacle as the largest, most well-planned national public event of their lives. The public excitement that surrounded the planning and preparations for the tour was elevated by the fact that it was the first time a reigning monarch would visit Canada. Before then, as Eirik Brazier explains in this volume, royal representatives such as imperial officers were cast in opposition to Canadian values or Canadian autonomy. There had been royal visits to Canada in 1860, 1901, 1919, and 1927, but this royal tour bore additional symbolism.[12] Further, a cult of celebrity had emerged around Edward, the Prince of Wales, in the interwar period.[13] Historian Laura Nym Mayhall argues that by the early 1930s the Prince of Wales had already transcended national boundaries and had become a "male sensation of Hollywood." Instead of being popular for his status as a future King, he captured hearts because he was handsome, photogenic, and often profiled in *Vanity Fair* as a prime arbiter of English fashion and celebrity style.[14] Following the abdication crisis in 1936, the cult of the celebrity shifted focus to King George VI and Queen Elizabeth during the 1939 royal tour, particularly to the Queen because of her beauty. This cult of celebrity and respect for the Crown likewise motivated Canadians to engage in the royal tour by creating their own records of events and by attending parades to catch a glimpse of the royal celebrities. King George VI himself helped fuel their interest, as he was anxious to return to the period of his father, George V, and participate in grand ceremonies.[15] The tour lasted just over a month, from May 17 to June 15, with a six-day stint in the United States. After arriving in Quebec aboard the *Empress of Australia,* the King and Queen travelled by train across Canada and stopped in most major cities from coast to coast.[16] Although the tour may be considered a story for predominantly English Canada, it was hoped that the King and Queen's ability to speak French fluently would help inspire all Canadians to share the momentous occasion.[17] While the tour was carefully crafted for national purposes and methodically planned to ensure the best display of Canada – its people, industry, and landscape – individual Canadians were more concerned with how they could claim a piece of the tour for themselves.

Even prior to Their Majesties' arrival, the tour headlined in the media and became the focus of businesses wanting to fulfill Canadians' appetite for commemorative and decorative items. Rather than merely wishing to profit from the tour, the producers of such items presupposed a level of engagement among consumers. Although the trend of producing commemorative china began in the 1780s, it was usually reserved for royal weddings, coronations, and deaths.[18] This royal tour, for the first time, was captured in china. China manufacturer Alfred Meakin designed a commemorative plate and a cup and saucer that profiled the King and Queen under a crown, flags, and a banner that clearly marked the memorable occasion as the "Royal Visit to Canada."[19] Although the Princesses Elizabeth and Margaret Rose did not accompany the monarchs on the tour, the manufacturer used the opportunity to point towards the future of the monarchy by including them on commemorative items. China mugs and cups and saucers, usually of poor to fair quality, were the most popular items for Canadians to purchase; they required an investment but were not too wasteful for those who still had the Depression on their minds.[20]

Canadians were also able to purchase Canadian-mined silver and bronze medallions designed by Emmanuel Hahn at the local post office. One side featured the monarchs' portrait while the other depicted a map of Canada with an etched line illustrating the tour route. That these medallions still survive in personal collections and can be found for sale on eBay indicates that Canadians purchased them. Even Canadian children were not overlooked; the prime minister approved the distribution of over 2.5 million smaller medallions for school children.[21] Well-known Canadian jeweller Birks likewise produced a medallion to "commemorate the visit of their majesties to Canada."[22] If one had the disposable income, customers at Ontario Furniture Limited could order a ninety-seven-piece Maddocks "Royal Blue" dinnerware set for $24.95. The set included a free souvenir plate, which, the advertisement noted, came with a picture of the King and Queen.[23] For those unable to afford such expensive items, local businesses enabled Canadians to engage in the royal tour by providing "free" commemorative items with the purchase of ordinary goods. In Toronto, Weston Bakeries offered a complimentary souvenir plate with the purchase of a cake while, in London, a family-size pack of "Concentrated Super Suds" came with a "King and Queen Souvenir Book."[24] Thus, Canadian households of all economic standing had the opportunity to claim commemorative objects that mirrored the longevity of the monarchy and depicted Their Majesties.

One innovative way that Canadians created personal mementos of the tour was through the postal service. The royal train was specially equipped with a mobile post office capable of processing 250,000 pieces of mail each day.[25] Each letter was cancelled with a special Royal Standard design stamp. Using the opportunity to both write to the royals and create their own souvenir, Canadians sent mail to the train and enclosed six cents to have the envelopes returned with royal visit stamps and the special cancellation stamp. By May 11, almost a week before the royals arrival in Quebec, the post office in Ottawa had received over seventy thousand letters destined for the royal train.[26] Those letters that survived and are available to historians reveal that Canadians addressed the letters to themselves, turning the letter and postmark into a personal keepsake. Archibald Brayley, a British-born caretaker living in Winnipeg who had served in the First World War, mailed a letter to himself through the royal train on May 15, the day the tour arrived in Winnipeg.[27] The specially designed envelope displays a portrait of the King and Queen above "Canada Welcomes Their Majesties."[28] The emphasis placed on "Their" indicates how Canada claimed the monarchs. While Brayley may not have been particularly wealthy, as his employment and address would suggest, he like many Canadians found a way to create a royal souvenir for himself. Alan McKenzie Gammell, a Canadian-born assistant manager from Montreal, used the royal train to send himself an envelope with "Welcome" printed in both English and French. Gammell's envelope, stamped with the royal train cancellation, displays portraits of the King and Queen above a beaver and maple leaves. While Brayley's and Gammell's envelopes provide just two illustrations of how some Canadians created mementos for themselves,

thousands of Canadians shared their idea, and their letters can be equally revealing of the motivations behind their participation in the royal tour. Desirous of
an even bolder statement of loyalty and as a way to create a souvenir, the Blacks,
a couple from Fort William, Ontario, went so far as to name their newborn
twins after George and Elizabeth as a reminder of the tour.[29]

Canadians also consumed the tour by purchasing decorative items to adorn
their homes, an act that, in turn, transformed the tour into a participative event.
Across the country, businesses worked hard to meet the high demand for ban-
ners, flags, and other decorations. In Toronto, the Poppy Fund sold "beautiful
six-foot silk drapes" with a Union Jack design for $2.75.[30] Wool flags, small flags,
bunting, shields, or "patriotic decoration sets" were also available for $2.25.[31]
Auto and window transfers enabled Canadians to decorate their homes, cars,
trucks, and bicycles.[32] While the mere availability of these decorations does not
prove that Canadians purchased them, the *Globe and Mail* reported on June 17,
1939, in "Royal Tour Gives Spurt to Business," that the demand for such items
"stimulated sales in many specialized lines." One Toronto flag manufacturer
alone sold 2 million flags across the country while a Toronto men's tailor esti-
mated that sales of morning clothes increased by 20 percent. A women's clothing
retailer claimed a 25 percent increase in purchases. Even a "foot-appliances firm"
experienced increased demand as Canadians rushed to buy corn plasters and
arch support to prepare for or recover from participation in parades and
celebrations.[33]

The ability to purchase items depended on disposable income and, within
the shadow of the Depression, such purchases were unlikely to be frivolous,
reinforcing the importance and value that Canadians placed on these decorative
and commemorative objects. Even if they were unable to purchase a new item,
Canadians found creative ways to engage with the tour, including washing or
repurposing old flags or patriotic fabrics to use as new flags and decorations.[34]
By purchasing or creating an object, Canadians claimed a space for themselves
within the patriotic fervour and crowds. Even if individuals were unable to
physically attend a parade because of their location, these objects allowed them
to share in and capture a part of the royal tour to keep in their own homes. By
actively participating in adorning spaces, Canadians also hoped to make the
tour memorable for the King and Queen.

Canadians participated in the tour and claimed their view of the monarchs
by attending parades. In some places, the royal train would only stop for several
minutes. Despite stopping in Sioux Lookout in northern Ontario for only
seventeen minutes, the train drew a crowd of eight thousand spectators, waiting
to catch a glimpse of their monarchs.[35] Longer stops allowed for a royal procession, which was carefully mapped. In London, Ontario, the hub of western

Ontario, the city's program, distributed to spectators, included a strict schedule of events for the June 7 visit and incorporated a four-and-a-half-mile route timed perfectly between 10:21 and 10:49 a.m. The schedule informed spectators so they could claim their viewpoints accordingly. It even provided "hints for seeing the royal party," including standing at "the northerly end of the route ... to obtain the best view of Their Majesties, as the space is less likely to be congested." The expectation was that London would be flooded with two hundred thousand visitors from surrounding areas as well as thousands of residents.[36] Organizers provided community groups such as veterans, Boy Scouts, and school children with designated spaces along the route, often enabling them to get the best views of the event.[37] Because the royal tour was declared a holiday, only one thousand Londoners had to sacrifice their view of the royals to maintain their duties as hospital workers, firemen, and Bell telephone operators.[38]

Other Canadians with means could afford to claim their view by purchasing tickets. In Toronto, tickets for bleacher seats and window space along the twenty-eight-mile route sold for one to fifty dollars, depending on the quality and duration of the view of the royal couple.[39] In London, one party rented a private property along the route for one hundred dollars, and the owner had already sold out of reservations a month before the tour.[40] The York Hotel offered Londoners a "20-minute view" of the royals for three dollars per spot on their grandstand.[41] An entrance ticket to the London Municipal Offices for June 7, Royal Visit Day, is inscribed with the name "Mr. Calvin Hodgins." The stipulations on the ticket – it was only valid for admission until 10:00 a.m. and only at the rear entrance – suggest that Hodgins was not an employee and purchased the ticket to access a window space to view the procession. Hodgins, born in 1883 and raised in London, was the son of a labourer moulder. By the age of seventeen, he had become a labourer and bookkeeper. At the time of the royal tour, he was fifty-six. Although of a working-class or lower-middle background, Hodgins felt compelled to pay a likely considerable sum to claim his own view of the King and Queen.[42] The ticket's number, "20," equally illustrates Hodgins' enthusiasm to claim his view. While age (children's groups and veterans) and wealth (the ability to purchase a view) guaranteed some access to a view of the royal couple, most Canadians were forced to rely on careful planning and stamina. The huge crowds that showed up for the royal processions are evidence of high-level consumption of the tour.

From coast to coast, Canadians prepared themselves for the arrival of Their Majesties by decorating the streets; devising viewing plans; reviewing the strict city regulations for parking, traffic, and pedestrians; and consuming media coverage in anticipation of the royal arrival. By decorating city streets, residents created a space of patriotism, hospitality, and enthusiasm for the monarchy. A month before the royal visit, the city of London, Ontario, started "dressing up streets" – erecting new street signs, repainting fire hydrants, improving roads and railway crossings, and hanging bunting, flags, and shields.[43] London's streets, like those in cities across the nation, turned from grey buildings and green trees to vibrant reflections of red, white, and blue. One seven-year-old girl in Sioux Lookout, Ontario, even learned to walk on a twelve-foot pair of stilts to claim the best view of the royal couple.[44] So anxious were Canadians to claim their space that thousands journeyed into cities or camped out overnight to secure a viewing spot.

Forging a strong connection between the monarchs and Canada's future, children were encouraged to consume the tour, and many created their own mementos. Although children might not have purchased commemorative items, they were encouraged to participate actively and to create a personal relationship with the monarch by creating their own mementos, reaching out to the royal couple, and writing their own narratives of the events. In preparation for Their Majesties' arrival, children across the country received lessons on the monarchy. One class in Sarnia, Ontario, even made a large card the size of a table for the King and Queen. The moment students lined up in the classroom to sign the card was encapsulated in a photograph. The card signing was evidently part of the lesson, as flags hang on the chalkboard, framing a "GR" symbol above "Welcome" and a Union Jack shield. A portrait of the King and Queen was also displayed to help students identify their monarchs.[45]

Eight-year-old Basil Hepplestall was fortunate enough to see, speak to, and touch the Queen in Washago, Ontario. Hepplestall was lifted up to the back of the royal train to give the Queen an album made by students from Washago School for the royal princesses. Not only did the Queen thank the boy, but she caringly wrapped her arm around him as he clung to the outside of the train railing.[46] At each stop along the tour route, children were taken to viewing points, given flags, and instructed to sing songs such as "God Save the King." In London, Ontario, children were even given a special pin with a picture of the King and Queen.[47] After experiencing the visit, some youth clearly felt compelled to form their own narrative of the event in their school yearbooks. Students at the boys' boarding school, St. Andrew's College, in Aurora, Ontario, crafted a two-page article titled "The Royal Visit" in their yearbook. It is highly likely that the students attended the Toronto parade and, for them, the tour represented didactically the "ideal of Democracy": "The acclaim of a democratic nation for its democratic rulers is a fitting tribute to the freedom, independence and security of our great British Empire, of which Canada and her peoples are proud to form a part."[48] Meanwhile, at Branksome Hall, a girls' school in Toronto, students commemorated the royal tour by planting two beautiful spruce trees in the front of the school and recording the event in their yearbook. Not simply a physical reminder of the royal visit, the trees were supposed to inspire the girls with "the spirit of loyalty and good-will."[49] Like adults, Canadian children claimed their own role in the tour. Yet, for children, the tour also became a cultural exchange as they made mementos to give to the King and Queen and reflected on the experience in a way that emphasized their willing participation in the imperial relationship.

News media also made the tour accessible to Canadians, regardless of their physical access to the festivities, through radio broadcasts and print reporting. By methodologically shifting our view to examine the media coverage of the tour, the reception of media, and individuals' films and scrapbooks, it is possible to capture the alternative ways Canadians mediated their own versions of the historic event. Traversing ten thousand miles across five time zones over the course of a month made the CBC's ninety-one broadcasts a major accomplishment.[50] Most broadcasts were bilingual, and the royal arrival in Quebec alone required thirty engineers and eighteen commentators (nine French and nine English speakers). The total cost for radio coverage of the tour amounted to approximately $100,000.[51] The broadcasts, however, meant that Canadians were able to participate throughout the duration of the tour rather than for just one day, which would have been the case if their town or city was a tour stop. For those distanced from the route and unable to travel to see a royal "stop," radio enabled Canadians to bring the tour into their homes. The RCA Victor Company proclaimed the CBC's "broadcasts of Royal Visit to be Greatest Radio Event in History of Canada" and that their new model of radios would enable Canadians to "follow their majesties across Canada."[52] By listening, Canadians could be transported from their living rooms across the country, to every stop along the route. One broadcast, transmitted as the royal party arrived in Winnipeg, spoke of spectators being drenched by a heavy rainstorm yet noted that "people [were] suffering it gladly." The broadcaster used imagery to share the sight: "The view from this point is a fine one. The parliament buildings are located in a park, the lawns are beautifully kept." Interrupted by an eruption of cheers, the broadcaster himself became elated, exclaiming, "Here they are. They're out now on the balcony."[53] The sights of cities and landscapes were shared with the nation, and listeners were able to learn about parts of the country they had never been able to visit. Through the medium of radio, Canadians accompanied the royals as tourists themselves.

On May 24, 1939, the King's official birthday, the King made his longest radio broadcast, and it was shared around the Empire. Hearing the King speak and, later, on the last day of the tour, hearing the Queen speak delighted Canadians and fostered a deeper connection to the monarchy, a hoped-for result of the tour. Anxious to catch the last sounds of the tour on June 16, three thousand people "jammed" the intersection of York and King Streets in Toronto to catch the monarchs' last broadcast on Canadian soil. The *Globe and Mail* noted: "The rumble of street cars was the only noise to be heard as the King began his brief but moving message ... there were many wet eyes among the densely packed throngs ... then came the brief address of the Queen. Cheers went up in a mighty roar." The article concluded by recounting the story of an elderly couple who remained standing underneath the loudspeaker for fear that they might miss a final word. When it ended, the woman, with tears in her eyes, turned to her companion and said, "That's all."[54] In a letter to the editor, *Globe and Mail* reader Florence Burns Cashion commended the broadcast for striking "the imagination of the people."[55]

Some Canadians with means and access were able to create their own record of the royal tour through film. Cinematography is a possessive activity; those behind the lens subjectively choose what to capture and the narrative they wish to create. Even if little is known about the author of a film, the content reveals something about what the recorder wanted to capture. As public celebrations, processions during the royal tour involved other participating Canadians, and they were frequently captured on film, sometimes unsuspectingly. These films suggest that Canadians were struck by the cult of celebrity, but they also used the opportunity to capture local and regional identities. Film footage of the royal tour captured by the National Film Board and British Pathé were well crafted to emphasize the importance and symbolism of the tour. The Pathé clip, "The Royal Tour in Western Canada," for instance, proclaimed that the tour had exemplified the "vastness of the Dominions" and the "unity of all nationalities under the British flag."[56]

Home footage more accurately reflected the viewpoints of individual Canadians. In 2013, the University of Manitoba Archives acquired films of the Winnipeg royal procession from an auction house that had purchased them as part of the estate of Rudolph Storch. Storch had graduated from the University of Manitoba in 1927 and became a teacher and, later, vice-principal of various Winnipeg schools. He recorded the royal procession in his role as teacher. Of the approximately eight minutes of footage over two films, only twenty seconds record the procession and catch a clear view of the King and Queen. The remainder captures students from Cecil Rhodes School lined up along Sherbrook Avenue. While the objective was most certainly to film Their Majesties to capture their images for posterity, Storch also took the opportunity to emphasize the children's role as spectators of a historic event. By focusing on the students, filming them walking, lining up for buses, and waiting curbside for the procession, Storch offered the students the opportunity to express their own agency. While younger children stared blankly into the camera's direction (perhaps it was their first experience being filmed), waved their flags, or smiled while remaining in their positions, older children displayed greater autonomy, playing up to the camera, merrily waving their hats, making silly faces, or joking around with one another. As Storch filmed the crowds dispersing after the procession, he revealed the vast number of people who, even on a residential street, had gathered to catch their own view of Their Majesties.[57]

A two-minute clip from Burnaby, British Columbia, intended to record the King and Queen's procession, likewise captures residents preparing to claim their own view: a bus arrives with people, individuals gather on the streets, girls sit on a blanket on the curbside, and two small children carry chairs. In the film, the cinematographer turns to a banner that reads "The Oak Salutes You" then to a man walking in a garden and, finally, to the procession. The King raises his hand as the procession passes in front of the camera. While the view of Their Majesties lasts only five seconds, somehow the cameraman managed to reposition himself further along the procession among much larger crowds and to catch another sight of the King and Queen, this time for only four seconds. The film ends with a view of a massive traffic jam of cars, decorated with flags and trying to return home. That this film is housed at the City of Burnaby Archives is fortunate, because the man behind the lens was fifty-two-year-old, British-born Andrew Digney.[58] Digney was the man walking in the gardens, and the "Oak" referenced in the welcome sign was his theatre.[59] While Digney wanted to capture priceless views of the royals, he also wanted to ensure that he embedded himself within the narrative.

Although unidentified, the cinematographer of another film recorded in British Columbia created a different kind of narrative. The film captures a remarkable view of the King and Queen as they drive through a rural area, so close that the Queen's pearl necklace and broach are distinguishable. The film includes a more obstructed view of Their Majesties, this time recorded from a crowded Vancouver street, but it is followed by another clear view, now of the King's face, as the royals drive down another rural road. The film captures three young girls in traditional Japanese dress holding Union Jacks and then pans to a view of a bridge, the mountains, and glistening water as the royal boat sails for Victoria. The cinematographer used the film not only to capture views of Their Majesties and enthusiastic crowds but also to reflect regional pride by capturing the scenic and identifiable natural landscape of British Columbia. Despite being from different parts of the country, these films illustrate the desire of Canadians to capture a view of the King and Queen to create a permanent record of the tour and Their Majesties.[60]

Canadians also used scrapbooks as a creative medium through which individuals could construct their own narrative of the royal tour. Although scrapbooks do not usually record their author, scrapbooking is a traditionally middle-class activity for females to record family events.[61] By using a family-oriented medium, scrapbookers were in some sense claiming the King and Queen as part of their own family as they collected, clipped, and compiled their volumes. Unlike claiming a view of the monarchs in a procession, creating a scrapbook did not depend on proximity to a stop on the royal tour. Although the examples offered here are from cities Their Majesties visited, Canadians throughout the country could have made their own scrapbooks from newspaper coverage of the tour. In addition, Canadian magazines such as the *Star Weekly* and *The Standard* provided large, glossy, and sometimes coloured photos perfect for scrapbooking. Even if scrapbooking was traditionally a middle-class endeavour, with newspapers the activity was accessible to all social standings and, more importantly, all ages.

Some scrapbookers started compiling a scrapbook before the royal tour. One of a two-volume series of scrapbooks commences with the death of King George V in 1936; empty pages silently point towards the abdication of Edward VIII. The second volume (with matching cover), however, records the royal tour, commencing with Their Majesties' departure from London. Analyzing the scrapbook alongside original copies of the magazines and newspapers illustrates that the author exercised agency to create their own narrative of events by organizing clippings thematically rather than retaining the associations within the original publications. For instance, rather than including a photo of the King and Queen aboard their ship, which was printed below a photo of Their Majesties' departure from Westminster Bridge in the May 27 edition of the *Star Weekly*, the scrapbooker chose to pair the Westminster photo thematically with one of Their Majesties leaving Buckingham Palace. The photo of Their Majesties aboard the ship, however, is recycled and used in the pages that follow, where the scrapbooker records the royals' voyage to Canada. The scrapbook ends with events in Quebec City, yet eight clippings about the journey through Quebec tucked in latter pages suggest that the scrapbooker intended to continue her record. Unfortunately, the scrapbooker removed all the clippings' dates and names in the volumes. Those that can be sourced came from the *Star Weekly* and the *Globe and Mail*. As both publications had wide distribution, it is difficult to establish exactly where the individual lived.[62]

Scrapbookers sought to create a personal reflection of the tour. On the cover of another scrapbook, the scrapbooker pasted a large photo of the King and Queen in regal clothing, standing in front of Canada's Houses of Parliament. The scrapbooker's hope for the monarchy was reflected in the title, "Long May

They Reign!" Like the previous scrapbook, this scrapbooker began their narrative of the tour with clippings of the royal family, Their Majesties' departure from London, and stops from Quebec City to Three Rivers, Montreal, and Ottawa. Uniquely, on the inside page, the scrapbooker used a ruler to pencil out in block letters "ROYAL." However, the "Y" has been partially erased and is waiting to be redrawn, suggesting that the scrapbooker had not completed their creation. To correspond with the decorations adorning city streets across the country, the scrapbooker painted red, white, and blue stripes to resemble patriotic bunting. These creative additions to the scrapbook suggest that its creator may have been young, perhaps even an adolescent. That a front cover of *The Masonic Sun*, displaying the King wearing his Masonic apron and gloves, is tucked inside the book suggests that the young scrapbooker may have obtained the cover from their father. Regardless, the scrapbooker sought to produce a narrative of the tour that captured and emphasized patriotic decorations and celebrations.[63]

A scrapbooker from London, Ontario, took a different approach. Rather than displaying a photo of the Their Majesties, the cover depicts the French flag and Union Jack draped behind a bulldog with "World Events Scrap Book" written above; the tour was not just a historic event for the British world but for the *whole* world. The scrapbook's coverage begins late, commencing in Toronto on May 23, a whole week after the royal arrival. The majority of the scrapbook relies on *London Free Press* articles to chronicle the preparations for and visit of the King and Queen to London, including images of the crowds and decorated spaces in London as a way to show civic pride. However, the scrapbooker's interest in the tour did not wane upon the monarchs' departure; they continued to include clippings from other tour stops, even in the United States and, finally, Halifax. For the scrapbooker, the tour was a national event but also a world event, especially important for Anglo-American relations.[64]

A second scrapbook from London provides a nearly complete narrative of the tour. Purpose-made and bearing a painted portrait of the King, Queen, and two Princesses on the cover, the scrapbook commences with five pages of coloured images of the royal family. Even though the royal tour had already stopped in Montreal and Toronto and on the West Coast, the book is dominated by coverage of the London visit. Photographs clipped from newspapers show the royal couple inspecting the Royal Canadian Regiment's guard on their arrival in London, visiting with local veterans, and passing in front of the offices of the *London Free Press*. Only after coverage of London does the scrapbooker include clippings of other tour stops, disregarding chronology to make London the most important stop on the tour. The name "Helen," written in cursive in the top-left corner of the front cover, hints at the author. The slant of the writing suggests that the name might have been written for the scrapbooker, perhaps by a mother. This may explain why the first clippings of the tour in the scrapbook was a collage of photos from Londoners who came out to see the procession. Instead of starting with a photo of London's decorated and crowded city hall, with the King and Queen in front (which is utilized on the second page), the scrapbooker chooses to begin the narrative with an image of Londoners. One photo in the collage shows five women and one young girl waiting at a fence. The young girl is identified as Helen Rodger, standing beside her mother, Mrs. J. E. Rodger. Although this may be a coincidence, the name on the front cover and placement of the photo reasonably suggests that the girl in the photo, Helen Rodger, may be the creator of the scrapbook.[65] If the scrapbook did belong to Helen Rodger, it clearly illustrates that Canadian children also consumed the royal tour and used scrapbooks to create their own narratives.

On September 3, 1939, mere weeks after Their Majesties returned from their Canadian tour, Britain declared war on Germany. Exercising its autonomy, Canada followed Britain a week later; as a sovereign Dominion, Canada chose to fight *with* the Empire. To solely attribute the declaration to the impact of the royal tour would be naive, yet the royal visit did stir up Canada's British heritage and strengthen public interest in the monarchy and Canadians' ties with Britain. Importantly, Canadians could consume the royal tour and engaged with *their* King and Queen irrespective of age, sex, ethnicity, class, or location.[66] Rather than simply ascribing to the nationally projected narrative of the tour, individual Canadians alone decided what to record, how to record it, and how to capture and bring a symbol of the monarchy into their own homes. Canadians exercised agency in choosing their mode of participation in the royal visit and crafted their own narratives of the tour. Commemorative items, radio broadcasts, mail, parades, films, and scrapbooks were created and consumed by individual Canadians to satisfy a desire to own a piece of the historic event and the royals themselves. In these personalized mementos, Canadians created narratives that included themselves and their local communities. For many Canadians, no longer were King George VI and Queen Elizabeth remote figures living in distant palaces; they had, over the course of a month, become humanized, kind, beautiful individuals who wanted to see Canada and Canadians as much as Canadians wanted to see them. In that regard, the royal tour fulfilled one of the organizers' goals. Rather than viewing them as subjects, Their Majesties saw Canadians as welcoming hosts. It is little wonder, then, that upon the outbreak of war, thousands of Canadians across the country publicly called for British children to be evacuated to safe homes in Canada.[67] That over four thousand British evacuees arrived in Canada in 1940 and were feted for the next five years was an immediate expression of the sentiments of sovereignty, patriotism, and loyalty that were excited during the royal tour.

Notes

1 "The King and His People," *Globe and Mail*, June 24, 1939.
2 Much more has been written on the American leg of the tour. See Tony McCulloch, "Roosevelt, Mackenzie King and the British Royal Visit to the USA in 1939," *London Journal of Canadian Studies* 23 (2008): 81–104. A detailed popular book on Canada is Tom MacDonnell's *Daylight upon Magic* (Toronto: MacMillan, 1989).
3 Heather Metcalfe, "It's All about War: Canadian Opinion and the Canadian Approach to International Relations, 1935–1939" (PhD diss., University of Toronto, 2009), 35.
4 Simon Potter, "The BBC, the CBC, and the 1939 Royal Tour of Canada," *Cultural and Social History* 3, 4 (2006): 424.
5 Mary Vipond, "The Royal Tour of 1939 as a Media Event," *Canadian Journal of Communications* 35, 1 (2010): 149.
6 Molly Pulver Ungar, "Nationalism on the Menu: Three Banquets on the 1939 Royal Tour," in *Edible Histories, Cultural Politics: Towards a Canadian Food History*, ed. Franca Iacovetta, Valerie J. Korinek, and Marlene Epp (Toronto: University of Toronto Press, 2012), 351–58.
7 J. William Galbraith, "Fiftieth Anniversary of the 1939 Royal Visit," *Parliamentary Review* 12, 3 (1989): 7.
8 "Behind the Diary," Library and Archives Canada (accessed February 17, 2016), https://www.collectionscanada.gc.ca/king/023011-1070.06-e.html.
9 Galbraith, "Fiftieth Anniversary," 7.
10 MacDonnell, *Daylight upon Magic*, 9.
11 Ibid., 14.
12 For more on the 1860 royal tour of Canada, see Ian Radforth, *Royal Spectacle: The 1860 Visit of the Prince of Wales to Canada and the United States* (Toronto: University of Toronto Press, 2004).
13 Laura Nym Mayhall, "The Prince of Wales versus Clark Gable," *Cultural and Social History* 4, 4 (2007): 529–43.
14 Ibid., 531.
15 David Cannadine, "The Context, Performance and Meaning of Ritual," in *The Invention of Tradition*, ed. Eric Hobsbawm and Terence Ranger (Cambridge: Cambridge University Press, 1992), 101–64.
16 Canadian National Railways/Canadian Pacific Railway, *Visit of Their Majesties the King and Queen to Canada: Itinerary*, 1939, 10.
17 "King Moved by Display of Loyalty: Responds in Clear and Heartfelt Tones and in Both Languages to Luncheon Addresses," *Globe and Mail*, May 18, 1939.
18 Jacques Lavoie, "The King and Queen of Hearts," *Rotunda* 31, 3 (1999): 14.
19 "Alfred Meakin Astoria Marigold English Plates," eBay (accessed February 24, 2016), http://www.ebay.ca/itm/alfred-meakin-astoria-marigold-english-plates-cup-king-george-queen-elizabeth.
20 Lavoie, "The King and Queen of Hearts," 14.
21 "Medals to Mark Royal Visit," *London Free Press*, April 27, 1939.
22 "1939 Royal Visit (Birk's)," eBay (accessed February 25, 2016), http://www.ebay.ca/itm/1939-Royal-Visit-Birks.
23 "Maddocks 'Royal Blue' Dinnerware Ensemble," *London Free Press*, May 24, 1939.
24 Lavoie, "The King and Queen of Hearts," 14, and "Concentrated Super Suds," *London Free Press*, May 11, 1939.
25 Jonathan Vance, *Maple Leaf Empire: Canada, Britain, and Two World Wars* (Don Mills, ON: Oxford University Press, 2012), 145.

26   "Royal Train Letters Reach 70,000 Total," *London Free Press,* May 11, 1939.

27   "Canada, Voters Lists, 1935, 1945, A. Brayley," *Ancestry,* https://www.ancestry.ca.

28   "1939 Royal Visit Train," eBay (accessed March 2, 2016), http://www.ebay.ca/itm/1939 -Royal-Visit-Train-RPO-Machine-Flag-Cancel-Beaver-Crown-Bilingual-CachetEbay, and "Canada, Voters Lists, 1949, A. Gammell," *Ancestry,* https://www.ancestry.ca.

29   "Twins to Get Names of King and Queen," *London Free Press,* May 9, 1939.

30   "Classifieds," *Globe and Mail,* May 19, 1939.

31   "Burroughes," *London Free Press,* May 31, 1939.

32   "Classifieds," *Globe and Mail,* May 19, 1939.

33   "Royal Tour Gives Spurt to Business," *Globe and Mail,* June 17, 1939.

34   "Correspondence," *Globe and Mail,* May 30, 1939.

35   "Still Clings to Flower Leaving Platform at Sioux Lookout," *Globe and Mail,* June 5, 1939. Two ten-minute stops in Cornwall and Brockville scheduled for May 20 were cancelled to "give Their Majesties more opportunity for rest": "Cancel 2 Stops on Royal Trip," *London Free Press,* May 9, 1939.

36   "Stage Full Rehearsal for Royal Visit to London as Thousands Expected," *London Free Press,* June 5, 1939.

37   "Royal Visits," box L7, London Public Library, London Room.

38   "Welcome to London," *London Free Press,* June 3, 1939.

39   "Royal Route 'Bleachers' Becomes Big Business," *London Free Press,* May 11, 1939.

40   "Rule to Include School Pupils," *London Free Press,* May 11, 1939.

41   "20 Minute View of the King and Queen," *London Free Press,* June 2, 1939.

42   "1901 Census of Canada, Calvin Hodgins," *Ancestry,* https://www.ancestry.ca.

43   "Rule to Include School Pupils," *London Free Press,* May 11, 1939.

44   "See Royalty from atop Stilts," *London Free Press,* June 5, 1939.

45   "Students in Classroom in 1939," Flickr (accessed February 25, 2016), https://www.flickr.com/photos/34370769.

46   "Boy Clings to Royal Train," *London Free Press,* June 6, 1939.

47   John McFerran, *Tecumseh Public School, 1914–1988* (n.p.: n.p., 1989).

48   St. Andrew's College, *St. Andrew's College Review* (Aurora, ON: St. Andrew's College, 1939): 20–21. Internet Archive, https://archive.org/details/msstandrewscolle1939stanuoft.

49   Branksome Hall, *The Slogan* (Toronto: Branksome Hall, 1939): 19. Internet Archive, https://archive.org/details/theslogan1931bran.

50   Potter, "The BBC," 438.

51   Ibid., 433.

52   "Be Ready with a New 1939 RCA Victor Radio," *Globe and Mail,* May 16, 1939.

53   "1939 Royal Tour Rolls through Winnipeg," CBC Radio Special, May 24, 1939, CBC Digital Archives, http://www.cbc.ca/archives/entry/royal-tour-rolls-through-winnipeg.

54   "3,000 Jam Intersection to Hear Royal Farewell," *Globe and Mail,* June 16, 1939.

55   "Thrilled by a Voice," *Globe and Mail,* June 22, 1939.

56   British Pathé, "The Royal Tour in Western Canada," 1939, http://www.britishpathe.com/video/the-royal-tour-of-western-canada/query/royal+tour+canada.

57   "U of M Archives Releases Historical Film of 1939 Royal Visit," *UM Today News,* May 20, 2014, http://news.umanitoba.ca/university-of-manitoba-archives-releases-historical -film-of-1939-royal-visit/; and Wayne Chan, "Rare Footage of the 1939 Royal Visit," *Manitoba History* 75 (2014): 59–61.

58   "Royal Visit," 1939, Heritage Burnaby, https://search.heritageburnaby.ca/permalink/archivevideo85203.

59   "The Great Days of the Movies," *Brandon Sun,* September 29, 1969.

60 "1939 Royal Visit to Vancouver," *BC History*, YouTube, https://www.youtube.com/watch?v=CFeU8CP7A3U.

61 For more on scrapbooks, see Glen McGillivray, ed., *Scrapbooks, Snapshots and Memorabilia: Hidden Archives of Performance* (New York: Peter Lang, 2011).

62 Two-volume scrapbook, Ley and Lois Smith War, Memory and Popular Culture Research Collection, University of Western Ontario.

63 Single-volume scrapbook, Ley and Lois Smith War, Memory and Popular Culture Research Collection, University of Western Ontario.

64 Scrapbook, box L7, London Public Library, London Room.

65 Scrapbook, author's collection.

66 Much more could be written on participation of different ethnic groups in the tour.

67 Claire Halstead, "'Dangers Behind, Pleasures Ahead': British-Canadian Identity and the Evacuation of British Children to Canada during the Second World War," *British Journal of Canadian Studies* 27, 2 (2014): 163–80.

Part 3
Hardly British

7

For King or Country?
Quebec, the Empire, and the First World War

Geoff Keelan

THE OUTBREAK OF war in August 1914 was a momentous event for Canadians. The world suddenly seemed a lot closer to Canadians in the young British Dominion. In Parliament, their political leaders pledged that the nation would support their European allies against the menace of Germany and Austria-Hungary. The global nature of the conflict became quickly apparent, as Africa, the Middle East, and Asia became sideshows to the brutal war unfolding across Europe. Nations large and small joined the Allies and the Central powers, and each in turn sent out a national *cri de coeur* for their citizens and soldiers: fight in this war, fight for your nation, and we will all be the stronger for it. This appeal to a national collective resonated in European nation-states, where societal mobilization proved the power of national communities to fight in the all-encompassing total war of 1914–18.[1] The same process occurred in Canada, but as a settler colony of the British Empire, it was unclear if Canadian appeals to fight for the nation referred to the contiguous provinces and territories that formed the Dominion of Canada or to the larger collective of Greater Britain, signifying a fight for the Empire. This geographic distinction raised deeper questions about whether Canada was a monocultural, anglophone nation within the Empire or a bicultural and bilingual one that reflected its two founding European cultures: France and Britain.

Ringing the bell of nationalism inhibited coherent opposition to the war among the belligerent nations in 1914. In France, the *union sacrée* symbolized a French determination to oppose the oncoming German menace that super-seded normal political concerns.[2] The Spirit of 1914 took hold of German citizens, who entered the war believing their country was threatened by Russia and its Western allies. *Feinde Ringsum*, "Enemies Surround Us," was the motto of the war.[3] On August 4, British opinion supported intervention, and crowds cheered news of Britain's declaration of war. After news of the British retreat from Mons on August 25 and accounts of German atrocities in occupied Belgium, British enlistment surged alongside support for the war.[4] In the young Dominion of Canada, it was no different. At least, a survey of the public sphere suggested that Canada stood united in support of the British Empire and fighting the European war, though it is probable that the most vocal outbursts were from British immigrants to the former colony.[5] It is more likely that although some immigrant and native-born Canadians celebrated the chance to fight for the Empire, as was popularly recorded in newspapers and in Parliament, a silent majority acceded to the conflict as their dissent was erased from the historical record. Regardless, a shift occurred in how Canadians understood their place in the world.[6] Nowhere was that more apparent than in French Canada, where previous imperial entanglements had roused serious opposition.[7] In the first months of the war, however, French Canada joined English Canada in supporting the war. The divide between French and English Canadians that had characterized the half century since Confederation seemed momentarily healed in the first few months of the war, but no one knew if it could last. Could the war's appeal to a national purpose unite Canada's two communities of English and French?

The last two decades had been particularly tense. Although Wilfrid Laurier became the country's first French Canadian prime minister in 1896, his tenure was marked by walking a middle ground between the two sides of Canadian identity – imperialism and nationalism. The political ideology of Canadian imperialism emerged in the late nineteenth century as the British debate over the purpose and utility of its Empire spread to Canada.[8] Canadian imperialists believed that participation in the British Empire would ensure Canada's future prosperity. They fashioned their own ideological worldview centred on a beneficial relationship between Canada and Britain, creating what Carl Berger termed a "nationalism unto itself."[9] In opposition to imperialism, Canadian nationalists desired either greater autonomy within the Empire or complete independence. Its chief proponents, English Canadian lawyer J.S. Ewart and French Canadian politician-cum-journalist Henri Bourassa, argued that separation was the natural path for the country to follow.[10] During his time as prime minister, between 1896 and 1911, Laurier sat perilously between the two as he balanced his own belief in a cautious progression away from empire with a national imperative to preserve unity between Canada's two cultural communities.[11]

Imperialists and nationalists disagreed over many issues on the political battlefield, ranging from education to economic policy, but it was imperial defence that set the stage for Canada's entry into the First World War in 1914. Britain faced a changing international situation in the late nineteenth century as new powers such as Russia, Germany, and the United States all vied for global power. In response, the Empire asked more of its Dominions and colonies than it ever had. Thus, when Britain declared war on the Boer Republics of present-day South Africa on October 11, 1899, it asked the Dominions to come to its aid.

While imperial-minded Canadians affirmed that they had a duty to answer the Empire's call, nationalists believed that Canada had no reason to send troops to far away Africa for British colonial interests. The most vocal critic was Liberal MP, Henri Bourassa, who argued that any involvement in imperial affairs that were not in Canada's direct concern would set a dangerous precedent of providing soldiers for a conflict that did not directly involve Canadians. He distinguished two key problems with Canadian participation: a question of fact and a question of law. Not only was Britain's justification for the war faulty, if not immoral and unjust, but Canada had no legal obligation to follow its lead.[12] Bourassa perceived that British demands had resulted from an unstable international situation that would not improve and a failed global policy, compelling them to turn towards the colonies and Dominions for help. In the future, he predicted, Britain would enter other wars that it could not fight without help, necessitating further Dominion contributions. Coming to Britain's aid now would effectively result in colonial conscription for British interests.[13] Laurier ignored Bourassa's warning and sent Canadian volunteers to the Boer Republics as a necessary compromise between English Canadian demands for action and the nationalists' reluctance. While the Boer War was not quite a prelude to the First World War, as historians once believed, it did prove to be a catalyst for Henri Bourassa's political career.[14] His open dissent led him to leave the Liberal Party in 1899 to sit as an independent and to seek out other allies who also believed in his nationalist cause.

Bourassa was undoubtedly the most prominent nationalist and Canada's most famous critic of the British Empire and imperialism. Bourassa helped create the Ligue nationaliste along with Olivar Asselin, Armand Lavergne, Jules Fournier, and Omar Héroux in 1903. Although he would never officially join the league, Bourassa still served as its de facto leader.[15] Together, the founders expressed a uniquely French Canadian form of Canadian nationalism, *nationalisme*. Historian Yvan Lamonde has termed their ideas a "dérivatif nationaliste" of Laurier's liberalism, since they, too, supported the collective national values of equality, democracy, and economic intervention.[16] Although they founded a primarily a Quebec-based movement, the nationalistes possessed a coherent set of economic and political ideas about the future of the Canadian nation.[17] In the context of imperialism and nationalism, the nationalistes were committed to a confederation in which French Canada could coexist with English Canada in a bicultural and bilingual compact. French Canada was the natural vehicle for the nationalistes' ideas. "Les Canadiens-français du peuple n'ont d'autre patrie que le Canada," Bourassa wrote in 1903. "Ils sont prêts à lui rendre tout ce qu'ils lui doivent; mais n'estimant rien devoir à l'Angleterre ni à aucun autre pays, ils n'en attendent rien."[18] Thus, imperialism was antithetical to the French Canadian experience in North America. It called on and reinforced cultural connections that simply did not exist for the descendants of French colonial endeavours.

Calls to defend the Empire rang particularly hollow for French Canadians. During the ongoing debate over the creation of a Canadian navy and the subsequent 1911 election, the nationalistes again confronted the question of whether Canada was obligated to join imperial commitments. In 1909, Britain feared that German increases in ship production might one day overcome Britain's naval supremacy. In Ottawa, the Opposition Conservatives demanded that ships or money be offered to Britain, but Laurier refused the gesture as an expensive "imperial obligation." On January 12, 1910, Laurier presented the Naval Service Bill in the House of Commons, proposing a small fleet of ships – five cruisers and six destroyers.[19] Seeking to still the fears of nationalistes, Laurier promised that only Parliament could commit the fleet to war. Yet the nationalistes were not convinced that Laurier's guarantee had much value, especially after he proclaimed in the House of Commons that "when Britain is at war, Canada is at war; there is no distinction."[20] It was clear that if Britain went to war, Parliament would volunteer the naval force without question.

This fact was not lost on Bourassa and the nationalistes, who claimed that Canada would again have no choice but to contribute to British military endeavours. In January 1910, Bourassa dismissed the possibility of naval conscription but emphasized that the Canadian *people* and not solely their government ought to decide whether to commit its forces to a British war.[21] Things changed during the crucial 1910 Arthabaska by-election and the 1911 federal election, when the nationalistes told voters that the Naval Act represented unquestioning involvement in imperial wars for the Canadian citizen, that conscription was a natural by-product of Laurier's continuing decision to side with British imperial policy.[22] Laurier's acceptance of imperialism became the primary focus of the nationalistes' attacks against him. Their determination to supplant the Liberals' power in Quebec even saw them ally with Quebec's federal Conservatives in the belief that a bloc of "conservative-nationaliste" MPs could assure parliamentary representation for their concerns.[23] The Liberals lost the Drummond-Arthabaska by-election and the federal election the next year, but the true impact of the nationaliste campaign is uncertain. Historians Patrice Dutil and David Mackenzie point out that 71 seats, a third of the 221 total, were decided by less than 5 percent of the vote in 1911.[24] Most Canadians who had voted Liberal once voted Liberal again. Almost all of the Quebec MPs elected as conservative-nationalistes (save one, Paul-Émile Lamarche) joined the new Conservative government and followed the party line. Bourassa had merely helped to place Robert Borden and his imperialist allies in power.[25] The question of Canadian obligations to Britain no doubt convinced some Québécois to change.

The two elections serve as a backdrop for 1914, when French Canadians once more had to assess the legitimacy of Britain's demands for Canadian help. The outbreak of war in August 1914 seemed to overwhelm older concerns about French Canada's political leanings as the public sphere erupted with French Canadian commentators voicing their support. Crowds gathered to hear news of the declaration of war on August 4.[26] A reader of urban newspapers would have seen pages of articles endorsing the defence of Britain, France, and Belgium. These editorials offered support for Canada's two motherlands, though primarily France over Britain, but a headline from Quebec's largest daily newspaper, *La Presse*, epitomized attitudes in the province: "Pour la France et L'Empire."[27] Other important stories, such as the need to defend Beligum appeared, especially after the burning of Louvain by German forces on August 25, but almost every article emphasized the war as a moment of national unity.[28] *Le Pays* reached out to English Canadians to underline this point, translating an article into English:

> The very fact of seeing English and French united upon the field of battle; the simple fact of the English being excited on receiving intelligence of French victories, and of us rejoicing on the receipt of news of the success of English arms, cannot help but cement an everlasting union between the two races who populate our country. This cannot help but lead to greater esteem, union, goodwill, toleration, as well as greater affection between the English and French speaking peoples of Canada ... If the two peoples are drawn closer together in a lasting friendship, then this was will appear less savage to us, less bloody, much less horrible.[29]

In contrast to the Boer War and the creation of the Canadian navy, the wave of public enthusiasm that swept through Quebec mirrored the rest of Canada. In English Canada, the outpouring seemed natural. In Quebec, it suggested that imperialism had become an acceptable ideology – at least as much as it related to Canada's international obligations. Even though protecting France and Belgium had no direct link to imperialism, they nonetheless represented a justification of Canada's imperial relationship. In 1914, the Empire was worth defending, and few raised whether Canada ought to fight the war.

That attitude mirrored the impassioned speeches of political leaders. During the parliamentary session of August 19, the prime minister, Sir Robert Borden, and the Liberal leader, Sir Wilfrid Laurier, spoke of Canada's duty to join the war, defend Britain, and uphold Canada's honour. Laurier famously proclaimed on August 19, "When the call comes our answer goes at once ... 'Ready, aye, ready.'"[30] Borden declared that the Dominion had entered the war "for the cause of honour, to maintain solemn pledges, to uphold principles of liberty, to with-stand forces that would convert the world into an armed camp."[31] Thousands showed up at Parc Sohmer in Montreal on October 15 to hear speeches from some of the country's most famous French Canadians – including Quebec premier Lomer Gouin, Sir Wilfrid Laurier, Conservative MP Thomas Chase-Casgrain, and Liberal MP Rodolphe Lemieux – urging their comrades to enlist.[32] They were supporting Arthur Mignault, a Montreal doctor who had offered the government $50,000 to form a French Canadian battalion in September. With the enthusiastic support of *La Presse*, the campaign eventually helped form the only fully French-speaking unit of the war, the 22nd Battalion.[33] Throughout the public sphere, Canadians in English or French would have seen the same message in 1914: the war had to be fought, and Canadians were vital to ensuring it ended in victory.

Canada's war effort also received approval from the Catholic hierarchy. Since the mid-nineteenth century, the Catholic Church had been one of French Canada's most significant institutions. Catholicism was a crucial aspect of French Canadians' cultural identity.[34] In August 1914, the upper echelons of the church aligned themselves with English Canada and the federal govern-ment. The official organ of the church in Quebec, *L'Action Social*, moved to fully support the Canadian war effort. Its editor, Abbé Joseph Prio Arthur D'Amours, penned an editorial despite the absence of Cardinal Bégin (who was in Rome electing the successor to Pope Pius X). D'Amours's words repre-sented the voice of the church in Quebec. His support of imperialist arguments was absolute: "Nous avons le devoir de donner à l'Angleterre ce qu'elle a droit de nous réclamer en toute équité et toute justice, pour le maintien et la défense de l'Empire dont nous faisons partie comme colonie britannique."[35] The bishops of Quebec eventually released a pastoral letter on September 23 that echoed Amours words.[36] In October, they confirmed their support for the war, since "the destiny of every part of the Empire is bound up with the fate of her armies."[37] It is difficult to evaluate how much these displays influenced support for the war, but it certainly signalled the direction of the majority of Quebec's elite in 1914.

Among the traditional opponents to British wars – namely, the nationalistes – there was a crisis of faith over support for the war. Less mainstream elements, such as Quebec socialists, opposed the war from the beginning.[38] But they did so having already rejected what Bourassa termed the thousand ethnic, social, intellectual, and economic ties between Canada, Britain, and France.[39] Instead, the nationalistes had acknowledged these elements as intrinsic to the brand of Canadian nationalism they espoused. Unsurprisingly, the immensity of the conflict and the call to defend Britain and France caused disagreement among the movement's most prominent members, reflecting the war's impact on Quebec attitudes towards the Empire even among its harshest critics.

Bourassa initially supported moderate Canadian contributions in sharp contrast to his previous position on imperial conflicts. He took heed of Canadians' support for the war and offered his own cautious endorsement while promising to fulfill his duty to explore the unreported, the ignored, and the unpopular news of the war.[40] The war had, he believed, created a space for an intelligent critique that was not simply a criticism of Canada's participation. Bourassa was in German Alsace-Lorraine when the war broke out visiting Europe to study linguistic minorities. He fled first to Belgium, then to France, before returning safely across the Atlantic.[41] In Paris, he witnessed firsthand the union sacrée that united France against the invading enemy. In his first published editorial after his return to Canada, he praised the national purpose that brought together the disparate sides of French politics. Bourassa wished to see the same harmony in Canada.[42] If Canada's fighting for Britain fashioned a war effort that unified French and English Canadians at home and on the battlefield, then Bourassa was willing to accept fighting for the British Empire. Although other public commentators attacked Bourassa's initial reaction, on the ground he did not offer the total support demanded by the majority of the public sphere, it remains a brief moment of potential peace between the poles of nationalism and imperialism.

Others within the nationaliste movement questioned the paradoxical nature of Bourassa's position in 1914. Jules Fournier disagreed and remained loyal to previously established nationaliste views on the Empire. He opposed any participation in the war and openly condemned his leader for offering a nationalist critique of the war while supposedly supporting it.[43] In an unpublished article written in 1916 and aptly titled "La faillite (?) du nationalisme," Fournier summarized his rejection of Bourassa's equivocation.[44] By sanctioning imperialism, even in part, Bourassa was disavowing the movement itself. There was every reason in the world for Canada to abstain from the conflict, Fournier wrote, and nothing justified its participation as Bourassa argued in 1914.[45] Instead, Bourassa's vacillation between criticizing the war and ostensibly supporting it harmed their future goals.

Because Bourassa was the foremost voice of the nationalistes, his qualified support offers a glimpse into changing views on the British Empire in Quebec. The journalist dissected Britain's entry into the war and justifications of its actions in a five-part series. Titled "Une page d'histoire," each editorial examined the British *White Papers,* which contained Foreign Secretary Sir Edward Grey's communications with the great powers of Europe in July and early August. Bourassa explored the British refusal to go to war for Serbia in July and their attempts to persuade Germany that Britain would stay out of an eastern European war. As late as August 2, he noted, Britain had committed to defending its coasts from the German navy but not the protection of France or Russia. In his explanation, only the August 3 invasion of Belgium and King Albert I's request for British intervention had secured English entry into the war. Bourassa concluded that war with Germany had been unavoidable by August 4, given rising British sentiment and the threat that Germany posed to the English Channel.

His outline of English efforts to sidestep the conflict exudes admiration for Sir Edward Grey, whose diplomatic machinations revealed a foreign secretary who wanted to preserve peace only for Britain's benefit so that the country could enter the war under the most favourable circumstances. Bourassa invoked Grey's actions as a blunt refusal to compromise on issues of national self-interest. Grey was "courageux, inlassable, dont toute l'action n'est inspirée que par ce seul mobile: l'intérêt de *son* pays," Bourassa wrote.[46] Bourassa's articles portray Britain's entry into the war as a failure to secure British interests by avoiding the continental conflict. The declaration did not stem from a moral obligation to defend Belgium, as most other Canadians believed in 1914. Once it was clear that participation was necessary, Britain entered the war. The British declaration of war was an act of self-interest for Great Britain – a national policy that Bourassa wished to see in Canada.

British actions in 1914 allowed Bourassa to endorse the war because they were a rational foreign policy, unlike the colonial adventures he had once opposed. He argued that Canada ought to mirror British policy and adjust its involvement according to its national interests. He believed that, like their British counterparts, Canadians should have a clear vision of those interests and what they entailed. The nation of Canada should have no interest in European concerns, only national ones, just as Grey's careful manoeuvring for Britain had demanded the same distance. Defending Britain and France fell under national interests, but to follow the British example, Canadians ought to consider carefully the scale and extent of its contributions. As he promised, Bourassa wrote much about why Canada ought to do less for the war, even as he repeated that it was a worthwhile endeavour. Even though the chief nationaliste praised the war, the reaction among his critics proved that the intensity of the conflict allowed little room for anything but black-and-white interpretations.

Other criticisms of Bourassa reveal the intensity of support for the war in Quebec. Newspapers demanded total support for the Empire during wartime and discarded prewar understandings of Quebec's relationship to Canada. While Bourassa's critics agreed that Canada's interests lay in its historical and cultural

obligations to England (and France), they argued that those obligations super-
seded national ones rather than accented them, as Bourassa believed. *La Patrie,*
the second largest French-language newspaper in Montreal, responded to
Bourassa on August 31 and throughout the ensuing month. Its editors dismissed
the idea that England had acted out of self-interest in July and August, as
Bourassa alleged, and instead argued that England had saved the countries of
France and Belgium from the German menace. *La Patrie* also denied that the
war required a compromise between nationalism and imperialism.[47] Those
ideologies, it argued, represented positions that were no longer relevant during
the war. Its editors demanded the dismissal of divisions for the sake of political
unity and argued that Bourassa should abandon his partisan position.

Editorials in smaller papers, such as *Le Pays, Le Clairon,* and *Le Soleil,* mirrored those in the larger papers. To their French Canadian editors, Bourassa
was naively unaware of the seriousness of the European war and the consequences of defeat – he was a political agitator to be pitied.[48] Quebec's English-
language papers, such as Montreal's *Daily Mail* and the *Montreal Star,* also added
their voices, though in far stronger terms than did their French Canadian
counterparts. Later in September, a few presses tempered their criticism of
Bourassa. *Le Canada* responded reasonably by undertaking another interpretation of Grey's diplomacy, one that rejected Bourassa's arguments; *Le Pays*
defended the nationaliste chief's right to offer his opinion.[49] Yet these exceptions
were rare. Most newspapers continued their unequivocal support for the war
and their attacks on its only vocal critic. English Canadian newspapers were
even worse. They denounced Bourassa as a traitor, and the journalist faced an
unruly mob when he tried to deliver a speech about his views in Ottawa that
December.[50]

Criticisms of Bourassa foreshadowed the return of animosity between French
and English Canada that had marked the years before the war. The unity of 1914
did not last as Canadians gradually begun to understand the war through their
own specific cultural experiences. By the spring of 1915, the "Great Adventure"
of 1914 had been transformed into the "Great Crusade."[51] Canadian soldiers
experienced their first serious taste of trench warfare at Ypres in April. The use
of poison gas by the Germans at Ypres seemed to prove the uncivilized nature
of the enemy. The sinking of a civilian liner, the RMS *Lusitania,* by a German
U-boat in May further emphasized that belief. For English Canadians, these
events imbued their contributions to the war with new seriousness. Now, they
were fighting to save the world from an evil, militaristic Germany. For French
Canada, however, the first year of the war reminded them little of its significance
except that once again they were being asked to fight while being mistreated at
home. Ontario's Regulation 17, originally enacted in 1912, was targeted by French

Canadians still angry over its restrictions on French-language schooling in the province. During the war, it worked its way through the appeals process and turned into a rallying point for Franco-Ontarians and Québécois.[52] Growing hostility among Canadians also chipped away at the national purpose welcomed in the first months of the war. The works of anti-Quebec writer Robert Sellar, who accused French Canadians of being cowards who were letting English Canadians die in their place, continued to sell well.[53] Equally important, disaffected French Canadians were reading fewer and fewer positive stories about the war, while English Canadian stories cemented the belief that the war was necessary at any cost.[54] Two separate narratives of the war emerged in English and French Canada. Outside of Quebec, Canadians seemed more certain that national sacrifice was required. Within the province, they grew less convinced that it was worth the cost.

These divisions deepened throughout the war, but it is less clear when the transition from the enthusiasm of 1914 to outright rejection started among French Canadians. Although historians have traditionally referred to faltering enlistment numbers as a sign of diminishing enthusiasm, alongside opposition to Regulation 17, French Canadians might have joined the army at a similar rate to native-born English Canadians throughout the war. Enlistments did drop; however, recent work by historian Jean Martin suggests that French Canadians enlisted at a similar rate as other native-born Canadians, if estimates include French Canadians outside of Quebec. Instead of the 25,000 to 35,000 French Canadians who were once believed to have enlisted, the number may in fact be between 55,000 and 61,000.[55] Martin's numbers show that although qualitative sources suggest an attitude shift in 1915 or 1916, enlistment numbers suggest that French Canadians continued to believe the war was worth fighting beyond these years. At the very least, the same percentage of French Canadians as native-born English Canadians was willing to join the fight in Europe. Regardless, falling enlistment rates across the country pushed the federal government to introduce conscription legislation in 1917. Fewer and fewer in Quebec believed that it was worth fighting a war for the British Empire. Many within and outside of the province believed that conscription targeted French Canadians over English Canadians, for better or for worse, because Quebec was not sufficiently supporting the war.[56]

By the time Prime Minister Robert Borden announced conscription on May 18, 1917, rumours of its enactment had been swirling for months, causing unrest in French Canada. Various alternatives had failed to raise enlistments rates, a problem that had become especially significant since Borden had expanded the Canadian army to five hundred thousand in January 1916.[57] The need for more soldiers became increasingly dire, but only a few Conservative voices in Quebec, such as Thomas Chase-Casgrain (before his death in late 1916) and Albert Sévigny, supported conscription. Most Quebec elites could no longer accept Borden's wartime policies. The Catholic Church opposed the war after the federal government announced conscription.[58] Bourassa, who had rejected the war entirely in January 1916, marshalled his followers against conscription through his newspaper and books.[59] Sir Wilfrid Laurier rejected the Borden government's decision to press for conscription, demanding instead that it hold a referendum. Borden announced an election in December, which was ultimately a contest between Laurier's Liberals and a union of pro-conscription Liberals and Conservatives called the Unionist Party. Effectively a referendum on Borden's wartime policies, the Liberals' defeat everywhere outside of Quebec in December 1917 underlined the separation between Canada's two peoples.[60] The shift in French Canadian attitudes towards the war marked a return to resisting – if not outright objecting to – Canada's ties with the British Empire.

The intellectual elite expressed these sentiments, and it is clear that the general populace mirrored and absorbed them. At the dawn of the new year, French Canadians actively opposed the Canadian war effort. A motion put forward by Joseph-Napoléon Francoeur in Quebec's Assemblé nationale in December 1917 asked if Quebec ought to leave the Canadian federation in light of three years of denigration at the hands of English Canada.[61] The motion was retracted in January, but the point was clear. Quebec no longer felt it was an equal partner in the nation of Canada. The actual process of enforcing conscription on an unwilling populace further heightened tensions. Riots broke out in Quebec City after the imprisonment of two men for not providing their exemption papers on March 28, 1918. The police eventually released them, but a crowd of about two thousand gathered and stormed the police station. The next evening, a crowd of eight thousand civilians looted the offices of two pro-conscription newspapers and burned down the offices of the Military Service Act Registrar. On March 30, Prime Minister Borden declared that the federal government would take charge of peace and order in Quebec City. Rioting continued through to April 1 as clashes broke out each night between rioters and soldiers. Over the entire Easter weekend, four civilians were killed, and sixty-two soldiers and an unknown number of civilians were injured.[62]

French Canadian views on the Empire fundamentally changed in the last years of the war as a result of the home front experience. The war years exacerbated traditional French Canadian criticisms of the Empire and isolationist tendencies.[63] These attitudes had been present, but the war intensified them. In 1899 or 1910, nationaliste critiques focused on the relationship between the

Empire and Canada. The nationalistes desired Canadian autonomy and French Canadian autonomy; they did not separate the two. In 1914, French Canadians celebrated the connection to Britain and France, albeit briefly, through a national war effort. By 1917–18, the focus had turned solely to French Canada's relationship to the Empire rather than the Canadian one. By war's end, Quebec was isolated from English Canada in a way unlike anything seen in Canadian history to that point. After the December 1917 election, Henri Bourassa lamented "l'isolement des canadiens-français" in Canada. The victorious Unionist party had almost no French Canadian representatives, meaning they were shut out of decision-making power in Ottawa.[64] Other nationalistes condemned the "new imperialism" that championed the supremacy of one people over all others.[65] As early as 1916, Bourassa wrote polemics against the "imperialist revolution" that had taken place after the outpouring of support in 1914 for a Canadian war effort. The profound transformation of Canada's place within the British Empire favoured English Canadians over French Canadians, and the Canadian nation that emerged from the war seemed much less friendlier to the latter.[66] Canada, nationalistes believed, was now bound to serve the Empire no matter the cost. It was a relationship of servility and slavery, wrote L.O. Maillé, rather than the nominally equal or beneficial relationship once championed by imperialists before the war.[67] Even the supporters of the war in Quebec found themselves adopting a different conception of empire. Ferdinand Roy's response to the war's critics acknowledged French Canada's diminished place but made the case that the problem would be resolved only if French Canadians proved willing to fight.[68] In his 1918 history of the "sang français," A.H. de Trémaudan reminded readers that the French Canadian nation could preserve its identity even under the British flag in Europe.[69] It was a drastic transformation from the attitude of 1914, and the tone shifted from emphasizing the Canadian nation to talking about the French Canadian people. These ideas had been present before the war, but they had not dominated the public discourse as they did in 1918. Over the next decade, postwar Quebec politics reflected these changes. The rise of Quebec nationalism under the leadership of Abbé Lionel Groulx owed little to the nationalistes of 1903. Groulx's followers remembered 1917 and 1918, not 1899 or 1910, as had Bourassa and his comrades.

Thus, by war's end, English Canadians believed they existed in partnership with the British Empire while French Canadians believed they had survived in spite of it. In 1914, the war began with appeals to Canadian nationalism and Canada's historical connections to Britain and France. The intensity of the war's beginning overpowered previous divisions between French and English Canadians, but unity faded over time as French Canadians perceived that the nationalist rhetoric of 1914 ultimately communicated an imperialist understanding of the war for English Canadians. Rather than feeling a valued part of the Empire, as did English Canadians, French Canada saw only the difference between itself and other Canadians. It was a stark contrast to what French Canadians would experience during the Second World War under the very different leadership of Prime Minister William Lyon Mackenzie King, as Robert Talbot outlines in his contribution to this volume. Talbot reveals that a focus on Canada rather than the Empire provided a common frame of reference for the sacrifices that came with conflict. In the First World War, however, political rhetoric reinforced exclusionary cultural boundaries that could not include French Canadians.[70] Grievances against English Canadian intransigence were an important instigator of the shift in attitude that took place between 1914 and 1917, whether it was among nationalistes or Liberals, as there was no compromise on issues such as Regulation 17 and conscription. For French Canada, the war touched on this shared cultural experience with English Canadians but not on a shared wartime experience. Since 1867, French Canadians had witnessed the loss of their rights outside of Quebec and had been ignored by the growing English Canadian majority. The two major events of the war for them, Regulation 17 and conscription, echoed those historical and cultural problems with English Canada. They were not celebrations of ties to Britain and France. In response, French Canadians saw themselves as a unique and isolated people within the Empire as well as the nation. As was the case in so many other belligerent nations during the First World War, the public unity of Canada's early days could not last. Instead, the pressures of wartime undid the brief moment when French Canada fully supported the Empire and volunteered to fight in its wars.

Notes

1 John Horne, "Introduction: Mobilizing for 'Total War,'" in *State, Society and Mobilization in Europe during the First World War,* ed. John Horne (Cambridge: Cambridge University Press, 1997), 1.
2 Leonard V. Smith, Stéphane Audoin-Rouzeau, and Annette Becker, *France and the Great War, 1914–1918* (Cambridge: Cambridge University Press, 2003), 9–41.
3 Roger Chickering, *Imperial Germany and the Great War, 1914–1918* (Cambridge: Cambridge University Press, 2004), 16. For the Spirit of 1914, see 13–17.
4 Adrian Gregory, *The Last Great War: British Society and the First World War* (Cambridge: Cambridge University Press, 2008), 9–39.
5 Desmond Morton, *When Your Number's Up: The Canadian Soldier in the First World War* (Toronto: Random House, 1993), 9.
6 For more on how Canadians understood the war within the public sphere, see R. Matthew Bray, "'Fighting as an Ally': The English-Canadian Patriotic Response to the Great War," *Canadian Historical Review* 61, 2 (1980): 141–68; Paul Maroney, "'The Great Adventure': The Context and Ideology of Recruiting in Ontario, 1914–17," *Canadian*

Historical Review 77, 1 (1996): 62–98; and Robert S. Prince, "The Mythology of War: How the Canadian Daily Newspaper Depicted the Great War" (PhD diss., University of Toronto, 1998).

7 This essay alternates between referring to French Canada and Quebec. While Quebec was distinct from the larger population of French Canadians, prior to and during the conflict commentators often discussed a collective community that included both.

8 E.H.H. Green, "The Political Economy of Empire, 1880–1914," *The Oxford History of the British Empire*, vol. 3, *The Nineteenth Century*, ed. Andrew Porter (Oxford: Oxford University Press, 1999), 347.

9 Carl Berger, *The Sense of Power: Studies in the Ideas of Canadian Imperialism, 1867–1914* (Toronto: University of Toronto Press, 1970), 250.

10 J.S. Ewart, *The Kingdom Papers* (Ottawa: n.p., 1912). The *Papers* were a series of articles examining Canada's legal obligations to Britain that were eventually published together.

11 The best overview of this period remains Robert Craig Brown and Ramsay Cook, *Canada, 1896–1921: A Nation Transformed* (Toronto: McClelland and Stewart, 1974).

12 James I.W. Corcoran, "Henri Bourassa et la guerre sud-africain (suite)," *Revue d'histoire de l'Amérique Française* 19, 1 (1965): 84.

13 Henri Bourassa, *Grande-Bretagne et Canada: Questions actuelles* (Montreal: Imprimerie du Pionnier, 1901), 26–27.

14 On the Boer War as prelude, see Carman Miller, "Framing Canada's Great War: A Case for Including the Boer War," *Journal of Transatlantic Studies* 6, 1 (April 2008): 16–17.

15 Joseph Levitt, *Henri Bourassa and the Golden Calf: The Social Program of the Nationalists of Quebec, 1900–1914* (Ottawa: Les Éditions de l'Université d'Ottawa, 1969), 2.

16 Yvan Mason Wade, *Histoire sociale des idées au Québec*, vol. 2, *1896–1929* (Quebec: Éditions Fides, 2004), 194–95, 226.

17 See the *Program of the Nationalist League – 1903*, as reprinted in Levitt, *Henri Bourassa and the Golden Calf*, 148–49.

18 "French Canadians have no other homeland than Canada ... They stand ready to offer it all they owe; but consider nothing owed to England nor any other nation, and French Canadians expect nothing of them." All translations provided by the author. Henri Bourassa, *Les Canadiens-français et l'empire britannique* (Quebec: Imprimerie S.A. Demers, 1903), 40.

19 Patrice Dutil and David Mackenzie, *Canada 1911: The Decisive Election That Shaped the Country* (Toronto: Dundurn, 2011), 39–52.

20 Canada, House of Commons, *Debates*, 11th Parl., 2nd Sess., January 12, 1910, 1735 (Hon. Sir Wilfrid Laurier). He later qualified his statement as simply stating a matter of international law. See Canada, House of Commons, *Debates*, 11th Parl., 2nd Sess., February 3, 1910, 2964–965 (Hon. Sir Wilfrid Laurier).

21 Henri Bourassa, *Le project du loi navale: Sa nature, ses conséquences* (Montreal: Le Devoir, 1910), 87.

22 Robert Rumilly, *Henri Bourassa: La vie publique d'un grand Canadien* (Montreal: Éditions Chantecler, 1953), 392. Oscar Skelton writes that canvassers actively campaigned on the idea that all Quebec children would be sacrificed by Laurier's Naval Act, though there is little evidence this actually happened. Still, Skelton sums up the elections of 1910 and 1911 with the only question that mattered in Quebec: "For Laurier, or against the navy?" See Oscar Skelton, *Life and Letters of Sir Wilfrid Laurier*, vol. 2 (Montreal/Kingston: McGill-Queen's University Press, 1965), 339.

23 For Bourassa's thoughts on allying with the Conservatives, see Réal Bélanger, *Henri Bourassa: Fascinant destin d'un homme libre (1868–1914)* (Quebec: Les Presses de l'Université de Laval, 2013), 302–9.

24 Dutil and Mackenzie, *Canada 1911*, 252, 278–79.
25 Bélanger, *Henri Bourassa*, 378–81. See also Réal Bélanger, *Paul-Émile Lamarche: Le pays avant le parti (1904–1918)* (Quebec: Presses de l'Université Laval, 1984), for his exploration of Lamarche's career as a "conservative-nationalist" MP.
26 "Un enthousiasme indescriptible salue à Québec l'attitude de l'Angleterre," *L'Action Sociale,* August 5, 1914, 2.
27 "Pour la France et L'Empire," *La Presse,* August 6, 1914, 8.
28 A brief sampling of articles bears this out: "Pour nos freres de France," *La Presse,* August 22, 1914, 8; "Belgique heroique," *La Presse,* August 29, 1914, 4; "Ce qui se passe dans la capitale française," *La Presse,* September 5, 1914, 2; "Soyons patriotes," *La Presse,* September 14, 1914, 8; "Pour la France," *L'Action Sociale,* August 12, 1914, 1; "La ténacité anglaise," *L'Action Sociale,* August 29, 1914, 1; "M. Bourassa et la guerre," *Le Pays,* September 5, 1914, 1; "La destruction de Louvain," *Le Pays,* September 5, 1914, 2; "Comment venger Louvain," *Le Pays,* September 19, 1914, 2; Thomas Chase-Casgrain, "Le role du Canada Français," *La Patrie,* September 14, 1914, 4; "De la Canadienne a la Française," *Le Devoir,* October 26, 1914; and "Le devoir du Canada est tout Indique," *Le Clairon,* August 21, 1914, 1.
29 "An Entente Cordiale between French and English of Canada at Hand," *Le Pays,* August 22, 1914, 7. Printed in French as "L'avers de la médaille," *Le Pays,* August 15, 1914, 2.
30 Canada, House of Commons, *Debates,* 12th Parl., 4th Sess., August 19, 1914, 10 (Hon. Sir Wilfrid Laurier).
31 Ibid., 19 (Hon. Sir Robert Borden).
32 J. Castell Hopkins, *Canadian Annual Review 1914* (Toronto: Canadian Annual Review Limited, 1918), 514.
33 Jean-Pierre Gagnon, *Le 22e bataillon (canadien-français), 1914–1919: Étude socio-militaire* (Ottawa: Presses de l'Université Laval, 1986), 38–41.
34 Sylvie Lacombe, "French Canada: The Rise and Decline of a 'Church Nation,'" *Quebec Studies* 48 (Fall 2009–Winter 2010): 135–58.
35 *L'Action Sociale,* September 11, 1914, 1. D'Amours repeatedly wrote of Canada's "national duty," a direct reference to an article from Bourassa on September 8, titled "Le devoir nationale." For more on Catholic responses, see Rumilly, *Henri Bourassa,* 508–9, and Elizabeth Armstrong, *Crisis of Quebec, 1914–1918* (Toronto: McClelland and Stewart, 1937), 61–62.
36 *Lettre pastorale de NN. SS les archevêques et évêques des provinces ecclésiastiques de Québec, de Montréal et d'Ottawa sur les devoirs des catholiques dans la guerre actuelle,* September 23, 1914, 4.
37 Hopkins, *Canadian Annual Review 1914,* 288.
38 Claude Larivière, *Albert Saint-Martin, militant d'avant-garde (1865–1947)* (Laval, QC: Éditions coopératives Albert Saint-Martin, 1979), 118–19. See also the denouncement of the war in "To the Workers of Canada," *The Voice,* August 28, 1914. The socialist movement was not particularly strong in Quebec as it represented a vehement rejection of Catholicism, see Jacques Rouillard, *Histoire du syndicalism au Québec: Des origines à nos jours* (Montreal: Les Éditions du Boréal, 1989), 305–12. Like the nationalistes, Quebec labour was also tied to a Catholic French Canadian identity and moved to support the war.
39 Henri Bourassa, "Le devoir national," *Le Devoir,* September 8, 1914, 1.
40 Henri Bourassa, "Après la guerre," *Le Devoir,* September 2, 1914, 1.
41 Bélanger, *Henri Bourassa,* 528–30; Rumilly, *Henri Bourassa,* 503; and Andre Bergevin, Cameron Nish, and Anne Bourassa, *Henri Bourassa: Biographie, index des écrit, index de la correspondance publique, 1895–1924* (Montreal: Les Éditions de l'Action Nationale, 1966), 47.

42 Henri Bourassa, "En France et en Alsace," *Le Devoir*, August 22, 1914, 1.

43 Yvan Lamonde, *Histoire social des idées au Québec*, 2:40–41; René Durocher, "Henri Bourassa, les évêques et la guerre de 1914–1918," *Canadian Historical Association Historical Papers* 6 (1971): 252.

44 Jules Fournier and Therese Fournier, *Mon encrier* (Montreal: Fides, 1922). The title harkens to an article Asselin had penned, Le Kronzprinz [Olivar Asselin], "Simple briques," *L'Action* 4, 173 (1914): 1. The article was eventually published as a booklet of Fournier's writing by his wife in 1922, four years after he died of influenza.

45 Jules Fournier, *Mon encrier*, 460.

46 Bourassa described Grey as "courageous, untiring, a man whose every action is only inspired by one motive: the interests of *his* country": Henri Bourassa, "Une page d'histoire – IV: L'Angleterre et l'Allemagne," *Le Devoir*, September 12, 1914, 1. For the entire series, see September 9–14, 1914. The *White Papers* were first publicly published on August 5, 1914, when they were presented to the British House of Commons "to inform Parliament as to the events which had brought about the war and the part taken in them by the British Government." See G.P. Gooch, D. Litt, and Harold Temperley, *British Official Documents on the Origins of the War, 1898–1914* (London: H.M.S.O, 1926). Other governments had already published similar collections of the official documents concerning their entry into the war, such as the *French Yellow Book* or the *German White Book*.

47 *La Patrie*, September 11, 1914, 4. See also Mason Wade, *The French Canadians 1760–1945* (Toronto: MacMillan, 1956) 648–49.

48 These articles are reviewed in Wade, *French Canadians*, 652–53, and Rumilly, *Henri Bourassa*, 507–11.

49 *Le Pays*, September 19, 1914, 1.

50 Rumilly, *Henri Bourassa*, 521–22. For Bourassa's account of the incident and the speech he was to give, see Henri Bourassa, *The Duty of Canada at the Present Hour* (Montreal: Le Devoir, 1915).

51 Ian Miller, *Our Glory and Our Grief: Torontonians and the Great War* (Toronto: University of Toronto Press, 2002), 15–66; see also Maroney, "The Great Adventure."

52 Margaret Prang, "Clerics, Politicians, and the Bilingual Schools Issue in Ontario, 1910–1917," *Canadian Historical Review* 41, 4 (December 1960): 281–307; see also Gaétan Gervais, "Le règlement XVII (1912–1927)," *Revue du Nouvel Ontario* 18 (1996): 123–92.

53 Kevin P. Anderson, "'This Typical Old Canadian Form of Racial and Religious Hate': Anti-Catholicism and English Canadian Nationalism, 1905–1965" (PhD diss., McMaster University, 2013), 53–56, 71. See also Craig Brown and Cook, *Canada, 1896–1921*, 255.

54 Jérôme Coutard examines the occurrence of war coverage in Quebec newspapers and the shift towards "negative stories" in "Des valeurs en guerre: Presse, propagande et culture de guerre au Québec, 1914–1918" (PhD diss., Université de Laval, 1999), 96–116, and offers a perceptive deconstruction of the values projected onto the war by newspapers in the rest of the work. See also Prince, "The Mythology of War."

55 Jean Martin, "La participation des francophones dans le Corps expéditionnaire canadien (1914–1919): Il faut réviser à la hausse," *Canadian Historical Review* 96, 3 (September 2015): 405–23; see also Chris Sharpe, "Enlistment in the Canadian Expeditionary Force, 1914–1918: A Re-evaluation," *Canadian Military History* 24, 1 (2015): 17–60.

56 For the national discussion over French Canadian enlistment, see, for example, Castell Hopkins, *Canadian Annual Review 1915* (Toronto: Canadian Annual Review Limited, 1918), 216–18, and Castell Hopkins, *Canadian Annual Review 1916* (Toronto: Canadian Annual Review Limited, 1918), 309, 566–67, 571.

57 J.L. Granatstein and J.M. Hitsman, *Broken Promises: A History of Conscription in Canada* (Toronto: Oxford University Press, 1977), 40–49.

58 Robert Rumilly, *Histoire de la province de Québec*, vol. 22, *"La conscription"* (Montreal: Fides, 1940), 99. See also *L'Action Catholique*, July 28, 1917, 1. For an overview of the Quebec Catholic response to the war, see Simon Jolivet, "French-Speaking Catholics in Quebec and the First World War," in *Canadian Churches and the First World War*, ed. Gordon L. Heath (Eugene, OR: Pickwick Publications, 2014), 75–98.

59 Henri Bourassa, *La conscription* (Montreal: Éditions du Devoir, 1917).

60 John English, *The Decline of Politics: The Conservatives and the Party System, 1901–20* (Toronto: University of Toronto Press, 1993), 186–203. Out of the 264-seat Parliament, the Unionists took 152 seats, and the Liberals took 82. Sixty-two of Quebec's 65 seats went to the Liberals, and they garnered 73 percent of the popular vote. Of the 67 ridings with French Canadian majorities, the Liberals won 65.

61 Jean Provencher, *Québec sous la loi des mesure de guerre 1918* (Trois-Rivères: Les Éditions de Boréal Express, 1971), 34–37.

62 Martin F. Auger, "On the Brink of Civil War: The Canadian Government and the Suppression of the 1918 Quebec Easter Riots," *Canadian Historical Review* 89, 4 (December 2008): 508–20.

63 Robert Comeau, "L'opposition à la conscription au Québec," in *La Première Guerre mondiale et le Canada*, ed. Roch Legault and Jean Lamarre (Montreal: Éditions du Méridien, 1999), 109.

64 Henri Bourassa, "'L'isolement' des Canadien-Français: Fausses manoeuvres de conciliation," *Le Devoir*, December 26, 1917, 1. On the Unionist Party and French Canadians, see English, *Decline of Politics*, 199–201.

65 Jean Vindex [Hermas Lalande], *Halte-là! "Patriote" que penser de notre école politico-théologique? De l'impérialisme qu'elle professe? Du nationalisme qu'elle censure?* (Rimouski, QC: Le Progrès du Golfe, 1917), 136.

66 Henri Bourassa, *Hier, aujourd'hui, demain* (Montreal: n.p., 1916), 110. Bourassa repeatedly refers to the imperialist revolution in his writings after rejecting the war in January 1916.

67 L.O. Maillé, *Réponse de M.L.O. Maillé aux articles "Où allons nous?" et à M. l'Abbé D'Amour* (Montreal: n.p., 1917), 7.

68 Ferdinand Roy, *L'appel aux armes et la réponse canadienne-française* (Quebec: J.P. Garneau, 1917).

69 A.H. de Trémaudan, *Le sang français* (Winnipeg: Imprimerie de La Libre Parole, 1918), 223–24.

70 Though, at the time, these would have been referred to as racial differences. See, for example, a contemporary examination of French and English Canadians as different races: André Siegfried, *The Race Question in Canada* (London: Eveleigh Nash, 1907).

8

Anti-fascist Strikes and the Patriotic Shield?
Canadian Workers and the Employment of
"Enemy Aliens" in the Second World War

Mikhail Bjorge

AT THE ONSET of the Second World War, the Canadian prime minister, William Lyon Mackenzie King, was deeply concerned with issues of social stability and his own electoral chances with the Canadian public. To this end, King enacted a wartime strategy of limited liability, which prioritized maintaining social cohesion and his future electability by contributing more material than men to the war effort.[1] King was, writes historian W.A.B. Douglas, "reluctant to see Canada committed to a major contribution of soldiers. He feared that casualties might be as great or greater in a second European war," potentially causing mass social destabilization similar to that which had erupted following the First World War.[2] The Canadian state therefore focused on feeding the industrial and caloric needs of its allies generally, and Britain specifically. On the industrial front, Canada quickly retooled its Depression-riddled economy onto a war footing.[3] Indeed, by 1940 the war effort constituted essentially the entirety of all federal government expenditures. In all, "Canada produced 400 naval and 391 cargo ships, 50,000 tanks, 16,000 military aircraft, 850,000 military vehicles, 1.5 million rifles and machine guns, 72 million artillery and mortar shells, and 4.4 billion rounds of small arms ammunition" for its own military and for the Allies.[4] By 1941 "94 percent of British wheat flour imports originated in Canada, along with 76 percent of bacon, 63 percent of pork, 20 percent of cheese, 16 percent of egg, and 99 percent of apple imports."[5]

To keep Canadian factories working, the King government invoked the War Measures Act before officially declaring war on Germany; the act gave cabinet "extraordinary powers, unprecedented in Britain or the United States."[6] Among these powers was the ability to declare any strike illegal and arrest and detain Canadians for any reason. However, Canadian workers during the war proved to be both active and essentially ungovernable, and both organized and unorganized workers ignored the legal position of their job actions with *relative* impunity. One ramification of the wave of wartime strikes was the demonization of unions and working people as unpatriotic, even treasonous.

Evidence pertaining to the series of anti-"alien" strikes that erupted in Ontario, Quebec, and particularly Nova Scotia reveals that some strikers took action against the employment of their fellow workers because of their real or imagined ethnicity, despite a governmental position of patriotic egalitarianism and a long, and deeply uneven, struggle by unions against racism and xenophobia.[7] If workers were born in geographies or "descended from" peoples with which Britain was now officially at war, some were painted as "enemy aliens" (despite their legal status) by their co-workers, and in the cases under consideration, they were forced from employment by illegal strikes that lacked union sanction.[8]

These job actions, which included the loss of hundreds of thousands of man-hours, received little attention in the Canadian media and almost none from the security services. Unlike other wartime strikes, these actions were justified using the language of empire, loyalty to Britain, and anti-fascism. In juxtaposition to other workers who attempted to make various gains through industrial action in pluralistic proletarian formations, these strikes were internally divisive, directed against fellow workers. This added a patriotic gloss to a situation that was, broadly speaking, a vitiating force within the workers' unions. Although there has been a tremendous amount of scholarship written on wartime Canada, and specifically the Canadian home front, these "patriotic" strikes have been ignored, even though they make up a significant portion of industrial activity in the early war period.[9] Although the Canadian labour movement certainly had a complex, difficult, and often ugly relationship with issues of "race," the Canadian movement had largely overcome overt racism by the Second World War. In many instances, the labour movement was a driver in social anti-racism and demands for equality and justice. These ethnicity-oriented strikes represent some of the last vestiges of such activity in the unions, and were denounced by union leadership. The onset of war in 1939 and the entry of Italy in 1940 presented an opportunity for agitators to revive their demands for xenophobic exclusions under the guise of wartime security, but they engaged these tropes mainly out of Depression-era desperation in an effort to secure employment for their kin.

In his study of industrial unrest in the Nova Scotia coalfields, historian Michael Earle argues that labour historians have understudied coal slowdowns and other examples of worker rebellion. Most historians of the Second World War have focused on the industrial relations system and large unions. The activity of workers themselves has seen far less examination. Although the Second World War saw the most intense period of industrial unrest since the workers' revolt following the First World War, much of the examination of the home front looks at institutions rather than people, at ideas rather than action, at culture rather than activity.[10] For historians of capitalism and the working class, much of this stems from source bias. Indeed, historian Jeremy Webber noted that for strikes before 1944, "virtually every file was destroyed" that related to state conciliation.[11] Ergo, the examination of wartime strikes can be difficult, but it is far from impossible.

Historians of capitalism and the proletariat have long had an interest in wildcat strikes. Free from the bureaucratism of the union, the unsanctioned strike emerges as the true or unfettered representation of workers' self-activity, as some sort of distilled class struggle. And, being fair minded, most wildcat strikes are something akin to this. This study, however, looks at the darker potential of spontaneous uprisings of opportunistic xenophobia. Far from being a simple hagiography of wartime unions or workers' militancy, it presents a more complicated picture. Nativism, patriotism, opportunism, and anti-fascist rhetoric all cloaked a movement that ripped at the heart of unionism: solidarity. Moreover, most illegal strikes were treated with some form of discipline, whether from the state, media, courts, or the Royal Canadian Mounted Police (RCMP). In the case of the strikes against aliens, the patriotic rhetoric of the strikers and their alarmist claims of enemy infiltration or sabotage disarmed the strong arm of the state, which favoured conciliation rather than confrontation.

The vast majority of these strikes occurred in Nova Scotia's coalfields, an area where workers had seen their wages actually decline since the 1920s and where "perhaps an unmatched record of poisoned labour relations" ruled the day.[12] And although the relatively conservative United Mine Workers of America (UMWA) eventually forced its locals to cease these unsanctioned work stoppages, such action was not immediate, and it was done with some reticence. The union, in these examples, did not live up to its constitutionally mandated goals of inclusivity and anti-racism. Moreover, the strikes themselves went against both state propaganda regarding inclusiveness and the relatively commendable work that unions had done in regard to anti-racism. The strikers' motives, as well as the state's reluctance to confront workers who struck in favour of ethnoracial exclusion, reveal a curious path that allowed for the instrumentalization of British race patriotism in Canada.

Although Canadian elites were slowly constructing Canadian nationalism during the interwar period, the prevailing notion of Canada was still predominantly Anglo-Celtic.[13] Indeed, "the worship of the monarchy and the British Empire enjoyed almost cult status in Canadian society," as Claire Halstead explores in this volume in her chapter on the 1939 royal tour.[14] Far from the ideas of "defending Canada" or "protecting democracy," a great deal of wartime propaganda (in both French and English) was oriented towards British nationalism, imperial pride, or both. Canada's place within the Empire generally was often represented as that of a junior partner. In school, children were reminded that "they were 'Britishers first, last, and all the time.'"[15] A poster that exclaimed "Let's Go Canada!" showed a soldier fighting in front of a Union Jack.[16] Even a poster that reminded Canadians that "Smith? Kelly? Cohen? Svoboda?" all died on the battlefield as Canadians and "fought Canadian ... died Canadian" concluded with the exclamation that one must "BE CANADIAN – Act British."[17] For the Canadian state and many Canadians, to be Canadian was to be British, if not in ethnicity, then at least in thought and deed. But Canada was self-evidently not a mono-ethnic state. Apart from the obvious divisions among English, French, and First Peoples, there were gradations of "whiteness" and race within the Canadian polity.

In the mines, fields, factories, and workshops of Canada, the interplay of race, ethnicity, wartime patriotism, and localized unemployment played a role in dividing workers from one another. Issues of whiteness were of concern as well, as most people in Canada, including those from Europe who were not Anglo-Celtic, were not considered white and often faced discrimination (although, this was less the case in union culture than in the wider society).[18] The question was, however, were these strikes ethnic, racist, patriotic in origin, or something altogether different? There were, of course, multiple precedents for strikes against the inclusion of racialized or "ethnic" workers in North American history. Early unions, often organized around craft protection, almost always had exclusionary practices. Organized labour in Canada generally stood "against the importation of cheap labour," largely because of fear of wage degradation rather than on purely biological or racial grounds.[19] The first industrial union in North America, the Knights of Labor, was more inclusive yet still excluded members of Asian extraction.[20] Although the Knights were willing to organize racialized and female workers, they generally did so in segregated locals.[21]

Canadian unions were only occasionally willing to organize with ethnic workers. With some evidence, craft unions had long seen immigration as a scheme to lower wages for skilled labourers. As historian David Goutor argues, "With few exceptions ... labour leaders insisted that a restrictive and racially discriminatory immigration policy was essential for protecting both the standards of living for Canadian workers and the social, moral, and medical vitality of Canadian communities."[22]

There was some precedent within Canada for striking against the employment of (or working alongside) enemy aliens. During the First World War, the executive of the Trades and Labour Congress (TLC) had embraced so-called patriotic dismissals based on ethnic grounds.[23] During that same war, the UMWA in Alberta and British Columbia threatened employers with strikes if all "enemy alien miners" were not dismissed.[24] In Nova Scotia, the Dominion Steel Company, which ran nearly all the mines in the province, resisted demands to dismiss enemy aliens during the Great War. It feared that Nova Scotia workers would not work as cheaply as foreigners. Only when it was allowed to import even cheaper labour from Newfoundland was it willing to "join in the patriotic crusade" against the employment of foreigners. Like the Second World War, the lead up to the Great War was marked by depression, and high unemployment rates were as much a factor as war fever. The new industrial unions that later formed in the crucible of the Great Depression (and the society in which they organized) would continue to grapple with issues of race and ethnicity.[25]

The Congress of Industrial Organizations (CIO), although much more inclusive than its craft-based brethren (and certainly more progressive than mainstream non-proletarian organizations), was no paragon of racial equality. Indeed, the CIO witnessed wildcat strikes against the integration of locals despite its attempts to promote racial egalitarianism.[26] The UMWA, which organized most miners in Nova Scotia, was a distinctly anti-racist union, even more so than the CIO, let alone the craft-oriented American Federation of Labor (AFL).[27] Therefore, the strikes against the employment of enemy aliens were not manifestations of deeply held feelings of racial or ethnic antagonism, they were opportunistic attacks on fellow workers that employed wartime xenophobia as an accelerant and imperial patriotism as a shield. Wartime strikes against the employment of aliens occurred during a time when Canada, and specifically Cape Breton, was still reeling from massive structural unemployment. Eliminating a fellow worker and giving his job to someone seemingly more deserving, or more similar, was the new reality. Indeed, the UMWA had been organized in an intrinsically multiethnic milieu, and the strikes were targeted at workers who were perceived to be associated, by virtue of their ethnicity or race, with the Axis cause.[28] Although these strikes have overtones of anti-fascism (and there certainly was tremendous anti-fascist sentiment in the Canadian working class and militant anti-fascism within large sectors of organized labour), they were populist outbursts that quickly subsided once full employment arrived in Canada in 1941.[29]

In the days before Canada's official entry into the war, anti-alien strikes were launched, mainly in Nova Scotia's coalfields and particularly in Glace Bay.[30] In the first months of the war, Nova Scotia miners were arguably the most militant section of Canada's working class. Internationally and historically, coal miners had always had a predilection towards militancy and strikes, but the miners were particularly combative.[31] In Canada during the early war period, no other group launched as many strikes, as often, and with as many concomitant sympathy strikes as the coal miners of Nova Scotia.

In Nova Scotia, three mines in particular faced strikes by workers attempting to compel their employers to expel the "foreign element."[32] Canada did not declare war on Germany until September 10, 1939, but after Great Britain declared war on September 3, anti-alien strikes began the following day. In these strikes against the foreign element, the language of anti-fascism was invoked, particularly in Springhill, traditionally the most militant area in Nova Scotia.[33] Reserve and New Waterford saw strikes on September 4 or 5. In Springhill, it was the midnight shifts at two Cumberland Coal and Railway Company mines that struck first. The miners were all members of the UMWA, a union with comparatively strong anti-racist tendencies and a relatively centralized structure. Although UMWA officials were on site, it was a wildcat strike. Neither the local nor the international sanctioned the action, which was called despite a contract being in place.[34] Four hundred miners refused to work with any employee who they deemed either a potential saboteur or genotypically suspect.

Fifteen hundred miners eventually joined (or were affected) by the strike. Miners claimed it "wasn't safe" to work with the "foreigners." They noted further that they refused to work with "enemy" or "foreign-born" employees since "hostilities broke out between Germany and Great Britain."[35] Given that it was officially an issue of safety and fear of "German treachery," the mine manager at Springhill offered "to have all men searched before they entered the pit." The men rejected the offer, repudiating any measures that were not expulsion.[36] The strike halted when the manager agreed to "stop the lamps" of fifteen foreign-born workers. The miners targeted not only Germans and Austrians but also, among others, Czech-Slovaks and Hungarians. That the latter were likely anti-fascist and British subjects was not accounted for. When the company agreed to temporarily relieve the foreign workers of their positions, some men returned to work, but many refused.[37] The miners would not return to work until "suitable precautions" for their safety had been met.[38] Eventually, sixty foreign workers were temporarily suspended before the workers returned to work.

Strikes at mines, particularly coal mines, are always tricky affairs. Even during particularly dire strikes, often accompanied by violence and scabbing, skilled workers often did maintenance work in the mines. An unkempt coal mine was liable to floods, cave-ins, fire, and explosions. In the history of Canadian mine strikes, withdrawal of maintenance work was exceptionally rare, as it was tantamount to burning down the factory to spite the boss. These prewar strikes against the employment of "enemies" were the same. Although over one thousand miners at Springhill were refusing to work, the employer still allowed UMWA members to maintain the shafts. Needless to say, the first anti-alien strike was a quickly stymied affair. The RCMP came the next morning and interviewed and catalogued the foreigners, who numbered about sixty.[39] At a union meeting, the leadership spurned the miners, who in turn "lifted their objections and decided to work with the aliens, including naturalized Canadians and those not naturalized."[40]

In Reserve, just outside of Glace Bay, eight hundred UMWA miners also struck against co-working with Germans. On September 5, the company sensed trouble and "ordered all Teutonic employees to remain out of its mines." Despite the order from management, five Germans showed up for underground work. The night shift at the Dominion Coal Company demanded that five "German-born employees" be relieved. Although the company's order was supposed to apply only to non-naturalized workers, naturalized workers who had been in Canada for decades were not allowed to work because they were born in Germany.[41] The company might have wanted to maintain order and stability through limited discipline and restrictions, but job action turned this manoeuvre into a licence for capricious enforcement. The RCMP registered all Germans, but they noted that "as long as they obeyed the laws of this country, there was nothing that could be done."[42] At a UMWA meeting on the night of September 6, the union leadership declared that the members' place of birth was "not a union matter," and all agreed to go back to work.[43]

The strikes calmed for the remainder of the week. But when Canada declared war, anti-alien sentiment emerged again in the coal pits. Sensing trouble, the UMWA held a meeting specifically related to working with foreigners.[44] It passed a motion that allowed all members to go to work despite status or place of birth, and a district-wide notification to this effect was distributed widely. However, on September 11, the New Waterford miners struck, demanding the discharge of 172 men based on their status, naturalization, or birth. Though the strike did not include the majority of the workforce, it was of sufficient strength that the mine was shuttered. With Nova Scotia mines tied up in wildcat strikes, the government sent ever more RCMP agents out to the pits to talk with Great War veterans and the UMWA.[45] At a union meeting on September 13, the UMWA (alongside representatives from the Canadian Legion and the Army and Navy Veterans' Association) passed a resolution asking the RCMP to survey all Germans in order to ascertain whether they were naturalized.[46] At New Waterford, the strike continued until September 19, when it was called off. The company agreed that the only foreign-born workers welcome in its employ were those who had fought in the Great War.[47] Direct action had gotten the goods, but the goods were odd, indeed.

At Glace Bay, a similar strike was keeping four hundred miners from the pits. Two brothers "of German origin" who had resided in Glace Bay for "many years" were the source of the stoppage. Despite their "excellent reputations," the UMWA had advised them to "remain away" from work during the first days of the war. In late September, the local advised the men to return to work. When the brothers arrived at the mine, a small minority of miners refused to work alongside them. Even this relatively minor reduction in the number of employees shuttered the mine.[48] Following the incident, D.W. Morrison, the district president of the UMWA, attended a special meeting to talk about the German-born brothers. Morrison noted that they were "good citizens" and that their presence at work should not shutter the entire mine. Morrison thought that the well-attended union meeting "seemed pretty well in favour of the [German] men concerned." A motion was passed to allow the brothers back into the colliery until such time that someone could produce some, or any, evidence against them. When the strike at Glace Bay officially ended on September 22, nearly all workers were officially back at the job. However, the following day, only 146 men showed up for work, causing the mine to operate at only partial capacity.

These early strikes in Nova Scotia were not parochial affairs involving insignificant numbers of miners in forlorn communities. The Nova Scotia coalfields were some of the largest in North America and employed tens of thousands of workers. The strikes involved at least five thousand workers and hundreds of thousands of mine hours.[49] Furthermore, the anti-alien strikes accounted for the plurality of strikes in the fall of 1939.[50] When the initial waves of war fever subsided, so too did strikes against enemy aliens.

On April 9, 1940, the Wehrmacht marched into Denmark and Norway. Germany's renewed offensive revived paranoia against foreign workers. With Hitler's armies marching into the heart of western Europe, and with chunks of Scandinavia well under German control, workers deemed of Axis or fascist descent – no matter how tenuous the connection – became targets once again. Shortly after the Netherlands fell, 275 miners at Glace Bay went on strike and demanded the elimination of enemy aliens. When five German-born miners showed up for their shift, miners held a vote at the pithead. Although three of the men were naturalized Canadians, "a majority opposed going down with the foreign-born men."[51] The workers' committee informed the men, and the "aliens" left for home. While the workers were voting, so many native workers absconded for home that the mine could not operate.[52] The owners of the mine took no part in this vote, and they told the union that it was "a matter for the men themselves."[53] With German-born or -descended miners staying home, the mine reopened the following day.

It was not only Nova Scotia coal miners who took job action against their fellow workers. In Windsor, Ontario, on May 22, 1940, around sixteen hundred non-unionized workers struck against the Chrysler Corporation's employment of Germans. Facing a union drive of its own, Chrysler was surely ecstatic that its workforce was focusing its anger inwards and stoically agreed to fully consider the strikers' arguments.[54] The government responded that although "public feeling may be understandable" in regard to working alongside German workers, "in the present crisis it may harm the nation's cause through slowing up essential work."[55]

A day after the strike, Chrysler fired all German employees until they could produce evidence of citizenship. The plant also banned oral communication unless it was in French or English, "the two official languages of Canada."[56] Never wasting an opportunity to spy on its employees, Chrysler forced them to fill out a "detailed questionnaire giving particulars of date and place of birth, citizenship, etc."[57] N.A. McLarty, minister of the Department of Labour, responded. In a telegram he noted, "Those who propose not to work alongside citizens of German descent are doing what they believe to be in the interests of our country[;] it would be a matter of greatest regret if production in the country ... were impeded.[58] With the anti-German strikes emerging from their original habitat in the notoriously strike-bound collieries of Nova Scotia, the government replied with a notification for workers. They informed them that the state had everything under control, that anyone who was sympathetic to Nazism or fascism had been interned (a dubious claim), and that the majority of foreign-born people were "fervently anti-Nazi" (assuredly true).[59] The government closed by noting that stopping production would be tantamount to "aiding the enemy" and that "any persecution of racial minorities in this country is unworthy of our people, and foreign to our national spirit." This was advice that the government failed to follow less than a year later in regard to Canadians of Japanese origin, and the government was failing to acknowledge its own "none is too many" policy on Jewish refugees.[60]

Action against German workers in Ontario waned under a government propaganda campaign that emphasized domestic unity. However, as the war in Europe raged, so too did tensions in the mines. Earlier, the RCMP had guaranteed miners that they would watch foreign workers for any sign of treason or sabotage and act on any finding. Rather than threatening the miners for their illegal actions, the RCMP once again sided with the strikers, an anomaly in the history of Canadian industrial relations, let alone wartime ones.

In Springhill, the site of the first mass strike against the employment of enemy workers, stalling by the RCMP came to a curious crescendo. On May 30, 1940, fourteen hundred members of UMWA Local 4514 at Cumberland Coal Company went on strike, refusing to work with foreign-born employees.[61] That night, the workers met for a union meeting at the Miners' Hall. With local and regional bureaucrats in attendance, the workers "voted to return to work" on "assurances that their grievances" would be heard.[62] The strike had allegedly been precipitated by a nefarious sabotage plot, evidence of which the RCMP said it would need in order to intern, arrest, or remove foreigners. A "bottle containing some shotgun powder" had been found in the No. 2 coal mine. On learning of the device, almost all workers left immediately.[63] On hearing of the "conspiracy," management suspended the lamps of twenty-seven miners because of their German ancestry. However, the department noted that it was not only Germans and Austrians who were affected but also Czechs and Poles. The UMWA did not sanction the strike, but it also did not seem terribly interested in truncating it. Wary of sabotage, the RCMP investigated and believed that the bottle had been "put there by a native to accomplish demand of having all foreigners removed from the mine." The Department of Labour concurred and argued, "This whole business proceeds from a selfish desire to get places in mines now held by foreigners." Ever more blunt, it continued, "The demands of the miners ... at Springhill or other mines, are not actuated by fear of sabotage or danger to their persons of acts by fellow workmen of alien descent, but are actuated solely by the desire to secure the positions presently held by the latter."[64]

The Department of Labour was worried but not about the "bomb." With the exception of some miners, everyone involved, including the UMWA, seemed to have doubted the veracity of the bomb's existence. However, department officials were particularly worried about what would happen if and when Britain declared war on Italy: "[If] similar action is taken by the miners in respect to the Italians ... there will not be a single mine working in the province."[65] Department reports noted that "Italians are all good workers and have the best positions in the mines, and rightly so by reasons of merit." If the animosity shown to the Germans was turned against the Italians ("good citizens" who "own their own homes" and who were almost all "naturalized Canadian citizens"), the latter would be thrown from work, shuttering the mines. The minister of labour responded by sending the union propaganda that had been written by the Department of Labour; it stated that all workers must "get along" to win the war.[66]

The Department of Labour could not simply break the strikes – let alone quell anti-Axis sentiment – through crude violence. Workers had wrapped themselves in patriotic support for the Empire. Furthermore, there was not enough police, militia, or jail space in Nova Scotia (let alone Cape Breton) to simply imprison all of the striking miners. Finally, the government desperately needed coal for the war effort. It opted for the softest resistance. Officials begged capitalists and the unions to ensure that "no industry is to be tied up during the war period by reasons of discrimination by labour against fellow workers of alien descent." The problem was not that there were nativist or xenophobic sentiment and activity but that the results could hamper the war effort.

The UMWA remained curiously quiet throughout the affair. The American-based leadership was aghast at the miners of Nova Scotia, but not necessarily because of the alien strikes. The anti-foreign strikes notwithstanding, the miners had essentially turned Nova Scotia into an industrial civil war. Workers withheld their labour with incredible regularity, making up a massive percentage of Canada's total strikes. In response, the leadership threatened to pull charters from locals for wildcat activity.[67] Unrelated to the anti-alien strikes, it threatened to put local unions into receivership.

By 1940, the leadership was no longer silent. That summer, D.W. Morrison, president of District 26, penned an illuminating letter to the minister of labour.[68] He had been in Springhill during the supposed bomb incident and commented that it had caused "quite a stir."[69] He seemed unconcerned that his "foreign" union members were being forced out and, knowing the desires of the government, emphasized that production would not be impacted in any meaningful way. Well aware that this sounded crass, he noted that it was an "extremely delicate matter for the union," because "under the constitution of the UMWA a member cannot be disqualified on account of creed, color, or nationality. However, in times such as we are passing through, it is rather difficult to carry out the provisions of our constitution."[70] The government's primary concern was maintaining production, and Morrison reassured the government on this front. On the issue of the complete removal of aliens, he argued that he could not "agree that production would be affected in Nova Scotia if all aliens were removed from the mines, *as there are many hundreds seeking employment at this present time.*" "In the event of Italy declaring war," he posited that it would be "far more difficult" to control workers, as "our men would refuse to work with them [Italians] in the mines." Morrison continued, "From the viewpoint of production ... it could be maintained at the present level ... by the younger men now employed and hiring others to take their place." Morrison's concern was neither sabotage nor racism but local unemployment levels and union coherency. For Morrison, the anti-foreign strikes would not affect production. Morrison knew that because local unemployment was high, there would be plenty of Anglo-Celtic workers to fill all positions.

The state might have had tremendous breadth of power under the law to prevent strikes and criminalize strike activity, but their actual enforcement powers were limited. Without challenge, Morrison contended that he did "not know at this time of any further steps that might be taken by the police to control the situation." He closed with a veiled threat: "If the miners of Nova Scotia refuse to work with these enemy aliens, it is going to be a serious matter and one, which I am afraid, will be beyond the control of the Union Executive and the police."[71] Judging by the rhetoric of the district's union leadership, the state's assessment of the strikes was essentially correct. Miners were not afraid for their lives in the pits. Although they might have been anti-fascist in their political convictions, their main goal was to gain employment, and their means to achieve it was opportunistic wartime xenophobia.

The UMWA was intrinsically multiethnic, and because of the nature of mining, it was organized by industry rather than by craft. Miners' living conditions in Nova Scotia were marked by high unemployment, desperate poverty, and low wages, in an area with few job opportunities outside of the mines. As late as 1940, the ghost of the Depression continued to haunt the pits, and there were many miners still out of work.[72] Although the UMWA's constitution specifically opposed racism, nativism, and xenophobia, the Depression had spiked unemployment levels in some areas well past 30 percent, and these strikes were driven, in large part, by the dominant ethnic group's desire to procure intra-ethnic employment at the expense of those viewed as outsiders. Although politics, patriotism, and wartime fervour played a role in driving the strikes, the cold reality of unemployment was a harsh, if effective, impulse. The RCMP were largely unable to exercise the hefty powers the state had extended them primarily due to logistics, but also because the miners wrapped themselves in the rhetoric of the flag and, to a much lesser extent, anti-fascism.

When Canada declared war on Italy on June 10, the colliers exploded anew, with over five thousand miners going out on strike in that month alone. The strikers targeted workers of Italian birth or descent while simultaneously reinvigorating activity against workers perceived as potentially Axis-aligned. Nova Scotia coal miners in the Glace Bay District, New Waterford, and Florence all struck. In Halifax, 135 unorganized, non-union construction workers followed their lead and demanded the expulsion of enemy aliens from their ranks.[73] Halifax was not an Italian town; there were thirty-eight Italian-born citizens, of whom at least twenty-one were naturalized Canadians.[74] The strike ended when the three "Italians" in question were discharged.[75]

The first strike erupted in three coal pits in Glace Bay, only minutes after the declaration of war on Italy. New Waterford miners quickly slowed down in sympathy, cutting their mine to half capacity.[76] The UMWA hurriedly stepped in and organized a meeting on the night of June 11. At that meeting, the UMWA local decided that "no enemy aliens would be permitted to work in the mine," and it named a five-man committee to make sure that the motion was adhered to.[77] The committee was further charged with procuring residency and registration papers from the RCMP to ensure that no aliens passed for native. The UMWA's regional director, however, was of a somewhat different mind. Morrison urged his members to allow the RCMP to deal with any problems with aliens and to allow their co-workers into the pits. Morrison had been in close contact with L.D. Currie, the minister of mines, who had decided to "keep all enemy aliens out of the collieries until officials had investigated the status of each."[78] The meeting adjourned with the miners agreeing to return to work, so long as "persons of any nationality now at war with Britain ... would not be permitted to work in the local mines."[79]

Another meeting was held in Dominion, and three executives from the district UMWA were in attendance. RCMP naturalization records had been released to the union. Clearly, the state was somewhat in concert with the union's anti-foreign crusade, even though the RCMP had long helped the coal bosses crush miners' unions, often with incredible violence.[80] For the RCMP, it was "communism, not nativism and white supremacy that was the real enemy."[81] By wrapping themselves in the flag, engaging in nativist rhetoric, and not challenging the normativity of capital, the strikers were once again treated with kid gloves. Whereas other strikes were "illegal" and "treasonous" and even carried the threat of imprisonment, these strikes were worthy of impartiality, even aid, from the security service.[82]

The committees charged with examining the RCMP records did so and found that they "had no trouble with Italians," who had all returned home "when the attitude of the men were made known to them."[83] Whereas the leadership was not in favour of banning the foreign-born from the mines, the "feeling of the members was that all foreign-born workers should be barred." Alex "Sandy" McKay, secretary-treasurer of the district UMWA, pressed them to definitively decide how the locals were going to proceed, and he related the "anxious" companies' wish that a definite understanding be reached as early as possible.[84] The mines were not running at full capacity even without the strikes because of the loss of labourers to enlistment and the availability of higher-waged employment available elsewhere. He noted that the companies were looking to fill the positions as soon as possible and wanted to know whom, exactly, the men *were* willing to work with. To answer this question, a racial tribunal was struck. Members decided that Canadian-born workers with Italian parents or workers with only one Italian parent would both be "an exception to the rule." Given that the UMWA members on the RCMP records committee had been both on strike and doing "union work" (of a kind), they asked for off pay. McKay, clearly disturbed, refused. After some prodding, he agreed to put it to a vote at a later meeting.

At the general meeting, the miners met with local and district union bureaucrats. A motion was passed to ban most foreign-born miners from the mines until a thorough government investigation had been undertaken and presented. Employers had representatives at the union meeting, another rarity. The employers' representatives' rhetoric, however, was nauseatingly familiar to the miners; they excused speed ups, low pay, and dangerous conditions as necessary to win the war. They wanted to learn what the miners would accept, to both ensure future stability (a Panglossian notion) and "so that the company could hire replacements."[85] Government representatives argued against replacing the men but cautioned that all aliens should "remain away from the colliery, or trouble was bound to arise." In all, over 122 men were put out of work based on their descent or place of birth, and the UMWA, to its credit, refused to pay the committeemen who had guarded the pits or policed the ethnicity of its work force.

Foreign workers fought back against the elimination of their employment. In Glace Bay and New Waterford, German and Italian miners insisted on going underground to work. The state responded by having a conference with the UMWA. In an unholy alliance, the UMWA and the RCMP decided that one RCMP officer would be stationed at each mine in the district to give local enforcement committees "any cooperation or assistance they might require in keeping enemy aliens out of the pits."[86] But as naturalization papers trickled in, the mood became less unwelcoming for Italian and German miners. Miners struck the Florence Colliery on June 21, 1940, because naturalized miners who had been cleared to work were not allowed in the pits. Although Nova Scotia miners were probably the most militant and strike-prone workers in Canada, the strikes were beginning to border on the absurd.[87] The strike carried on for three days, and on June 23 the miners returned to work, Italian comrades in tow.[88] Only two days later, over at Glace Bay, four hundred miners struck against the employment of three Italians who had been cleared to work under the terms agreed to by a union vote.[89] At a union meeting on June 22, the workers agreed to allow certain men underground. When the men showed up to work on Monday, June 24, some five hundred miners struck. After a sufficient show of force in the one-day strike, the Italians stayed home, and the mine returned to production.[90]

Strikes against the employment of foreigners were largely successful. By June, all foreign-born workers needed naturalization papers and clearance from the RCMP to return to work. The UMWA and the RCMP cleared all foreign men to return to work until charges had been laid against them."[91] However, these measures were not enough. Workers continued to strike every time Italians or Germans attempted to enter the mines, even after they had been cleared to work. Although the foreigners attempted to gain entrance to their workplace, they were continually stopped from doing so. The RCMP and mine owners essentially told them to stay home, but the union leadership told them that if they did not attempt to work, "their relief would be cut off." Privation loomed for the families of those put out of work. Adding to the pain, councils in these small mining towns denied foreign families relief, telling them to appeal to the provincial and federal governments instead.[92]

The situation quieted down for a few weeks, but at the beginning of July the pits erupted again. On July 3, just over 3,750 miners struck multiple collieries in and around Glace Bay. The number of "nationalities" that miners refused to work with increased. Not content with banning Italians, Germans, and Austrians, they expanded their taxonomy to include newly conquered Poles and, bizarrely, Belgians. A letter to the *Sydney Post-Record* conveyed the feelings of at least one miner. He argued that the Italian government had "set up schools" all over Canada. In these schools, the fascists had indoctrinated children of Italian descent and had been told (quoting a school book) to "think of Italy and make a vow to be ready to give her all of your blood ... Someday we may need even your life to become bigger. Be one of the first to answer the call."[93] The author noted that one could not be "sure there aren't any of these among our miners who would blow up one of our mines and a few hundred good Canadians in order that his people could say 'daddy or brother tried to win the war for Italy.' There are thousands of Italians in Canada schooled to die for their country."[94] Although the media paid little attention to the anti-foreign strikes, an editorial in the *Sydney Post-Record* had a different take on events: "The excuse for [the strikes] is worse than none. It was so silly, so utterly indefensible, as to render it difficult to believe that those who resorted to it were serious in the arguments with which they sought to justify their own wanton dereliction of duty."[95] Few took the threat of a "potential sabotage" seriously, and the strikes were increasingly likened to fifth column activities. The shield of xenophobic patriotism and anti-fascism was only so effective, and its effectiveness was increasingly threadbare.

Anti-fascist sentiment seemed to have shifting boundaries that were often articulated in uneven and self-interested ways. A dozen Canadian-born men of Italian parentage were allowed back in the mines by union decree, but when they showed up for work, they were refused entry by miners. A special report by the Department of Labour noted that there was some "apprehension of possible sabotage" by "some fanatical adherent of either Germany or Italy." The possibility of sabotage, the report concluded, was more imaginary than real, but what was real was the "unemployment problem" and how it "aggravated the enemy alien situation."[96] Clarence Gillis, a Co-operative Commonwealth Federation (CCF) MP for Cape Breton South, argued that "since the outbreak of the war their wages have remained stagnant, while their cost of living has increased by about 30 percent."[97] In many ways, the strikes were part of wider effort to exercise job control and hiring.

The UMWA had internal strictures against discrimination, but heretofore these strictures had seen limited enforcement. The state desperately needed the UMWA to maintain industrial discipline. If threats from the state could not control individual workers, the union was its best chance. In July, the UMWA officially ended any official or de facto support for agitation against working with aliens. Morrison argued that all men should be allowed back in the mines regardless of their status or nationality. Noting the illegal nature of the strikes, he invoked his own brand of war patriotism, arguing that the strikers were "taking the very dangerous procedure, in wartime particularly, of defying the law of the land."[98]

The wildcat strikes came to an end in June after a three-party conference between the UMWA, the province, and the Dominion Coal Company, and the decision was reaffirmed at the District 26 convention in the fall. In the end, the operators agreed to employ an unemployed native-born man for every foreigner on the payroll; to sequester all foreigners to one shift, from 11:00 to 19:00; and to ensure that the two groups did not work together at any time.[99] As the "foreigners" had been out of work for anywhere from several weeks to several months at this point, they agreed to the terms. In September, at the District 26 conference, the UMWA passed a motion to allow "any worker whose record is clear," regardless of nationality, back into the mines.[100] Three Nova Scotia locals held out against the motion, noting the "difficulty in securing employment for native youths," but the district told them to cleave to the convention's hearing or risk having their locals put into receivership. There was a spurt of strikes in the summer of 1940 in the jurisdictions of the obstreperous locals, but by fall the anti-alien outbursts in the mines had finally ceased.

Because the UMWA firmly adhered to its anti-racist constitution, the mines slowly reintegrated during the war. As the unemployment rate in Canada dipped into negative territory going into 1941 and as the unemployment rate in the collieries fell nearly to zero, strikes focused on the employment of enemies abated. By 1940, CCF MP Clarence Gillis echoed the quiet arguments of many strikers when he said the affair "was not a question of alienism, but of unemployment ... the last stand of desperate men."[101] By 1942, unemployment had vanished and with it actions of this kind. In the end, strikes against the employment of aliens primarily in Nova Scotia's coal mines involved at least 14,937 individual workers, causing time loss of 23,163 days.[102]

Although there were a small number of strikes against the employment of enemy aliens in Ontario and Quebec in 1940 and 1941, respectively, they were small affairs, never involving thousands of workers, multiple pickets, and weeks of active inactivity, as did the strikes in Nova Scotia. In fact, one of the last strikes against the employment of enemy aliens was a single-day affair in September 1941 in St. Remi d'Amherst, Quebec, when thirty employees struck against the employment of their fellow worker. The strike ended quickly when he was dismissed.[103] Another strike, in Wallaceburg, Ontario, erupted when a third-generation Canadian of German extraction precipitated a two-hour strike.[104]

Some employers attempted to instrumentalize the idea of foreignness to break strikes and demonize the CIO in general and communists in particular as foreign, or worse. In the midst of an illegal strike at the Pioneer gold mine in British Columbia, management threatened miners of German and Austrian extraction with deportation or internment. The International Union of Mine, Mill, and Smelter Workers (Mine Mill) was aghast at the prospect and successfully fought against the attempt to intimidate the foreign workers or sow disunity with the threat of extraction.[105]

The "patriotic" strikes against the employment of enemy aliens during the opening years of the Second World War are telling. Like most strikes during the war, the state had little ability to simply put the actions down by force. With so many men of fighting age involved in the war effort, they lacked the bodies to physically discipline the miners, let alone imprison them. However, wartime patriotism seems to have eclipsed wartime egalitarianism, and the security state was willing to occasionally aid the strikers in their actions, no matter how odious they were to the official stance on plurality. Historiographically and theoretically, the strikes stand as a corrective to historians who put forward a triumphalist notion of the CIO, or even labour, during the war. The good must be taken with the unsavoury, and militancy did not, necessarily, signify progressivism or an enlightened proletariat; it could be driven by material concerns. Whether from the point of view of an activist or a historian, it is clear that the struggle against racism and nativism continued during the war, if only in an uneven and haphazard fashion. The strikes ultimately stand as evidence of the workers' ability to instrumentalize notions of Britishness. Although they officially supported patriotic egalitarianism, the state and the RCMP were much more willing to allow a space for strikers, so long as they cloaked their actions in terms of loyalty and empire rather than material or socioeconomic concerns. In the end, the strikes fell off when full employment was achieved in 1942 and there was no further material reason for ethnocentric agitation for job control. The strikes were also some of the last ethnically or racially motivated strikes in Canada. Though the labour movement was often at the forefront of anti-racism in Canadian history, it was not immune to racist and xenophobic outbursts, ideas, or the ethno-racially defined structures in which they operated, whether determined by members or the leadership. But these strikes were among the last material manifestations of the instrumentalization of Anglo-Celtic superiority, a notion that slowly faded in the postwar era when civic nationalism elevated whiteness over ethnicity.

Notes

1 C.P. Stacey, *Arms, Men and Governments: The War Policies of Canada, 1939-1945* (Ottawa: Queen's Printer, 1970), 7. Stanley's seven-hundred-plus-page report is the standard treatment of the war on the home front. Stacy was given unprecedented access to the archives, and his tome is unmatched in breadth and scope.

2 W.A.B. Douglas, *The Creation of a National Air Force: The Official History of the Royal Canadian Air Force* (Toronto: University of Toronto Press, 1986), 192. King was further worried that the transition to peacetime would be "marked with massive unemployment and popular unrest." King was obsessed with the prospect of postwar instability. See Jack Granatstein, *Canada's War: The Politics of the Mackenzie King Government, 1939-1945* (Toronto: Oxford University Press, 1975), 250.

3 For more on the early industrial and political plans of Canada in the pre- or early war period, see Robert R. Bryce, *Canada and the Cost of World War II: The International Operations of Canada's Department of Finance, 1939-1947* (Montreal/Kingston: McGill-Queen's University Press, 2005), 11–85.

4 Jeffrey A. Keshen, *Saints, Sinners, and Soldiers: Canada's Second World War* (Vancouver: UBC Press, 2004), 43.

5 Ian Mosby, *Food Will Win the War: The Politics, Culture, and Science of Food on Canada's Home Front* (Vancouver: UBC Press, 2014), 212. The British Commonwealth Air Training Plan was also of particular importance and turned Canada into what American president Franklin Delano Roosevelt called "the aerodrome of democracy." Eventually, the scheme trained nearly two hundred thousand air force combat personnel in hundreds of locations across Canada; more importantly, it was (to that date) the largest industrial project undertaken on Canadian soil. F.J. Hatch, *The Aerodrome of Democracy: Canada and the British Commonwealth Air Training Plan, 1939-1945* (Ottawa: Directorate of History, Department of National Defence, 1983), iv.

6 Judy Fudge and Eric Tucker, *Labour before the Law: The Regulation of Workers' Collective Action in Canada, 1900-1948* (Toronto: University of Toronto Press, 2004), 229.

7 The Canadian government produced propaganda that specifically "told English Canadians of the loyalty of the ethnic community, even of enemy aliens," and that they would have to "widen the range of our nation-building to include ... a fuller knowledge of your fellow Canadians and particularly those who are not part of your race or creed." See William Young, "Mobilizing English Canada for War: The Bureau of Public Information, the Wartime Information Board, and a View of the Nation during the Second World War," in *The Second World War as a National Experience*, ed. Sidney Aster (Ottawa: Canadian Committee on Labour History, 1981), 191.

8 Prior to mass extermination, removal, repatriation, and national(ist) solidification following the Second World War, "area of birth" was far from akin to "ethnicity," let alone "race" or "nationality." However, because these words and phrases were used at the time, they are of importance as signifiers, however inaccurate. In many cases, "Italians" and "Germans" were neither, but for the sake of clarity, these terms are neither italicized nor put in quotation marks. As Donald Avery pointed out in his groundbreaking *"Dangerous Foreigners"*: "Any study of this type inevitably involves some problems of definition. Three terms that will be used frequently here are 'ethnic,' 'alien,' and 'foreigner.' These terms have unpleasant connotations, but the historian cannot avoid them: they were used in many ways and for many purposes in the period being studied. They are part of our history and must be accepted as such." This author shares Avery's reservations and his conclusions, and the use of "ethnic," "foreigner," and "alien" are used, not in a trajectory of acceptance but of commentary and critique. See Donald Avery, *"Dangerous Foreigners": European Immigrant Workers and*

Labour Radicalism in Canada, 1896–1932 (Toronto: McClelland and Stewart, 1980), 13–14.

9 For a broad overview of Canadian proletarian life during the Second World War, see Bryan Palmer, *Working-Class Experience: The Rise and Reconstitution of Canadian Labour, 1800–1980* (Toronto: Butterworth, 1983), 229–45; Craig Heron, *The Canadian Labour Movement* (Toronto: James Lorimer and Co., 1996), 58–75; Peter McInnis, *Harnessing Labour Confrontation: Shaping the Postwar Settlement in Canada, 1943–1950* (Toronto: University of Toronto Press, 2002); Desmond Morton, *Working People: An Illustrated History of the Canadian Labour Movement* (Montreal/Kingston: McGill-Queens University Press, 2007), 165–200; and Laurel Sefton MacDowell, *Renegade Lawyer: The Life of J.L. Cohen* (Toronto: University of Toronto Press/Osgoode Society for Canadian Legal History, 2001). More targeted studies include William Kaplan, *Everything That Floats: Pat Sullivan, Hal Banks, and the Seamen's Unions of Canada* (Toronto: University of Toronto Press, 1987); James Pritchard, "The Long, Angry Summer of '43: Labour Relations in Quebec's Shipbuilding Industry," *Labour/Le Travail* 65 (Spring 2010): 47–73; Laura Sefton MacDowell, *Remember Kirkland Lake: The Gold Miners Strike of 1941–1942* (Toronto: Canadian Scholars' Press, 2001); John MacFarlane, "Agents of Control or Chaos? A Strike at Arvida Helps Clarify Canadian Policy on Using Troops against Workers during the Second World War," *Canadian Historical Review* 86, 4 (December 2005): 619–40; Ruth Roach Pierson, *"They're Still Women after All": The Second World War and Canadian Womanhood* (Toronto: McClelland and Stewart, 1976); Ron Crawley, "What Kind of Unionism: Struggles among Sydney Steel Workers in the SWOC Years, 1936–1942," *Labour/Le Travail* 39 (Spring 1997): 99–123; and Sean Tucker and Brian Thorn, "Railing against the Company Union: The State, Union Substitution, and the Montréal Tramways Strike of 1943," *Labour/Le Travail* 58 (Fall 2006): 41–70. Institutionally oriented historians may be interested in Wendy Cuthbertson, *Labour Goes to War: The CIO and the Construction of a New Social Order, 1939–1945* (Vancouver: UBC Press, 2012).

10 For more on the workers' revolt, see Craig Heron, ed., *The Workers' Revolt in Canada, 1917–1925* (Toronto: University of Toronto Press, 1998).

11 Jeremy Webber, "The Malaise of Compulsory Conciliation: Strike Prevention in Canada during World War II," *Labour/Le Travail* 15 (Spring 1985): 69.

12 Michael D. Stevenson, "Conscripting Coal: The Regulation of the Coal Labour Force in Nova Scotia during the Second World War," *Acadiensis* 29, 2 (Spring 2000): 64. For more on the history of radicalism within the coalfields of Cape Breton, see John Manley, "Preaching the Red Stuff: J.B. McLachlan, Communism, and the Cape Breton Miners, 1922–1935," *Labour/Le Travail* 30 (Fall 1992): 65–114.

13 For elite attempts at the construction of a specifically Canadian nationalism in the interwar period, see Jeffrey Brison, *Rockefeller, Carnegie, and Canada: American Philanthropy and the Arts and Letters in Canada* (Montreal/Kingston: McGill-Queen's University Press, 2005).

14 Daniel Francis, *National Dreams: Myth, Memory, and Canadian History* (Vancouver: Arsenal Pulp Press, 1997), 53.

15 Charles Johnston, "The Children's War: The Mobilization of Ontario's Youth during the Second World War," in *Patterns of the Past: Interpreting Ontario's History*, ed. Roger Hall, William Westfall, and Laurel Sefton MacDowell (Toronto: Dundurn, 1988), 361.

16 A relatively comprehensive archive of posters is available online through McGill University Library's Canadian War Posters Collection. Henri Eveleigh, "Let's Go Canada!," WP2.R24.F4, Rare Books and Special Collections, McGill University Library, Montreal.

17 The poster also urged Canadians that "when you find anyone – yourself included – thinking, speaking, acting, with racial or religious prejudice – STOP IT! If Smith, Kelly, Cohen or Svoboda is good enough to die for us, he's good enough to live with us ... As an equal." *Winnipeg Tribune,* November 20, 1943.

18 For more on "whiteness" in general, see Theodore Allen, *The Invention of the White Race,* vol. 1, *Racial Oppression and Social Control* (New York: Verso, 2012); David Roediger, *The Wages of Whiteness: Race and the Making of the American Working Class* (New York: Verso, 1999); David Theo Goldberg, *The Racial State* (Hong Kong: Blackwell, 2002); Noel Ignatiev, *How the Irish Became White* (New York: Routledge, 1995); and Karen Brodkin, *How Jews Became White Folks and What That Says about Race in America* (New Brunswick, NJ: Rutgers University Press, 1998). For an international comparative study on the interplay of democracy and racism, see David Scott FitzGerald and David Cook-Martín, *Culling the Masses: The Democratic Origins of Racist Immigration Policy in the Americas* (Cambridge: Harvard University Press, 2014), particularly chaps. 1, 3, and 4. For specifically Canadian interpretations of race, racism, and "citizenship" (there were no citizens of Canada until 1947; before this, they were British subjects or, occasionally, Canadian nationals) during the war, see Ivana Caccia, *Managing the Canadian Mosaic in Wartime: Shaping Citizenship Policy, 1939-1945* (Montreal/Kingston: McGill-Queen's University Press, 2010); Pamela Sugiman, "Privilege and Oppression: The Configuration of Race, Gender, and Class in Southern Ontario Auto Plants, 1939 to 1949," *Labour/ Le Travail* 47 (Spring 2001): 83–113; Richard Day, *Multiculturalism and the History of Canadian Diversity* (Toronto: University of Toronto Press, 2000); and, to a lesser extent, Carmela Patrias, *Jobs and Justice: Fighting Wartime Discrimination in Wartime Canada, 1939-1945* (Toronto: University of Toronto Press, 2012).

19 Avery, *Dangerous Foreigners,* 41. The standard treatment on racism within the American labour movement, is Robert Zieger, *For Jobs and Freedom: Race and Labor in America since 1865* (Lexington: University Press of Kentucky, 2007).

20 Joseph Gerteis, *Class and the Color Line: Interracial Class Coalition in the Knights of Labor and the Populist Movement* (Durham: Duke University Press 2007), and Melton McLaurin, *The Knights of Labor in the South* (Westport: Greenwood Press, 1978). For the Knights in the Canadian context, see Gregory Kealey and Bryan Palmer, *Dreaming of What Might Be: The Knights of Labor in Ontario, 1880-1900* (Cambridge: Cambridge University Press, 1982).

21 At the 1886 Knights convention in Richmond, Virginia, the national leaders successfully insisted that the city's theaters and hotels accept African American delegates. See Michael Goldfield, "Race and the CIO: The Possibilities for Racial Egalitarianism during the 1930s and 1940s," *International Labor and Working-Class History* 44 (Fall 1993): 4. This contrasts with the Industrial Workers of the World (IWW), the most actively anti-racist political formation in North America's history, which combined revolutionary anarcho-syndicalism with a radical egalitarianism. For more on the IWW in Canada, see Mark Leier, *Where the Fraser River Flows: The Industrial Workers of the World in British Columbia* (Vancouver: New Star Books, 1990), and Peter Campbell, "The Cult of Spontaneity: Finnish-Canadian Bushworkers and the Industrial Workers of the World in Northern Ontario, 1919–1934," *Labour/Le Travail* 41 (Spring 1998): 117–46.

22 David Goutor, *Guarding the Gates: The Canadian Labour Movement and Immigration, 1872-1934* (Vancouver: UBC Press, 2007), 4.

23 The TLC campaigned on behalf of English workers who spoke out against the war. For example, John Reid, a socialist from Calgary, was sentenced to fifteen months hard labour for sedition. Following extensive protest from the TLC, he was released. This was

rarely, if ever, the case for foreign workers. See Helen Potrebenko, *No Streets of Gold: A Social History of Ukrainians in Alberta* (Vancouver: New Star Books, 1977), 110.

24   Avery, *Dangerous Foreigners*, 67.

25   In 1937, a group of largely eastern European workers held a sit-down strike at the Holmes Foundry near Sarnia, Ontario, under the auspices of the Congress of Industrial Organizations' (CIO) Steel Workers Organizing Committee. Local politicians and the employer capitalized on the split and hired the British workers and some allies (numbering around three hundred) to forcibly expel the strikers. During the assault, twenty strikers were injured seriously enough to require hospitalization, and sixty-six were arrested, resulting in fifty-five convictions. See Duart Snow, "The Holmes Foundry Strike of 1937: 'We'll Give Their Jobs to White Men,'" *Ontario History* 69, 1 (1977): 4–31.

26   Nelson Lichtenstein, *Labor's War at Home: The CIO in World War II* (New York: Cambridge University Press, 1987), 124–26.

27   Goldfield, "Race and the CIO," 7–10. For more on the history of the AFL in Canada, see Robert Babcock, *Gompers in Canada: A Study in American Continentalism before the First World War* (Toronto: University of Toronto Press, 1974).

28   The Dominion Coal Company owned nearly all Nova Scotia mines and had a multicultural workforce. The company retained files on the birthplaces of its workers. Apart from the majority, who were Anglo-Celtic, the company also had (in order from most to least common) Italian, Polish, Austrian, German, Ukrainian, Bohemian, Czech-Slovakian, Hungarian, Russian, French, Belgian, Romanian, Norwegian, American, Yugoslavian, Hungarian, Spanish, Syrian, Greek, Swedish, Danish, Dutch, and Serbian employees. In all, the company employed 916 men of "foreign birth." The UMWA local was far from monolithically Anglo-Celtic. As with many collieries organized during the interwar years, it was not organized in an "ethno-racially" monolithic fashion but one well within its polyglot, multiethnic reality. *Sydney Post Record*, September 2, 1939.

29   For a limited overview on the history of fascism and anti-fascism in Canada, see Martin Robin, *Shades of Right: Nativist and Fascist Politics in Canada, 1920–1940* (Toronto: University of Toronto Press, 1992); Lita-Rose Betcherman, *The Swastika and the Maple Leaf: Fascist Movements in Canada in the Thirties* (Toronto: Fitzhenry and Whiteside, 1975); Ivan Avakumovic, *The Communist Party of Canada: A History* (Toronto: McClelland and Stewart, 1975); and John Manley "From United Front to Popular Front: The CPC in 1936," in *R.C.M.P. Security Bulletins: The Depression Years*, Part 3, *1936*, ed. Gregory S. Kealey and Reg Whitaker (St. John's: Canadian Committee on Labour History, 1996), 1–24.

30   Traditionally, "Communist influence was greatest" in the area, but the Communist Party seems to have said little on the matter. See Michael J. Earle, "The Coalminers and Their 'Red' Union: The Amalgamated Mine Workers of Nova Scotia, 1932–1936," *Labour/Le Travail* 22 (Fall 1988): 105.

31   Clark Kerr and Abraham Siegel, "The Interindustry Propensity to Strike: An International Comparison," in *Industrial Conflict*, ed. Arthur Kornhauser, Robert Dubin, and Arthur M. Ross (New York: McGraw-Hill, 1954), 189–212.

32   *Toronto Telegram*, September 5, 1939.

33   Ian McKay, "Strikes in the Maritimes, 1901–1914," *Acadiensis* 13 (1983): 14. See also W.M. Baker, "The Personal Touch: Mackenzie King, Harriett Reid, and the Springhill Strike, 1909–1911," *Labour/Le Travail* 13 (Spring 1984): 159–76.

34   Strike and Lockout files, RG 27, vol. 402: 39–97, Library and Archives Canada (hereafter LAC).

35   Ibid., 39–110.

36   *Halifax Chronicle*, September 5, 1939.

37 *Toronto Telegram,* September 5, 1939.

38 *Winnipeg Tribune,* September 5, 1939.

39 *New Glasgow News,* September 6, 1939.

40 *Halifax Herald,* September 6, 1939.

41 Ibid.

42 *Halifax Chronicle,* September 6, 1939.

43 Ibid.

44 Strike and Lockout files, RG 27, vol. 402: 39–102a, LAC.

45 *Halifax Herald,* September 13, 1939.

46 The Legion in Nova Scotia mining communities was much more progressive than its compatriots elsewhere in the country owing to the demographic base of its miners. Clarence Gillis, the socialist Co-operative Commonwealth Federation (CCF) MP in the area, had long led the Legion. See Michael Earle and Herb Gamberg, "The United Mine Workers and the Coming of the CCF to Cape Breton," *Acadiensis* 19, 1 (1989): 21.

47 *Montreal Herald,* September 19, 1939.

48 Although it seems that only 60 of the over 1,040 men employed were active in demanding that the brothers be fired.

49 Strike and Lockout files, RG 27, vol. 402: 39–102a, LAC.

50 *Labour Gazette* (Ottawa: King's Printer, 1939), 989.

51 *Ottawa Journal,* May 16, 1940.

52 *Halifax Chronicle,* May 16, 1940.

53 *Sydney Post-Record,* May 16, 1940.

54 *Hamilton Spectator,* May 23, 1940.

55 *Toronto Telegram,* May 23, 1940.

56 *Windsor Star,* May 24, 1940.

57 Vice-President of Chrysler Corporation of Canada to the Deputy Minister of Labour, n.d., Strike and Lockout files, RG 27, vol. 402: 40–66, LAC.

58 *Windsor Star,* May 29, 1940.

59 The government and RCMP, in all reality, were much more concerned with interning communists, trade union leaders, leftist politicians, and Ukrainian progressives than Germanic Nazis, domestic fascists and anti-Semites, Italian fascists, or fascist or nationalist Ukrainians sympathetic to Hitler. See Reg Whitaker, "Official Repression of Communism during World War II," *Labour/Le Travail* 17 (Spring 1986): 135–66.

60 Irving Abella and Harold Troper, *None Is Too Many: Canada and the Jews of Europe, 1933–1948* (Toronto: Lester and Orpen Dennys, 1983).

61 RG 27, vol. 402: 40–74, LAC.

62 *Halifax Chronicle,* May 31, 1940.

63 L.D. Currie, Deputy Minister of Labour, to Norman McLarty, Minister of Labour, June 3, 1940, Strike and Lockout files, RG 27, vol. 402: 40–74, LAC.

64 Department of Labour, memo, June 4, 1940, Strike and Lockout files, RG 27, vol. 402: 40–74, LAC.

65 Ibid.

66 Norman McLarty to L.D. Currie, June 6, 1940, RG 27, vol. 402: 40–74, LAC.

67 In December 1939, the executive of District 26, in concert with the International leadership, stated that they "would no longer countenance or condone petty strikes, tie-ups or any other breaches of contract." Locals who ignored this order, they continued, would face individual fines or would have their charters revoked. See "Petty Strikes Banned by UMW Executive," *Sydney Post-Record,* December 22, 1939. The UMWA later made good on this threat during the war. For the latter, see Michael Earle, "'Down with Hitler

and Silby Barrett': The Cape Breton Miners' Slowdown Strike of 1941," *Acadiensis* 18, 1 (1988): 56–90.

68   Morrison was the relatively unpopular long-time leader of the UMWA in District 26. See Christina M. Lamey, "Davis Day through the Years: A Cape Breton Coalmining Tradition," *Nova Scotia Historical Review* 16, 2 (1996): 23–33.

69   D.W. Morrison to W.M. Dickson, June 10, 1940, RG 27, vol. 402: 40–74, LAC.

70   Ibid.

71   Ibid.

72   In early June, a four-day strike was called in Westville, Nova Scotia, because a miner enlisted, assaulted his commanding officer, was discharged, and then was refused his job because it had already been filled. Unemployment remained relatively high in 1940 in Nova Scotia.

73   *Labour Gazette* (Ottawa: King's Printer, 1940), 673.

74   *Halifax Chronicle,* June 12, 1940.

75   Strike and Lockout files, RG 27, vol. 402: 40–80, LAC.

76   *Halifax Herald,* June 11, 1940.

77   *Windsor Star,* June 12, 1940.

78   Ibid.

79   Strike and Lockout files, RG 27, vol. 402: 40–79, LAC.

80   Ian McKay and Suzanne Morton, "The Maritimes: Expanding the Circle of Resistance," in *The Workers' Revolt in Canada, 1917–1925,* ed. Craig Heron (Toronto: University of Toronto Press, 1998), 43–86.

81   Reg Whitaker, Gregory S. Kealey, and Andrew Parnaby, *Secret Service: Political Policing in Canada from the Fenians to Fortress Canada* (Toronto: University of Toronto Press, 2012), 106.

82   For more on the harsh treatment meted out to other unionists, see MacDowell, *Renegade Lawyer,* 161–70.

83   *Sydney Post-Record,* June 15, 1940.

84   Although, by the Second World War, McKay was seen as a conservative in the UMWA, he was elected in 1924 as a member of the Communist Party. See M. Earle and H. Gamberg, "The United Mine Workers and the Coming of the CCF to Cape Breton," *Acadiensis* 19, 1 (1989): 6.

85   *Sydney Post-Record,* June 15, 1940.

86   *Halifax Chronicle,* June 13, 1940.

87   Memorandum, n.d., Strike and Lockout files, RG 27, vol. 402: 40–85, LAC.

88   *Sydney Post-Record,* June 25, 1940.

89   Strike and Lockout files, RG 27, vol. 402: 40–87, LAC.

90   Special Report, n.d., RG 27, vol. 402: 40–87, LAC.

91   *Halifax Herald,* June 6, 1940.

92   *Halifax Chronicle,* June 11, 1940, and *Sydney Post-Record,* June 11, 1940.

93   *Sydney Post-Record,* August 28, 1940.

94   Hyperbole aside, the fascist government of Italy did sponsor the curriculum, and its embassies were arms of the state. Nonetheless, apart from the Italians, however numerous and sympathetic they were to fascism, there is little evidence that there was much in the way of active, useful support for Mussolini in Canada. Italians were interned in Canada for supporting fascism, but they were never pursued with the same vigour as the state pursued communists, the leadership of ethnic progressive organizations, militant trade union leaders, or left-wing politicians. See *Sydney Post-Record,* August 28, 1940, and Whitaker, "Official Repression." For more on Italian internment, see Franca

Iacovetta, Roberto Perin, and Angelo Principe, eds., *Enemies Within: Italian and Other Internees in Canada and Abroad* (Toronto: University of Toronto Press, 2000).

95 *Sydney Post-Record,* July 3, 1940.

96 Special Report, July 13, 1940, Strike and Lockout files, RG 27, vol. 402: 40–90, LAC.

97 *Edmonton People's Weekly,* July 13, 1940.

98 *New Glasgow News,* June 5, 1940.

99 Special Report, June 22, 1940, Strike and Lockout files, RG 27, vol. 402: 40–90, LAC.

100 *Sydney Post-Record,* November 1, 1940.

101 Ivana Caccia, *Managing the Canadian Mosaic in Wartime: Shaping Citizenship Policy, 1939–1945* (Montreal/Kingston: McGill-Queen's University Press, 2010), 48.

102 *Labour Gazette* (Ottawa: King's Printer, 1941), 248. This number is surely a minor underestimate. The *Labour Gazette* had a habit of underestimating the number of strikes and strikers and of discounting small strikes.

103 Ibid., 1222.

104 Wallaceburg Brass to Department of Labour, July 7, 1941, Strike and Lockout files, RG 27, vol. 402: 41–127, LAC. There was also a small strike in an automotive plant in Sarnia, Ontario, over the continued employment of an Austrian Polish worker who had been drafted into the "Austrian" army in the First World War. He had told his employer and fellow workers (over six years of employment) that he had known Adolf Hitler and had served in his regiment. After a half-day strike of some twenty-one men, the man was terminated. See Strike and Lockout files, RG 27, vol. 402: 40–99, LAC.

105 *Bridge River Miner,* January 10, 1940. That Mine Mill was actively anti-racist in the midst of wartime xenophobia is of little surprise. Mine Mill had been at the forefront of anti-racist policies.

9

First Nations and the British Connection during the Second World War

R. Scott Sheffield

WHEN CANADA MARCHED off to war in 1939, it did so primarily to aid its King and the British Empire, so suggests the bulk of the historical literature.[1] As Tim Cook argues, "Canada would never have gone to war unless Britain was threatened; nor was it able – even with control over its foreign policy – to stay out of the conflict, so deep were its ties to the British Empire."[2] In reality, the reasons behind Canadians' willingness to have their country join Britain's fight against the Axis powers were more complex and nuanced than blind loyalty.[3] While neither universal nor all-encompassing, loyalty to King and Empire was most evident among those of British heritage and least evident in French Canadian communities, as the contributions by Geoff Keelan and Robert Talbot in this volume demonstrate. Understandably, then, Anglo-Canadians' links to Britain and the Crown during the Second World War infringed on matters of national unity, and they have generally been examined within that framework. Anglo-Canadians, however, were not the only residents to foreground the British connection in their approach to the global crisis. Many First Nations across Canada also felt motivated to participate because of their historical relationship with Britain, often symbolically invested in the Crown or specific monarchs, past and present.[4] Many First Nations men and women demonstrated their loyalty and provided aid to the Empire in diverse ways, including, most profoundly, military service. More than four thousand enlisted or were conscripted, and of them, almost three hundred lost their lives.[5]

First Nations involvement in the war was much more complex than a simple urge to demonstrate loyalty and allegiance. Importantly, the connection between Status Indians and the Crown was distanced and mediated through agencies of the Canadian federal government, particularly the Indian Affairs Branch. By 1939, the relationship between First Nations and the Indian Affairs Branch varied from agency to agency but was generally marred by mutual distrust, poor communication, and occasional confrontation. Long-standing grievances and fractious dealings over lands, governance, education, and treaties, among other things, remained problematic during the war. To these would be added specific wartime concerns over new taxation, national registration, and conscription that ensured that First Nations communities confronted and resisted the state, even as they cooperated in pursuit of a shared war effort. The British connection and the Crown remained important as an avenue of appeal for First Nations in their efforts to defend themselves from an increasingly intrusive wartime state.

It is impossible to read through the archival records pertaining to Status Indians in the Second World War without recognizing how conceptually entwined First Nations engagement in the war was with their connection to Britain and the Crown.[6] The Indigenous voices that emerge from Indian Affairs documents and English Canadian newspapers reveal not only how genuine this connection was but also how malleable a tool the "Crown" proved to be for First Nations people as they sought to manage both their relationship with the Canadian state and their involvement in the Second World War. Whether as a rhetorical, a symbolic, or a legal instrument, the British connection was something First Nations people drew upon as they negotiated the enhancement or limitation of their participation, depending on circumstances. The exigencies and opportunities fostered by the Second World War consequently provide a lens through which to view the continuing significance of the British Crown to Indigenous peoples.

The historical military connection between First Nations peoples and Britain is both ancient and significant. Following contact, complex rivalries between Indigenous nations and confederacies and Euro-American imperial powers created a dynamic environment in which an Indigenous community could sometimes further its interests by allying with Europeans or their colonial offspring.[7] Evident in certain regions even before the conquest of New France in 1760, Indigenous relationships with the British subsequently diversified and solidified across the region in numerous conflicts through to 1815.[8] These years established traditions of alliance and cooperation between many First Nations and Britain in the central and eastern portions of Canada. After 1815, Indigenous men provided military aid and scouting on a smaller scale up to the end of the nineteenth century.[9] For those nations involved, these actions reaffirmed their alliance with the Crown, but even without such opportunities, oral traditions sustained Indigenous connections to past military relationships and cultural imperatives through to the twentieth century.

Most of the early agreements between the British and First Nations arose from a context of conflict, taking the form of military alliances or peace treaties. In the wake of the Royal Proclamation of 1763, as agreements shifted increasingly to land cession treaties, Crown pre-emption ensured that the Crown remained central to First Nations relationship with imperial authorities. Following Confederation in 1867, jurisdiction over First Nations transferred to Ottawa, which inherited the imperial legislative and administrative tool kit. Thus, the Canadian government acted as the agent of the Crown in negotiations of the land cession treaties known as the Numbered Treaties, which covered much of western and northern Canada from 1871 to 1921.[10] Indigenous ceremonies that marked the negotiations of many of these treaties "invoked the Great Spirit and effectively made it party to the proceedings. The terms that were then negotiated thus became a covenant – an agreement that involved First Nations, the Crown, and the diety."[11] Plains and northern First Nations peoples, through these holistic and sacred agreements, thus shared a profound sense of connection to the British Crown.

As First Nations found their vision of themselves, their lands, and their future increasingly in conflict with the narrow vision of the Canadian government in the later nineteenth and early twentieth centuries, they logically looked to the British Crown and government for intervention.[12] As early as 1860, royal visits became occasions for First Nations people to "claim public attention, affirm their loyalism and cultural integrity, and demand redress of political grievances."[13] In British Columbia, without treaties and with provincial officials obstinately refusing to acknowledge Indigenous rights and title, First Nations discovered the Royal Proclamation of 1763. Thereafter, many Indigenous leaders would position this key document at the centre of their arguments for political justice, and the "Royal Proclamation and the British monarch became and remained important political symbols."[14] The Nisga'a, the most active political campaigners among BC First Nations, even sent a famous petition addressed to "the King's Most Excellent Majesty in Council," in 1913, in hopes of obtaining British justice.[15] The Crown and British connection therefore became both a fond symbol with which many First Nations felt bonded and a potential stick with which to bludgeon recalcitrant Canadian governments.

That connection survived well into the twentieth century among First Nations peoples, even if it was progressively overshadowed in day-to-day dealings by the Canadian Department of Indian Affairs. By the later nineteenth and early twentieth centuries, however, opportunities to reaffirm alliances and demonstrate military prowess were hard to find. A new opportunity emerged when the Dominions began to send contingents of volunteer soldiers to join imperial military campaigns around the world. In 1885, 367 Canadian voyageurs, many of them Indigenous, joined the 1885 British Nile River expedition to the Sudan.[16] Some First Nations men might also have been able to participate in the Boer War, but because "no account of 'race' was registered on any military records, the precise number of Indians who served is not known."[17] By contrast, the Great War offered expanded opportunities for Status Indian youths to volunteer for military service and renew their people's sacred connection to the British Crown. Some caution is needed in generalizing here, as many Indigenous communities remained ambivalent about a war that was not their own, and engagement in the war effort varied widely.[18] Nevertheless, in those communities that culturally venerated warriors, military service reinvigorated ceremonial traditions and the social status connected to warriors.[19]

Though only a relatively small number of Indigenous men were able to enlist in the early stages of the war because of racial antipathies, by late 1915 restrictions were lifted, and First Nations recruiting accelerated.[20] By war's end, approximately four thousand Status Indian men had served with the Canadian army, their service the living embodiment of their communities' sense of allegiance and loyalty. The shabby treatment they received as veterans, however, corroded the sense of accomplishment they felt at having upheld their end of the relationship with Britain. Nevertheless, the Great War experience was an important one for First Nations populations, honouring and renewing treaties and traditions of alliance with Britain.

When war broke out in Europe once again in 1939, there remained a relatively unbroken line of connection that ensured the British Crown's continued relevance to many Canadian First Nations. This manifested most visibly in declarations of First Nations allegiance and willingness to contribute to the national war effort, as well as in subsequent claims for citizenship. Public statements and acts of loyalty were especially evident in the first years of the conflict, as the nation galvanized itself for war and rallied around the flag. Some of these statements and acts of loyalty were produced for public purposes and to appeal to a Euro-Canadian audience.

Two examples occurred in Alberta in 1940–41. The first was a prize-winning essay by a student from the St. Paul's Indian Residential School in southern Alberta: "Britain ... is fighting for liberty and free institutions for others, which she considers are their birthright. Her responsibilities are world-wide but everywhere they stand for the same principle, maintaining the force of decency against barbarian people ... So in the meantime let us pray, pray, pray, and at the last may God Save the King."[21] The second example came from Mike Mountain Horse, a Great War veteran and prominent Kainai (Blood) leader, who concluded a public lecture in Cardston by informing the audience "that his people were 100 percent behind us in the present conflict ... The Indians realize the freedom they enjoy under the British Flag, they can only tolerate one flag, 'British'; one language, 'English'; and one loyalty – 'to the King.'"[22] These types of public proclamations played very well to English Canadians, especially in 1940–41, when the war news was mostly grim and people appreciated hearing that every segment of the population was pulling together in a common cause.[23]

Such public acts and words might well have been designed to curry favour, or were at least articulated to achieve that end, but they should not be dismissed as simply pandering to Canadians' elevated wartime patriotism. First Nations peoples' genuine concerns clearly emerge in similar comments made in more private moments. For example, shortly after the collapse of French resistance in June 1940, Indian agent G.C. Laight included a comment from a chief in his agency in a letter to his superiors in Ottawa: "Chief James Peacock asked me to express to the Government of Canada their Loyalty to His Majesty The King and the British Empire, also to state that the Indians of the Enoch Band are willing to assist the Government of Canada in any way they can to bring the war to a successful conclusion."[24] In a similar vein, a news report from North Battleford, Saskatchewan, informed its readers about the treaty annuities ceremonies in the province: "The treaty party reported the Indians volunteered to contribute their annual allowance to help the national war effort. The Indians, aware of the current trend of the war, said they wanted Canada to give full aid to their 'glorious King and Queen.'"[25] These expressions of loyalty were clearly less polished and public, reflecting the sincere feelings of the individuals and communities involved. Driving home the heartfelt nature of the British connection was a pattern revealed in the latter example: words were frequently combined with actions and generosity.

Despite the often constrained fiscal situation of Indigenous communities in Canada after a decade of Depression, and the often limited nature of band funds held in trust for the community, First Nations peoples were moved by the suffering and stalwart stand of the British people in 1940–41. Many communities opted to donate money from their band funds to specific British causes and charities. For instance, in a Siksika (Blackfoot) Council meeting in 1941, "Councillor Yellow Fly broached the subject of giving help to the air raid victims of Britain through the Queen's Fund. The Council received this suggestion enthusiastically and Yellow Fly was detailed to draft the resolution asking for a payment of $200.00 to this fund, from the funds of the Band; all Councillors agreed to sign such a resolution.'[26] In the Maritimes, the Mi'kmaq people from the Whycocomagh Reserve, according to Chief Gabriel Holliboy, "having been born and brought up with Scotch people, we ask, that ... the above stated amount of our gift [$2,000] be used to aid the suffering children of Scotland."[27]

Many communities, however, had few band funds to draw upon or were refused permission by Indian Affairs to do so, and they actively raised funds to donate.[28] Even in the remote northern reaches of Yukon, the Vuntut Gwitchin (the Old Crow Band) cobbled together a donation of $432.30 for the London Orphans Fund.[29] Sometimes aid came in forms other than money, but the sentiments were similar. In March 1941, a Brockville newspaper noted: "Accompanied by a note saying 'Usually people are helping us; now we can help others not so fortunate as we are,' a hamper of clothes has been sent to Vancouver by 18 Indian women of a church circle at Hartley Bay, on the far north coast of British Columbia, to be given to needy evacuee children from the United Kingdom."[30]

Although First Nations mostly directed their efforts to humanitarian causes, they sometimes wished to aid Britain's military effort. Patriotic campaigns to purchase weapons were common across Canada, and few captured imaginations as much as the purchase of fighter aircraft. The *Winnipeg Free Press* reported on a remote Cree community in York Factory who sent a $240 cheque "for Wings for Britain ... York Factory Indians who have been enthusiastic in their subscriptions because of the prospects that the proceeds would be applied to the purchase of a fight [sic] plane for aid in the defence of Britain."[31] As early as 1940, a number of Salish communities proposed raising $25,000 among BC First Nations to buy a Spitfire.[32] Despite opposition from the BC Indian commissioner and Indian Affairs, these efforts continued over a year later. A *Vancouver Province* photo caption reveals: "INDIANS ON THE WARPATH – Helping to further Britain's war effort, residents of Capilano Indian Reserve at North Vancouver Wednesday staged a concert and bazaar to swell the total of the Squamish Spitfire Fund."[33] While Indigenous acts of generosity to Britain were clearly heartfelt and meaningful for those who made the offerings, they stemmed from more than simple altruism.

These actions reflected an implicit belief in the right of First Nations to participate in the collective war effort, a belief that, in some instances, was made explicit. Despite First Nations aiming their arguments in favour of their right to contribute to the war at Canadians and their government, the declarations often made reference to a British connection. For instance, a letter accompanying an $850 donation to the Canadian Red Cross from band funds contained the following words: "We the Blackfoot tribe of Indians desire to show our loyalty to Canada and to the Empire by our humble bit to help in the struggle for freedom against tyranny. Canada has, and always shall be, our home. The outlook of the Indian is purely Canadian in its nature and character."[34] In other instances, declarations of belonging could be twinned with assertions of the distinct identity and status of Indigenous peoples. Something of this can be seen in the Nishga Land Committee's reminder of their long-standing claims to Indigenous rights and title in a letter to the prime minister: "To show our loyalty to our country contributing $25 ... To protect our tribal rights and to strengthen his Majesties [sic] Forces ... We also pray that there always be an England and final victory."[35] Perhaps this final iteration of loyalty to the King and England debarbed an otherwise challenging statement.

The symbolism and philosophical foundation of the Empire and the war effort could amplify the impact of claims for citizenship rights. For instance, Chief Tibbetts from Burns Lake, British Columbia, wrote the following to the Indian Affairs Branch: "We are all on our feet marching with the soldiers. We Indians do not know what we are fighting for. King George [has] called up the boys to protect him. Our Indian boys have taken up a very difficult task they may not all return home at all." After arguing against wartime taxation and conscription being imposed on his people, he concluded that if "you are not going to give us the same privileges as the white then bring our Indian boys back to guard Canada only. If the Indians boys are going to stay overseas then we want to be mix with the white people like one."[36]

No one articulated these sentiments so powerfully as did the chiefs of the Kainai people in southern Alberta:

> Why should we be asked to go when we only live in the Empire and are not part of it. We are only wards of the government and have no voice in control-ling the affairs of government but are asked to submit like children and take full responsibility with those who are fortunate to be full citizens and subjects of the King ... We all know that the war must be fought and won for the Brit-ish Empire but why treat us like this and use our loyalty without giving us the thing the empire and the united nations are fighting for: "THE RIGHT TO RUN OUR OWN COUNTRIES AND HAVE OUR OWN LIBERTY IN THE WAY WE DESIRE IT" ... Surely if our young men are good enough to wear the King's uniform and take their place with others, they should have full right to say with the others when and where Canada should fight.[37]

Framed in the context of the Empire, their status as British subjects, and the philosophical ideals for which the war was being fought, such words would have moved most English Canadians. Many First Nations saw the Empire, Britain, and the Crown through the lens of loyalty and utilized those same concepts to express a sense of inclusion, to assert their right to participate in the war, and to argue for the rights earned by their sacrifices for the common cause.

While many First Nations people wished to take part in the war effort during the Second World War, the desire was not universal; not all communities aspired to join the crusade. Even those First Nations that wished to participate sought to do so on their own terms, which sometimes brought them into contestation with a Canadian state fixated on the exigencies of total war. Wartime changes such as increases in taxes, which were felt by the many First Nations now employed off reserve, provoked a sharp response from First Nations leaders from across the country at a meeting in Ottawa in 1943.[38] One of the men at that meeting, Andrew Paull, continued to challenge the government's right to tax Status Indians throughout the war: "The government makes us pay income taxes because they say we are British subjects, but when we demand the privilege of voting, or seek old age pensions, they say, 'Oh, you're just Indians, wards of the Government.'"[39] It was not simply the nebulous distinction between being British subjects and being citizens that bothered Paul and other delegates at the annual meeting of the Native Brotherhood of BC in December 1943: "We opposed the imposition of the Income Tax on the grounds that it was against the British principle of taxation, without representation, and because by the imposition of the Income Tax and the compulsory military training, the government of Canada had exceeded the orbit of their authority, by violation of the Treaties made and signed by England."[40] In this instance, a core tenet of Britain's democratic tradition was mobilized to attack the state's application of taxation to Status Indians despite their lack of parliamentary representation and the franchise.

For First Nations communities who were less enthusiastic about their young men serving in the armed forces, finding ways to limit or define the extent or nature of wartime contributions was also problematic. For example, in a meeting of the Homalco (Xwemalhkwu) Band in January 1942,

> Chief Tommy said they did not want their young men taken in the army as the Band is decreasing and the people are more useful at fishing and logging. They would do all they could to help the Empire in other ways by working hard at fishing to feed people and logging to provide lumber for building planes and other war things. They are collecting money for the war effort every month and do A.R.P. work and would be willing to join any local defence corps.[41]

Significantly, the chief did not wish the aversion to military service to be interpreted as disloyalty or a lack of interest in helping the Empire; he merely wished to redefine his people's contribution along avenues of their own choosing. First Nations leaders needed to be careful about the degree to which they committed their people to the cause in their pronouncements of loyalty. The chief of the Patricia Bay Band issued a statement to correct a news report of a speech he had made to the governor general pledging his people's "willingness to fight and die for the King and Empire." The *Victoria Times* reported:

> "It is not a question of loyalty of the Indians," said Pierre. "We are loyal to the King, loyal to the British flag and loyal to the government of Canada, which His Excellency represented. But the Chief feels that the report has put him in a false position with his followers ... The Indians are ready and willing to take arms for the defence of Canada. Many of them are being called for compulsory training. Others have volunteered for active service anywhere in the field. But the chief does not wish it thought he has pledged the entire tribe to fight on foreign soil.[42]

The chief's concerns showed foresight because, as the war progressed, the state incrementally imposed and extended compulsory military training, eventually sending conscripts overseas into combat. Status Indians would be included in the national registration beginning in the summer of 1940, and young men of military age would be called up for service.

The development of conscription, under the 1940 National Resources Mobilization Act, provoked strident, persistent, and nation-wide protest from First Nations peoples, often expressed in the context of the British connection.[43] Even communities that were supportive of voluntary service fought vigorously against compulsory training and service. For instance, in a lengthy petition to the prime minister, the Caughnawaga community looked to the ancient Iroquois alliance with Britain to protest the arrest of members who had refused to report for duty:

> Therefore, Right Honourable Sir, the Covenant Chain of Peace and Friendship, so solemnly renewed by your forefathers and ours should not be violated *ever*, as we were promised never to be molested. In the name of Her Most Gracious Majesty Queen Victoria, who observed that by the bloodshed of our forefathers, Canada is under British rule, and we, the undersigned members of the same Iroquois Tribe of Caughnawaga, earnestly request that you will take this matter into serious consideration.[44]

Others protested that their lack of citizenship rights should absolve Status Indians of the duty to serve. Mrs. Mary Greenbird, a Chippewa from the Kettle and Stony Point Reserves in southern Ontario, sought exemptions for her sons;

> We are classed as wards of the Canadian Government. We are classed as minors ... children of his Majesty the King, that is to say to be protected by the representatives of the King and his successors according to the Treaties made with the Indians. These treaties state that all Indians are exempt from compulsory military duties unless they want to do so by their own free will.[45]

That First Nations remembered a limited exemption from overseas conscription in 1918, based largely on their lack of the franchise, only strengthened their determined opposition.[46]

Traditionalist voices among the Six Nations in Ontario and Quebec added a unique argument in First Nations resistance to conscription. The words of a Cayuga woman expressed this passionately: "We are six nations Indians. We are not British subjects therefore never sign as British subjects on any paper we are Indian, belong to laygua longhouse we beleave. Both my son he belong to longhouse Cayuga."⁴⁷ No less passionately, a petition from members of the Longhouse movement argued that

> Joseph Brant ... received a message from King George III recognizing the rights of the five nations ... to be termed allies and not as subjects, as they would have us believe today. Our side of the controversy is that we are unconquered residents within the confines of Canada ...The Mohawks claim that they are allies of the British Crown and owe no allegiance to, and desire no vote from the government, such as British Subjects enjoy ... The British Government does not approve of Hitler's autocratic rule that take initiativeness away from his people, (why have it here?) Lest we forget now and forever, in Flander's field the poppies bloom between the crosses row on row and in other places lie many of our Indian braves ... They lie in honour, in order that the British Flag never fall, the sun never set, on the British empire, that Britannia rule the waves, and that the escuteons of the House of Windsor, be not desecrated but to blaze as always in all its splendant glory.⁴⁸

This last is quite striking, both in the forceful nature of the argument that Six Nations were never subjects of the King, but even more so in the fervent proclamation of loyalty and memory of past sacrifices with which it concluded. It is also significant that Six Nations traditionalists, even in rejecting British status, still defined their status in relation to the British, as unconquered allies. Despite Six Nations loyalty, Canadian government officials dismissed their nationalist claims out of hand.

Most common among the references to Britain in the extensive literature protesting conscription were references to treaty promises made during the reign of Queen Victoria. One mother wrote, "Asking you to send me papers for my 2 sons as I don't want them to be Soldiers. Queen Victoria had made a promise to all the Indians here in Canada that Indians shall never go and fight again."⁴⁹ Others urged "the Indian Dept to look up the North West Angle Treaty of 1873. Lord Simcoe representing Queen Victoria, regarding the compulsory military service for Indians."⁵⁰ One brief letter simply quoted from that treaty negotiation without any comment: "The English never call the Indians out of their country to fight their battles; you are living here and the queen expect[s] you to live at peace with the white man and your Red Brothers, and with other nations."⁵¹ Residents of the Basswood and Elphinstone Reserves in Treaty 3 held meetings and understood "that they are all exempt from military duty by the terms of the Treaty made years ago on their behalf with Queen Victoria."⁵² But it is clear that many First Nations people across the country were familiar with the terms of that and other treaty negotiations, even if they had not been a signatory to them.

On behalf of several West Coast First Nations, prominent Gitxaala (Kitkatla) chief Edward Gamble wrote the prime minister as the war ended:

> We have heard that the native people may be conscripted. We are all grieved, because we are not citizens. Our good Queen Victoria said that the Native people of Canada would never be called upon to bear arms in battle ... So I wish and pray that the heads of our Country would take this matter seriously and not make a law to conscript our Indian people. We will never forget the promise that was given by our good Queen Victoria to the native people as long as we live.[53]

The sacred nature of treaty agreements for First Nations added poignancy and conviction to First Nations protests.

When all efforts to gain a hearing from federal authorities failed, or at least failed to obtain the desired goal, some First Nations leaders appealed to the British government or to the King himself to intercede on their behalf. When Indian Affairs officials refused to meet with First Nations delegates in Ottawa for a national political meeting in October 1943, one of their strategies was to call at "the office of Sir Malcolm MacDonald, the British High Commissioner, asking that his government use their influence to cause the Canadian Government to honor the terms of the Treaties which England ... signed."[54] Earlier in 1943, the vocal activist Jules Sioui, of the Lorettville Wendat (Huron), took his people's opposition to conscription over the heads of the Canadian government, writing to the King and Queen.[55]

> I am compelled to inform you that the Canadian Government has decided that it had the rights and jurisdiction over the Indians, regardless of the treaties which you have entered into with the Indians. The Canadian Government compels us to undergo military training. I must say that we are not against the war effort, on the contrary. We are ready to do any kind of work and we have offered the Government our full co-operation. However, the Government does not find this sufficient and it claims that we are compelled to do our military service as any other citizens of the country. We refuse to admit this illegal right ... I have nothing to reproach to Your Majesty but still I wish to ask you to kindly instruct the Canadian Government to cease its threats against us, otherwise I shall be compelled to appeal to the courts and I shall even appear before Your Majesty's court, if necessary.[56]

Here was the Crown, the British connection, being accessed directly as a perceived higher authority that might act to curb the Canadian government's implementation of conscription.

Based on the evidence presented here, the British connection remained alive and real for many First Nations communities in the context of the Second World War. Because it clearly mattered to First Nations people, this connection was an important aspect of their individual and collective experiences of the Second World War. The depth and authenticity of that connection was evident in the words spoken and in the actions and generosity that backed them up. Importantly, Britain, the Empire, and the Crown remained important to First Nations because they provided leaders and communities with tools to influence Canadians and their government as Indigenous communities sought to manage their relationship with the settler state. First Nations peoples made remarkably varied use of their relationship with Britain. Early in the war, especially, proclamations of loyalty, combined with Status Indians' legal standing as British subjects, symbolically supported desires to participate in the war effort. In this sense, Crown and empire functioned as expressions of loyalty, belonging, and inclusion. As the war progressed, however, Status Indians increasingly drew on the British connection in diverse ways to limit, or (re)define the nature of, their participation in the war. In these instances, the Crown and British government provided a moral high ground or an avenue of appeal that could be deployed in defence against intrusive Canadian federal agencies and insensitive wartime policies.

The ways in which British connections manifested in First Nations voices and dealings with the state are relatively clear; the actual "success" of such efforts and the utility of the British connection is less certain. First Nations men and women were able to enlist in the army and, to a much lesser extent, the Royal Canadian Air Force, but the Royal Canadian Navy retained a colour line in its recruitment policy that barred anyone not "of pure European descent and of the white race" until spring 1943.[57] Though somewhat dubious to list it as a "success," Status Indians were also deemed British subjects who were liable under the National Resources Mobilization Act for compulsory military training and service "in the same manner as other people."[58] Regardless of how they were viewed at the time, or subsequently, the right to enlist, the gradual dropping of racial barriers, and the liability to be conscripted indicate a degree of inclusivity. The military service and other patriotic contributions of First Nations also drew significant positive media attention, garnering recognition and moral capital from Canadians that translated into postwar support for Indian policy reform.[59] The degree to which First Nations' utilization of the British connection contributed to the relative success of opening the door to wartime participation is impossible to determine. Nevertheless, that it was employed in various efforts to take part, and that First Nations people persevered in its use throughout the war, suggests that they believed in its efficacy.

Efforts to limit First Nations participation, especially in terms of conscription, were only partially successful. As it turned out, the door to wartime participation proved much easier to open than to close. From August 1940 until December 1944, both the Ministry of Justice and the Department of National War Services determined that Status Indians, as British subjects, fell fully under the terms of the National Resources Mobilization Act. As a result, young First Nations men received their call-up notices, reported for medicals, undertook compulsory military training, and were enrolled in the Active Militia for the duration of the war unless they could obtain deferment for essential war labour or family hardship. Despite all their opposition; despite the moral, legal, and philosophical arguments in their favour; despite their reference to the British connection, First Nations people were unable to gain any alteration of conscription in their favour, largely because the only government agency that might have interceded on their behalf was the Indian Affairs Branch, whose personnel mostly viewed Indian military service as a positive and assimilative experience for their charges. The Indian Affairs Branch claimed that compulsory home defence service was not actually conscription, which they interpreted narrowly as overseas combative service. The only line of argument that did eventually bear fruit was the constant reference to Crown negotiators' verbal treaty promises that the "English never call the Indians out of the country to fight their battles."[60] However, this argument's impact was felt only after the national conscription crisis of November 1944, when the federal government decided to send conscripts into combat overseas. The Indian Affairs Branch's hand was forced by this policy change, and it finally stepped in to press for an exemption for Status Indians in December 1944. This was clearly a victory for First Nations peoples who had fought so long to halt the imposition of conscription on their young men, but it was a partial victory at best. The Indian Affairs Branch sought exemption for only those First Nations covered by Treaties 3, 6, 8, and 11, the treaties that had written records documenting that such verbal promises had, indeed, been made. In the end, Indigenous efforts to use the British connection to help manage their relationship with the Canadian wartime state proved helpful, within the narrow parameters within which they could influence state agencies and policy.

Notes

The author is indebted to the University of the Fraser Valley and the Social Science and Humanities Research Council of Canada, whose support and funding enabled the research on which this chapter is based.

1   For example, J.L. Granatstein, *Canada's War: The Politics of the Mackenzie King Government, 1939–1945* (Toronto: Oxford University Press, 1975).

2   Tim Cook, *The Necessary War*, vol. 1, *Canadians Fighting the Second World War, 1939–1943* (Toronto: Penguin, 2014), 24.

3 C.P. Stacey provides an insightful breakdown of Canadian attitudes in the lead up to the war, as understood by then-prominent newspaper editor J.W. Dafoe, in *Canada and the Age of Conflict*, vol. 2, *1921–1948: The Mackenzie King Era* (Toronto: University of Toronto Press, 1981): 233–34.

4 Note on terminology: I have generally used "First Nations" to describe Status Indians, though the term "Indian" is occasionally used as well, a reflection of the time period under discussion. The term "Indigenous" is occasionally used to denote broader references, including to the Métis and Inuit.

5 The official Indian enlistment figure was 3,090. See P. Whitney Lackenbauer, John Moses, R. Scott Sheffield, and Maxime Gohier, *Aboriginal Peoples in the Canadian Military* (Ottawa: Department of National Defence, 2010), 139. The figures provided here are derived from estimates developed during the National Round Table on First Nations' Veterans Issues, 1999–2001, based on crossreferencing Defence, Veterans Affairs, and Indian Affairs personnel records, which identified between 4,200 and 4,300 Status Indian veterans. The process was not quite completed during my involvement in the round table; hence, there is no hard, final figure. But this is the most empirically convincing estimate.

6 The archival records are drawn from RG 10 (Department of Indian Affairs records at Library and Archives Canada) files relating to military service and a variety of home front war topics. The newspapers were collected for another project but include more than a thousand articles, editorials, advertisements, and satirical cartoons that mention Status Indians during the war years. For large and small urban dailies, several months for most years of the war were examined, while every edition of rural weeklies and monthly magazines was surveyed. The papers canvassed include the *Vancouver Sun*, the *Kamloops Sentinel*, the *Calgary Herald*, the *Cardston News*, the *Saskatoon Star-Phoenix*, the *Prince Albert Daily Herald*, the *Winnipeg Free Press*, the *Brantford Expositor*, the *Globe and Mail*, and the *Halifax Herald*. In addition, the *Canadian Forum*, *Maclean's*, and *Saturday Night* magazines were read for the entirety of the war years. These newspaper stories were augmented with a diverse range of newspaper stories included in Indian Affairs clippings files.

7 Tolm Holm, "American Indian Warfare: The Cycles of Conflict and the Militarization of Native North America," in *Companion to American Indian History*, ed. Philip Joseph Deloria (Malden, MA: Blackwell, 2002): 154–72.

8 There is an extensive literature on this era; important works include Richard White, *The Middle Ground: Indians, Empires, and Republics in the Great Lakes Region, 1650–1815* (New York: Cambridge University Press, 1991); Carl Benn, *The Iroquois in the War of 1812* (Toronto: University of Toronto Press, 1998); Gregory E. Dowd, *War under Heaven: Pontiac, the Indian Nations and the British Empire* (Baltimore: Johns Hopkins University Press, 2002); and Colin Calloway, *Crown and Calumet: British-Indian Relations, 1783–1815* (Norman: University of Oklahoma Press, 1987).

9 These events are covered in Lackenbauer et al., *Aboriginal Peoples in the Canadian Military*. On the Rebellions, see Mary Babcock Fryer, *Volunteers and Redcoats/Rebels and Raiders: A Military History of the Rebellions in Upper Canada*, Canadian War Museum Historical Publication No. 23 (Toronto: Dundurn Press/Canadian War Museum/Canadian Museum of Civilization, 1987). On the Fenian raids, see Hereward Senior, *The Last Invasion of Canada: The Fenian Raids, 1866–1870*, Canadian War Museum Historical Publication No. 27 (Toronto: Dundurn Press/Canadian War Museum/Canadian Museum of Civilization, 1991). On the Northwest Resistance, see Bill Waiser and Blair Stonechild, *Loyal Till Death: Indians and the North-West Rebellion* (Calgary: Fifth House, 1997).

10   The commissioners and lieutenant-governors who conducted the negotiations capitalized on the symbolism of the Crown and the person of Queen Victoria in their discussions with First Nations delegations. See J.R. Miller, *Compact, Contract, Covenant:
Aboriginal Treaty-Making in Canada* (Toronto: University of Toronto Press, 2009),
157–58.

11   Ibid., 179.

12   Brian Titley, *A Narrow Vision: Duncan Campbell Scott and the Administration of Indian
Affairs in Canada* (Vancouver: UBC Press, 1986). Scott was a long-time civil servant in
Indian Affairs, including taking the reins as director from 1913 to 1933, during the high-
water mark of coercive assimilation policies.

13   Ian Radforth, *Royal Spectacle: The 1860 Visit of the Prince of Wales to Canada and the
United States* (Toronto: University of Toronto Press, 2004).

14   Paul Tennant, *Aboriginal Peoples and Politics: The Indian Land Question in British Columbia, 1849–1989* (Vancouver: UBC Press, 1990), 71.

15   Ibid., 91.

16   Louis Jackson, *Our Caughnawagas in Egypt: A Narrative of What Was Seen and Accomplished by the Contingent of North American Indian Voyageurs Who Led the British Boat
Expedition for the Relief of Khartoum Up the Cataracts of the Nile, by Louis Jackson of
Caughnawaga, Captain of the Contingent* (Montreal: William Drysdale and Co., 1885),
and Roy MacLaren, *Canadians on the Nile, 1882–1898: Being the Adventures of the Voyageurs on the Khartoum Relief Expedition and Other Exploits* (Vancouver: UBC Press,
1978).

17   Timothy C. Winegard, *For King and Kanata: Canadian Indians and the First World War*
(Winnipeg: University of Manitoba Press, 2012), 38.

18   Robert J. Talbot, "'It Would Be Best to Leave Us Alone': First Nations Responses to the
Canadian War Effort, 1914–1918," *Journal of Canadian Studies* 45, 1 (Winter 2011):
90–120.

19   James L. Dempsey, *Warriors of the King: Prairie Indians in World War I* (Regina: Canadian Plains Research Center, 1999), 47.

20   On the notion of a "white man's war," see James W. St.G. Walker, "Race and Recruitment
in World War I: Enlistment of Visible Minorities in the Canadian Expeditionary Force,"
Canadian Historical Review 70, 1 (1989): 1–26. For enlistment numbers and shifts in
Indigenous recruitment, see Winegard, *For King and Kanata*, chaps. 4 and 5.

21   "Indians Are Loyal," *Calgary Herald*, July 4, 1940.

22   "Address by Chief Mike Mountain Horse," *Cardston News*, February 4, 1941. The
author was possibly paraphrasing rather than directly quoting Mountain Horse in this
article.

23   This is covered in more detail in R. Scott Sheffield, *The Red Man's on the Warpath: The
Image of the "Indian" and the Second World War* (Vancouver: UBC Press, 2004), chap. 3.

24   G.C. Laight to the Secretary, July 8, 1940, RG 10, vol. 6763, 452–5 Alta, Library and
Archives Canada (hereafter LAC).

25   "Treaty Money from Indians to Aid War," press clipping, RG 10, vol. 6763, 452–5 Sask,
LAC.

26   G.H. Gooderham, Blackfoot Agency Council Meeting, December 29, 1941, RG 10, vol.
6763, 452–5 Alta, LAC.

27   Chief Gabriel Holliboy and John S. Googas to the Secretary of Indian Affairs, June 10,
1941, RG 10, vol. 6763, 452–5, Maritimes, LAC, as cited in Roy Toomey, "Canadian
First Nations and the Second World War" (master's thesis, University of Northern British Columbia, 2002), 66. Toomey examines in detail the extraordinary giving by First
Nations, see chap. 2.

28 Eventually, the Indian Affairs Branch halted band councils' accessing band funds for this purpose because the extent of the generosity, officials feared, could undermine community well-being in the future. See Toomey, "Canadian First Nations and the Second World War," 68–69.

29 Letter to the Commissioner, RCMP, September 25, 1942, RG 10, vol. 6763, 452–5 NWT, LAC.

30 "Indian Women Aid Evacuees," *Brockville Recorder and Times*, March 18, 1941, RG 10, vol. 6768, 452–5, pt. 6, LAC.

31 "Indians Send $240 for Britain," *Winnipeg Free Press*, August 4, 1941, RG 10, vol. 6764, 452–6, pt. 2, LAC.

32 The first mention is an Indian agent's report, Vancouver Agency, September 1940, RG 10, vol. 6763, 452–5 BC, LAC, in which the chief and some councillors of the Klahoose Reserve mention their intention to start this fund. The Squamish Council also joined the effort. See Squamish Indian Council, May 26, 1941, RG 10, vol. 6763, file 452–5 BC, LAC.

33 "Indians Help to Raise Funds for Purchase of Spitfires," *Vancouver Province*, December 18, 1941. For official skepticism and opposition, see F.J.C. Ball to the Secretary, October 24, 1940, RG 10, vol. 6763, 45 2–5 BC, LAC.

34 "Indian Assist Red Cross Drive," *Calgary Herald*, August 3, 1940.

35 Peter Calder to Mackenzie King, March 6, 1941, RG 10, vol. 6763, 452–5 BC, LAC.

36 Chief Tibbetts to the Department of Indian Affairs, February 7, 1944, RG 10, vol. 6769, 452–20–3, LAC.

37 Shot Both Sides, Frank Red Crow, Percy Creighton, Fred T. Feathers, and Cross Child to the Honorable Minister of Defence, September 3, 1942, RG 10, vol. 6769, 452–20, pt. 5, LAC.

38 "Indians Ask Tax Exemptions," *Vancouver Sun*, October 21, 1943, and "11 Indians Ask for Army, Tax Exemptions," *Globe and Mail*, October 22, 1943.

39 Paull was quoted at a meeting of the Native Brotherhood of BC. See "Indians Say Taxes Unfair," *Kamloops Sentinel*, December 15, 1943.

40 Report of the Fourteenth Annual Convention of the Native Brotherhood of British Columbia, December 1–7, 1943, pp. 7–8, RG 10, vol. 6769, 452–20, pt. 6, LAC.

41 Homalco Band Minutes of Council Meeting, F.J.C. Ball, January 13, 1942, RG 10, vol. 6769, 452–20–3, LAC.

42 "Indians Willing to Defend Canada," *Victoria Times*, May 3, 1941, RG 10, vol. 6768, 452–20, pt. 4, LAC.

43 Indigenous opposition is most thoroughly covered in R. Scott Sheffield, "'… In the Same Manner as Other People': Government Policy and the Military Service of Canada's First Nations People, 1939–1945" (master's thesis, University of Victoria, 1995), chap. 3 and 4, as well as in Michael Stevenson, "The Mobilisation of Native Canadians during the Second World War," *Journal of the Canadian Historical Association* 7, 1 (1996): 205–26.

44 Petition from Caughnawaga Reserve to the Right Honorable Mackenzie King, October 29, 1941, RG 10, vol. 6768, 452–20, pt. 4, LAC.

45 Mrs. Mary Greenbird to the Honorable T.A. Crerar, September 14, 1942, RG 10, vol. 6769, 452–20, pt. 5, LAC. A similar protest about citizenship rights debarring First Nations from being conscripted was produced by Alphonse P. Picard, Maurice Vincent, and Jules Sioui and presented to the governor general on October 14, 1940. See RG 10, vol. 6768, 452–20, pt. 4, LAC.

46 This was based on PC 111, an Order-in-Council revising the Military Service Act, 1917. See PC 111, January 17, 1918, RG 10, vol. 6770, 452–26, pt. 2, LAC.

47 Miss Bessie Hess to unknown, January 10, 1944, RG 10, vol. 6767, 452–15, pt. 2, LAC.

48 Petition, members of the Six Nations Confederacy and Joseph L. Beauvais, Caughnawaga, included with a letter from Chief Peter Lazare to the Honorable Minister of Mines and Resources, May 18, 1942, RG 10, vol. 6769, 452–20, pt. 5, LAC.
49 Mrs. Paul Noon to Department of Indian Affairs, November 19, 1940, RG 10, vol. 6768, 452–20, pt. 4, LAC.
50 Resolution 1008, Caughnawaga Band Council, November 5, 1940, RG 10, vol. 6768, 452–20, pt. 4, LAC.
51 Mark Shabequay to unknown, undated, RG 10, vol. 6768, 452–20, pt. 4, LAC.
52 C.L. St. John to the Minister of Indian Affairs, April 24, 1943, RG 10, vol. 6769, 452–20–4, LAC. St. John was a lawyer who filed this complaint with the minister on behalf of Councillor George Shinnacap of Basswood Reserve and Councillor Burns of Elphinstone Reserve.
53 Chief Edward Gamble, OBE, to the Premier of Canada, March 9, 1945, RG 10, vol. 6769, 452–20, pt. 6, LAC.
54 "Report of the Fourteenth Annual Convention of the Native Brotherhood of British Columbia," December 1–7, 1943, pp. 7–8, RG 10, vol. 6769, 452–20, pt. 6, LAC.
55 Hugh Shewell, "Jules Sioui and Indian Political Radicalism in Canada, 1943–44," *Journal of Canadian Studies* 34, 3 (1999): 211–42.
56 Jules Sioui to His Majesty the King and the Queen, March 27, 1943, RG 10, vol. 6770, 452–26, pt. 3, LAC.
57 R. Scott Sheffield, "'Of Pure European Descent and of the White Race': Recruitment Policy and Aboriginal Canadians, 1939–1945," *Canadian Military History* 5, 1 (Spring 1996): 8–15.
58 Sheffield, "… In the Same Manner as Other People."
59 Sheffield, *The Red Man's on the Warpath*, chaps. 2, 4, and 6. Support for reform of Canadian Indian policy was diverse and widespread, with hundreds of letters and petitions sent to the postwar reconstructions authorities, Indian Affairs, and MPs from civil-rights groups, municipal governments, women's organizations, labour, and, especially, veterans. Though the ideas expressed were varied, most supported the idea of greater equality and citizenship rights for Status Indians. The wide pressure on the government provoked the creation, in 1946, of a special joint parliamentary committee to assess and reform the Indian Act and Canadian Indian policy more generally; the outcome of its report would be a new Indian Act in 1951.
60 Alexander Morris, *The Treaties of Canada with the Indians of Manitoba and the North-West Territories* (Saskatoon: Fifth House, 1991), 69. Originally published in 1880 by Willing and Williamson (Toronto).

Conclusion

Steve Marti

FOR THE FIRST eighty years of Confederation, the Dominion of Canada contributed to imperial defence because it depended militarily on Britain. The Statute of Westminster officially granted Canada the power to conduct its own foreign policy, independent from Britain, but the limited strength and capabilities of the Canadian armed forces restricted the Dominion's ability to operate independently overseas. Despite the Ogdensburg Agreement of 1940, which set the groundwork for Canadian-American cooperation in the defence of North America, and a few instances when Canadian forces deployed as part of a larger American formation during the Second World War, substantive Canadian military deployments during the Second World War contributed to the imperial war effort. In matters of war and security, Canadian participation in global affairs necessitated cooperation with Britain, while British military power relied, in no small measure, on contributions from Canada and the other Dominions.

This symbiotic relationship between Britain and its Dominions complicated the nature of the colonial attachment, as each relied on the other to display or exercise military power. Just like the economic union of imperial federation championed by Lord Milner's Kindergarten, the Round Table movement, and the writings of Richard Jebb, military cooperation between Britain and the Dominions was idealized as a complementary and reciprocal arrangement between Dominion and imperial interests.[1] The brand of imperialism that reconciled Canadian expansion as a contribution to the growth of British Empire was undone through the experience of successive Canadian military deployments overseas. The common bonds that united Canadian and British interests slowly dissolved as Canadians contributed to the imperial war effort, or as they participated in an imperial diplomatic delegation, all the while attempting to differentiate the national from the imperial. The contributions to this volume present long narrative arcs that reveal how the seemingly complementary nature of Canadian-British cooperation unravelled from Confederation and on through the half century of warfare between the Boer War and the end of the Second World War.

Amidst public commemorations of battles and the negotiations of Canadian statesmen, Canadian soldiers and civilians came to terms with the imperial relationship through the experience of imperial mobility or their efforts to mobilize resources for the imperial war effort. Canadian men who volunteered for the Boer War embodied British imperial masculinity as they donned their imperial uniforms, learned the precise movements of a British military drill, and rationalized their participation in the war as Canada's contribution to the British imperial mission. Yet in her contribution, Amy Shaw also shows how this duality frayed as Canadian soldiers embraced the nationalist symbols of their frontier identity, such as the Stetson hats that topped their uniforms, but recoiled at the violent atrocities committed by the "rougher types" who enlisted in the Canadian contingent. Canadian women mobilized their voluntary work for the imperial war effort, but organizing this work and allocating their contributions raised pressing questions about the needs of the nation versus those of the Empire. Steve Marti's chapter discusses how members of the Imperial Order Daughters of the Empire debated the merits of buying local versus buying imperial, contributing to Canadian collections or imperial appeals, and whether the exclusively British membership of the IODE should include non-British women. During both world wars, Canadian soldiers of British descent passed through Britain before moving on to fight on mainland Europe. William Pratt's study of Canadian soldiers' letters during the Second World War shows that Canadian soldiers thought of Britain increasingly as a travel destination, rather than as an ancestral homeland, and recognized the increasingly palpable differences between British and North American culture. Mobility and wartime mobilization within these imperial networks brought Canadians into closer contact with Britain and the Empire, but these colonial contacts challenged Canadians to question the extent to which they and their actions should be defined by their relationship to Britain or by connections made closer to home in Canada.

The Statute of Westminster afforded the Dominion of Canada legislative autonomy over all its affairs. The structures and symbols of imperial power in Canada, such as the Crown or the monarchy, remained fixtures in Canadian public life. The Canadian public's relationship to these structures of power, however, revealed an underlying transformation in imperial sentiment in Canada. Alongside the governor general, the British-appointed general officer commanding the Canadian militia represented the Crown as the head of the Canadian militia. Many of these imperial appointees raised the hackles of Canadian politicians by attempting to impose reforms on the militia, but Eirik Brazier's chapter reveals that the Canadian public's admiration for these imperial officers reflected an aspiration to graft the traditions and history of the British army onto the Canadian militia, just as other Canadian institutions were moulded by British traditions. Amidst the constitutional transformations of the interwar years, William Lyon Mackenzie King's Department of External Affairs prioritized domestic stability over imperial commitments. Robert Talbot's research on the Canadian diplomatic corps reveals that, in the context of growing concern over Nazi German aggression, these civil servants worked as part of a larger intellectual movement appealing to French Canadians to support another Canadian contribution to an imperial war effort. The looming conflict in Europe also necessitated the support of anglophones. Canadians welcomed George VI and Queen Elizabeth as their monarchs, and Claire Halstead's study of royal ephemera during the royal tour reveals that the souvenirs and memorabilia collected reflected Canadians' desire to frame a personal connection to the royal couple and to celebrate the ways in which the Dominion left its impression on the monarchs. These artifacts reflected Mackenzie King's intention to use the tour to shore up popular support in anticipation of another major war overseas. Compared to the reception of British officers appointed to command the Canadian militia, imperial pageantry moved from celebrating unity and conformity with Britain to asserting a more participative role in the Empire. The transition in Canadian ideas of empire become particularly evident in the rhetoric used to cultivate popular support, which relied less on appeals to imperial duty and more on arguments of collective security.

Examining the public perception of British symbols demonstrates the rhetorical shift in Canadian perceptions of the Dominion's obligations to the Empire. The meaning of British symbolism in Canada evolved with the Dominion's changing constitutional status, while Canada's diverse population remained at odds with symbols that defined Canada as a British nation. Britain's liberal tradition offered protections, such as freedom of religion, to the Dominion's multiethnic diaspora and shielded such communities from wartime zealotry. Geoff Keelan presents Henri Bourassa's sustained critiques of Canadian involvement in imperial entanglements such as the Boer War and the 1910 Naval Service Bill, which Bourassa framed against restrictive legislation threatening French-language instruction in Ontario and Manitoba. At the outbreak of war in 1914, Bourassa supported Canadian contributions to the imperial war effort after witnessing the inspiring accord of the *union sacrée* and the Franco-British Entente, but the imposition of conscription in 1917 provided the most cogent reminder that unquestioning imperial loyalty trampled on the principles of British liberalism. The Conscription Crisis ushered in a new brand of nationalism in French Canada. Mikhail Bjorge likewise demonstrates the tension between British patriotism and Canada's multiethnic population, as English Canadian miners attempted to force suspected enemy aliens out of work. While management, the union leadership, and the RCMP initially reacted with indifference to the exclusion of continental European miners, the needs of the war effort quickly overruled the strikers' appeal to British race patriotism, and the excluded miners returned to work. R. Scott Sheffield's chapter on Canadian First Nations' contributions to the war effort during the Second World War reveals the extent to which the legal entity of the Crown interfered with a homogenizing national effort. As the Dominion of Canada attempted to impose compulsory military service and universal income tax, the Crown provided First Nations communities with the legal leverage to contest these wartime policies that sought to pull more men and resources into the national war effort. Drawing contributions from all Canadians to produce a stronger national contribution eroded the pre-eminence of a racially British Canada by highlighting the contradictions between British values and British race patriotism.

The historical trajectory of Canada from a colony to a nation-state presents historians with a particular challenge: writing a history of Canada's development as a nation without producing a nationalistic narrative. Indeed, popular and academic histories that explicitly tied Canada's constitutional transformation to military exploits have been the subject of sharp criticisms.[2] While Canadians do not owe their existence as a nation-state purely to military actions, the role of conflict, diplomacy, and security cannot be discounted as forces that shaped Canadian ideas about their place within the British Empire. Writing a national history of Canada also runs the risk of flattening out the distinctions of region, class, gender, and race in shaping Canada's historical narrative.[3] Studying the impact of conflict and diplomacy on ideas of nation and empire among Canadians at home and overseas produces a more diverse and inclusive history than a study limited to soldiers in the Canadian military or the members of the civil service or diplomatic corps. Such an approach considers the role of women on the home front alongside the experiences of soldiers overseas. Examining the experience of French Canadians, Indigenous peoples, and European immigrants demonstrates how British ideals challenged the structures that compelled, discouraged, or disallowed them from participating in the war effort. George VI's visit in 1939 demonstrated the symbolic status of the monarch, but the occasion also offers an opportunity to view the tour through the eyes of school children that lined the streets during his visit. Examining attitudes and ideas of imperialism and nationhood, while moving the gaze away from the vainglorious exploits of the battlefield, reveals how the Canadians' social, cultural, and constitutional ties to Britain shaped their experiences of war and peace. More than asserting a new Canadian nationalism, the experience of war highlighted the contradictions of British imperialism in Canada.

The contributions to this volume present more subtle transformations as Canadians reassessed their relationship to Britain and the Empire through the experience of war. Major victories, both on the battlefield and at the imperial conference tables, provide useful signposts for Canada's trajectory from a

Dominion to an independent nation-state, but *Fighting with the Empire* presents a wider cast of actors – who participated in a broader collection of conversations, debates, dialogues, and negotiations – to understand the slow transformation of British imperial sentiment in Canada. National mobilization for war, or anticipation of war, forced Canadians to consider the symbols, people, and values that represented their nation as they contributed to the imperial war effort. The result of these debates increasingly highlighted the contradictions between a national identity determined by British ancestry and an identity defined by distinct liberal values. Matters of war, peace, and security challenged Canadians to consider Canada's place in the British Empire and re-evaluate their identity as a British nation.

Barely two months after Canadians celebrated Victory in Europe Day, diplomats gathered for the United Nations Conference on International Organization in San Francisco to draft the United Nations Charter. While Canadian diplomats had represented the Dominion at the League of Nations during the interwar years, the UN proved relatively decisive in its application of force. Canadians fought under the banner of the UN in Korea and pioneered the practice of UN peacekeeping, mending Egypt following an attempt to salvage Britain's imperial lifeline: the Suez Canal. In the aftermath of the crisis, British prime minister Anthony Eden resigned and his successor, Harold MacMillan, initiated a wave of British decolonization in Africa and Asia. Canadian soldiers wearing the blue berets of the UN stabilized Egypt after the failed invasion, staged by the two European powers whose imperial ambition in North America had created Canada as a modern state, forged a new national myth of Canadian martial masculinity, as peacekeepers rather than soldiers.[4] Prime Minister Lester B. Pearson's role in mending the Suez Crisis, which precipitated the permanent decline of the British Empire, perfectly captured the transition of Canadian military and security operations away from the bonds of Britain and the Empire.

The onset of the Cold War ushered in a new collection of military alliances in which Canadians could exercise their role as a middle power. Alongside the UN, the North Atlantic Treaty Organization (NATO) and the North American Air Defence Command (NORAD) provided new international frameworks in which Canada could participate in peace support and security operations, sometimes by contributing to a British force but increasingly by integrating into an American-led coalition. The conflicts that sent Canadian soldiers halfway around the world during the first eighty years of Confederation challenged Canadians to define and redefine their status as a nation within the Empire. After 1945, Canadians began to define themselves as a nation in the world.

Notes

1   Richard Jebb, *Studies in Colonial Nationalism* (London: Edward Arnold, 1905). See also John Eddy, Deryck Schreuder, and Oliver MacDonagh, *The Rise of Colonial Nationalism: Australia, New Zealand, Canada and South Africa First Assert Their Nationalities, 1880–1914* (Sydney: Allen and Ulwin, 1988).

2   Ian McKay and Jamie Swift, *Warrior Nation: Rebranding Canada in an Age of Anxiety* (Toronto: Between the Lines, 2012).

3   Philip Buckner, "Defining Identities in Canada: Regional, Imperial, National" *Canadian Historical Review* 94, 2 (2013): 303.

4   Michael K. Carroll, "Peacekeeping: Canada's Past, but Not Its Present and Future?" *International Journal: Canada's Journal of Global Policy Analysis* 71, 1 (2016): 168–76.

Selected Bibliography

Anderson, Kevin P. "'This Typical Old Canadian Form of Racial and Religious Hate': Anti-Catholicism and English Canadian Nationalism, 1905–1965." PhD diss., McMaster University, 2013.

Auger, Martin F. "On the Brink of Civil War: The Canadian Government and the Suppression of the 1918 Quebec Easter Riots." *Canadian Historical Review* 89, 4 (December 2008): 503–20. https://doi.org/10.3138/chr.89.4.503.

Auger, Martin F. *Prisoners of the Home Front: German POWs and "Enemy Aliens" in Southern Quebec, 1940–46*. Vancouver: UBC Press, 2006.

Avery, Donald. *"Dangerous Foreigners": European Immigrant Workers and Labour Radicalism in Canada, 1896–1932*. Toronto: McClelland and Stewart, 1980.

Bélanger, Réal. *Henri Bourassa: Fascinant destin d'un homme libre, 1868–1914*. Quebec: Les Presses de l'Université de Laval, 2013.

Bélanger, Réal. *Paul-Émile Lamarche: Le pays avant le parti, 1904–1918*. Quebec: Presses de l'Université Laval, 1984.

Belich, James. *Replenishing the Earth: The Settler Revolution and the Rise of the Anglo-World, 1783–1939*. Oxford: Oxford University Press, 2009. https://doi.org/10.1093/acprof:oso/9780199297276.001.0001.

Bell, Duncan. *The Idea of Greater Britain: Empire and the Future of World Order, 1860–1900*. Princeton: Princeton University Press, 2007. https://doi.org/10.1515/9781400827978.

Bell, Duncan. *Victorian Visions of Global Order: Empire and International Relations in Nineteenth-Century Political Thought*. Cambridge: Cambridge University Press, 2012.

Benn, Carl. *The Iroquois in the War of 1812*. Toronto: University of Toronto Press, 1998.

Berger, Carl. *The Sense of Power: Studies in the Idea of Canadian Imperialism, 1867–1914*. Toronto: University of Toronto Press, 1970.

Berger, Carl. *The Writing of Canadian History: Aspects of English-Canadian Historical Writing since 1900*. 2nd ed. Toronto: University of Toronto Press, 1986.

Betcherman, Lita-Rose. *Ernest Lapointe: Mackenzie King's Great Quebec Lieutenant*. Toronto: University of Toronto Press, 2002. https://doi.org/10.3138/9781442674592.

Bourne, Kenneth. *Britain and the Balance of Power in North America, 1815–1908*. Berkeley: University of California Press, 1967.

Bray, R. Matthew. "'Fighting as an Ally': The English-Canadian Patriotic Response to the Great War." *Canadian Historical Review* 61, 2 (1980): 141–68. https://doi.org/10.3138/CHR-061-02-01.

Brown, Robert Craig, and Ramsay Cook. *Canada, 1896–1921: A Nation Transformed*. Toronto: McClelland and Stewart, 1974.

Brown, Robert Craig, and Donald Loveridge. "Unrequited Faith: Recruiting the CEF, 1914–1918." *Canadian Military History* 24, 1 (Spring 2015): 1–28.

Bryce, Robert R. *Canada and the Cost of World War II: The International Operations of Canada's Department of Finance, 1939–1947*. Montreal/Kingston: McGill-Queen's University Press, 2005.

Buckner, Philip, ed. *Canada and the End of Empire*. Vancouver: UBC Press, 2005.

Buckner, Philip, ed. *Rediscovering the British World*. Calgary: University of Calgary Press, 2003.

Buckner, Philip, and R. Douglas Francis, eds. *Canada and the British World: Culture, Migration, and Identity*. Vancouver: UBC Press, 2006.

Caccia, Ivana. *Managing the Canadian Mosaic in Wartime: Shaping Citizenship Policy, 1939–1945*. Montreal/Kingston: McGill-Queen's University Press, 2010.

Calloway, Colin. *Crown and Calumet: British-Indian Relations, 1783–1815*. Norman: University of Oklahoma Press, 1987.

Campbell, Isabel. *Unlikely Diplomats: The Canadian Brigade in Germany, 1951–64*. Vancouver: UBC Press, 2013.

Campbell, Lara Michael Dawson, and Catherine Gidney, eds. *Worth Fighting For: Canada's Tradition of War Resistance from 1812 to the War on Terror*. Toronto: Between the Lines, 2015.

Carroll, Michael K. "Peacekeeping: Canada's Past, but Not Its Present and Future?" *International Journal* 71, 1 (2016): 168–76.

Champion, C.P. "Mike Pearson at Oxford: War, Varsity, and Canadianism." *Canadian Historical Review* 88, 2 (June 2007): 263–90. https://doi.org/10.3138/chr.88.2.263.

Champion, C.P. *The Strange Demise of British Canada: The Liberals and Canadian Nationality, 1964–1968*. Montreal/Kingston: McGill-Queen's University Press, 2010.

Cole, Douglas. "The Problem of 'Nationalism' and 'Imperialism' in British Settlement Colonies." *Journal of British Studies* 10, 2 (1971): 160–82. https://doi.org/10.1086/385614.

Colley, Linda. *Britons: Forging the Nation, 1707–1837*. New Haven: Yale University Press, 1992.

Copp, Terry. *Fields of Fire: The Canadians in Normandy*. Toronto: University of Toronto Press, 2004.

Cook, Ramsay. *Canada and the French-Canadian Question*. Toronto: MacMillan, 1966.

Cook, Ramsay, and D.B. Macrae. "A Canadian Account of the 1926 Imperial Conference." *Journal of Commonwealth Political Studies* 3, 1 (1965): 50–56. https://doi.org/10.1080/14662046508447011.

Cook, Tim. "The Politics of Surrender: Canadian Soldiers and the Killing of Prisoners in the Great War." *Journal of Military History* 70, 3 (July 2006): 637–65. https://doi.org/10.1353/jmh.2006.0158.

Cook, Tim. *Warlords: Borden, Mackenzie King and Canada's World Wars*. Toronto: Allen Lane/Penguin Canada, 2012.

Corcoran, James I.W. "Henri Bourassa et la guerre sud-africain (suite)." *Revue d'Histoire de l'Amerique Francaise* 19, 1 (1965): 84–105. https://doi.org/10.7202/302441ar.

Coutard, Jérôme. "Des valeurs en guerre: Presse, propagande et culture de guerre au Québec, 1914–1918." PhD diss., Université de Laval, 1999.

Couture, Claude. *Le mythe de la modernisation du Québec: Des années 1930 à la révolution tranquille*. Montreal: Méridien, 1991.

Cuthbertson, Wendy. *Labour Goes to War: The CIO and the Construction of a New Social Order, 1939–1945*. Vancouver: UBC Press, 2012.

Darwin, John. *The Empire Project: The Rise and Fall of the British World-System, 1830–1970*. Cambridge: Cambridge University Press, 2010.

Daschuk, James. *Clearing the Plains: Disease, Politics of Starvation, and the Loss of Aboriginal Life*. Regina: University of Regina Press, 2013.

Dawson, Michael. "'That Nice Red Coat Goes to My Head Like Champagne': Gender, Antimodernism, and the Mountie Image, 1880–1960." *Journal of Canadian Studies/ Revue d'Etudes Canadiennes* 32, 3 (1997): 119–39. https://doi.org/10.3138/jcs.32.3.119.

Dempsey, James L. *Warriors of the King: Prairie Indians in World War I*. Regina: Canadian Plains Research Center, 1999.

Dick, Lyle. "Sergeant Masumi Mitsui and the Japanese Canadian War Memorial." *Canadian Historical Review* 91, 3 (2010): 435–63.

Djwa, Sandra. *The Politics of the Imagination: A Life of F.R. Scott.* Toronto: McClelland and Stewart, 1987.

Donaghy, Greg, and Michael Kiernan Carroll, eds. *In the National Interest: Canadian Foreign Policy and the Department of Foreign Affairs and International Trade, 1909–2009.* Calgary: University of Calgary Press, 2011.

Donaghy, Greg, and Kim Richard Nossal, eds. *Architects and Innovators: Building the Department of External Affairs and International Trade, 1909–2009.* Montreal/Kingston: McGill-Queen's University Press, 2009.

Dowd, Gregory E. *War under Heaven: Pontiac, the Indian Nations and the British Empire.* Baltimore: Johns Hopkins University Press, 2002.

Eddy, John, Deryck Schreuder, and Oliver MacDonagh. *The Rise of Colonial Nationalism: Australia, New Zealand, Canada and South Africa First Assert Their Nationalities, 1880–1914.* Sydney: Allen and Ulwin, 1988.

Fedorowich, Kent. "Directing the War from Trafalgar Square? Vincent Massey and the Canadian High Commission, 1939–42." *Journal of Imperial and Commonwealth History* 40, 1 (March 2012): 87–117. https://doi.org/10.1080/03086534.2012.656493.

Fennell, Johathan. *Combat and Morale in the North African Campaign: The Eighth Army and the Path to El Alamein.* Cambridge: Cambridge University Press, 2011. https://doi.org/10.1017/CBO9780511921513.

FitzGerald, David Scott, and David Cook-Martín. *Culling the Masses: The Democratic Origins of Racist Immigration Policy in the Americas.* Cambridge: Harvard University Press, 2014. https://doi.org/10.4159/harvard.9780674369665.

Flanagan, Luke. "Canadians in Bexhill-on-Sea during the First World War: A Reflection of Canadian Nationhood?" *British Journal of Canadian Studies* 27, 2 (October 2014): 131–48. https://doi.org/10.3828/bjcs.2014.9.

Fudge, Judy, and Eric Tucker. *Labour before the Law: The Regulation of Workers' Collective Action in Canada, 1900–1948.* Toronto: University of Toronto Press, 2004.

Gagnon, Jean-Pierre. *Le 22e Bataillon (canadien-français), 1914–1919: Étude socio-militaire.* Ottawa: Presses de l'Université Laval, 1986.

Gentile, Patrizia, and Jane Nicholas, eds. *Contesting Bodies and Nation in Canadian History.* Toronto: University of Toronto Press, 2013.

Goutor, David. *Guarding the Gates: The Canadian Labour Movement and Immigration, 1872–1934.* Vancouver: UBC Press, 2007.

Granatstein, J.L. *Canada's War: The Politics of the Mackenzie King Government, 1939–1945.* Toronto: Oxford University Press, 1975.

Granatstein, J. L., and David Bercuson. *War and Peacekeeping: From South Africa to the Gulf – Canada's Limited Wars.* Toronto: Key Porter, 1991.

Granatstein, J.L., and Norman Hillmer. *Empire to Umpire: Canada and the World to the 1990s.* Toronto: Copp Clark Longman, 1994.

Granatstein, Jack, and Desmond Morton. *Canada and the Two World Wars.* Toronto: Key Porter Books, 2003.

Grant, Peter. *Philanthropy and Voluntary Action in the First World War: Mobilizing Charity.* New York: Routledge, Taylor and Francis Group, 2014.

Gravel, Jean-Yves. *Le Québec et la guerre, 1867–1960.* Montreal: Boréal, 1974.

Grayzel, Susan R. *Women's Identities at War: Gender, Motherhood, and Politics in Britain and France during the First World War.* Chapel Hill: University of North Carolina Press, 1999.

Halstead, Claire. "'Dangers Behind, Pleasures Ahead': British-Canadian Identity and the Evacuation of British Children to Canada during the Second World War."

British Journal of Canadian Studies 27, 2 (2014): 163–80. https://doi.org/10.3828/bjcs.2014.11.

Harris, Stephen. *Canadian Brass: The Making of a Professional Army, 1860–1939.* Toronto: University of Toronto Press, 1988.

Heath, Gordon L. *A War with a Silver Lining: Canadian Protestant Churches and the South African War, 1899–1902.* Montreal/Kingston: McGill-Queen's University Press, 2009.

Heron, Craig, ed. *The Workers' Revolt in Canada, 1917–1925.* Toronto: University of Toronto Press, 1998. https://doi.org/10.3138/9781442682566.

Higonnet, Margaret R., Sonya Michel, Jane Jenson, and Margaret Collins Weitz, eds. *Behind the Lines: Gender and the Two World Wars.* New Haven: Yale University Press, 1987.

Hobsbawm, Eric, and Terence Ranger, eds. *The Invention of Tradition.* Cambridge: Cambridge University Press, 1992.

Horne, John, ed. *State, Society and Mobilization in Europe during the First World War.* Cambridge: Cambridge University Press, 1997. https://doi.org/10.1017/CBO9780511562891.

Iacovetta, Franca, Roberto Perin, and Angelo Principe, eds. *Enemies Within: Italian and Other Internees in Canada and Abroad.* Toronto: University of Toronto Press, 2000. https://doi.org/10.3138/9781442674462.

Igartua, José E. *The Other Quiet Revolution: National Identities in English Canada, 1945–71.* Vancouver: UBC Press, 2006.

Kasurak, Peter. *A National Force: The Evolution of Canada's Army, 1950–2000.* Vancouver: UBC Press, 2013.

Keshen, Jeffrey A. *Saints, Sinners, and Soldiers: Canada's Second World War.* Vancouver: UBC Press, 2004.

Killingray, David. "Imperial Defence." In *The Oxford History of the British Empire*, vol. 5., *Historiography*, edited by Robin Winks, 342–53. Oxford: Oxford University Press, 2001.

Kordan, Bohdan S. *Enemy Aliens, Prisoners of War: Internment in Canada during the Great War.* Montreal/Kingston: McGill-Queen's University Press, 2002.

Lackenbauer, P. Whitney, and Craig Leslie Mantle, eds. *Aboriginal Peoples and the Canadian Military: Historical Perspectives.* Winnipeg: Canadian Defence Academy Press, 2007.

Lacombe, Sylvie. "French Canada: The Rise and Decline of a 'Church Nation.'" *Québec Studies* 48 (Fall 2009): 135–58. https://doi.org/10.3828/qs.48.1.135.

LaForest, Guy. *Trudeau and the End of a Canadian Dream.* Montreal/Kingston: McGill-Queen's University Press, 1995.

Lamonde, Yvan. *Histoire sociale des idées au Québec, 1896–1929.* Vol. 2. Quebec: Éditions Fides, 2004.

Levitt, Joseph. *Henri Bourassa and the Golden Calf: The Social Program of the Nationalists of Quebec, 1900–1914.* Ottawa: Les Éditions de l'Université d'Ottawa, 1969.

Lowry, Donal, ed. *The South African War Reappraised.* Manchester: Manchester University Press, 2000.

MacFarlane, John. *Ernest Lapointe and Quebec's Influence on Canadian Foreign Policy.* Toronto: University of Toronto Press, 1999. https://doi.org/10.3138/9781442674585.

MacLaren, Roy. *Canadians on the Nile, 1882–1898: Being the Adventures of the Voyageurs on the Khartoum Relief Expedition and Other Exploits.* Vancouver: UBC Press, 1978.

Mansergh, Nicholas. *The Commonwealth Experience*, 2 vols. Toronto: University of Toronto Press, 1982–83. https://doi.org/10.1007/978-1-349-16952-8.

Maroney, Paul. "'The Great Adventure': The Context and Ideology of Recruiting in Ontario, 1914–17." *Canadian Historical Review* 77, 1 (1996): 62–98. https://doi.org/10.3138/CHR-077-01-03.

Marshall, Dominique. *The Social Origins of the Welfare State: Quebec Families, Compulsory Education, and Family Allowances, 1940–1955.* Waterloo: Wilfrid Laurier University Press, 2006.

Martin, Jean. "La participation des francophones dans le Corps expéditionnaire canadien, 1914–1919: Il faut réviser à la hausse." *Canadian Historical Review* 96, 3 (September 2015): 405–23. https://doi.org/10.3138/chr.2966.

Mayhall, Laura E. Nym. "The Prince of Wales versus Clark Gable." *Cultural and Social History* 4, 4 (2007): 529–43. https://doi.org/10.2752/147800407X243514.

McCulloch, Tony. "Roosevelt, Mackenzie King and the British Royal Visit to the USA in 1939." *London Journal of Canadian Studies* 23 (2007–08): 81–104.

McKay, Ian, and Jamie Swift. *Warrior Nation: Rebranding Canada in an Age of Anxiety.* Toronto: Between the Lines, 2012.

Metcalfe, Heather. "It's All about War: Canadian Opinion and the Canadian Approach to International Relations, 1935–1939." PhD diss., University of Toronto, 2009.

Miller, Carman. "English-Canadian Opposition to the South African War as Seen through the Press." *Canadian Historical Review* 55, 4 (December 1974): 422–38. https://doi.org/10.3138/CHR-055-04-04.

Miller, Carman. "Framing Canada's Great War: A Case for Including the Boer War." *Journal of Transatlantic Studies* 6, 1 (April 2008): 3–17. https://doi.org/10.1080/14794010801916982.

Miller, Carman. *Painting the Map Red: Canada and the South African War, 1899–1902.* Montreal/Kingston: McGill-Queen's University Press, 1993.

Miller, Ian Hugh Maclean. *Our Glory and Our Grief: Torontonians and the Great War.* Toronto: University of Toronto Press, 2002. https://doi.org/10.3138/9781442678170.

Miller, J.R. *Compact, Contract, Covenant: Aboriginal Treaty-Making in Canada.* Toronto: University of Toronto Press, 2009.

Monière, Denis. *Le développement des idéologies au Québec: Des origines à nos jours.* Montreal, Québec: Amérique, 1977.

Morton, Desmond. *Canada and War: A Military and Political History.* Toronto: Butterworths, 1981.

Morton, Desmond. *Fight or Pay: Soldiers' Families in the Great War.* Vancouver: UBC Press, 2004.

Morton, Desmond. *Ministers and Generals: Politics and the Canadian Militia, 1868–1904.* Toronto: University of Toronto Press, 1970.

Morton, Desmond. *A Peculiar Kind of Politics: Canada's Overseas Ministry in the First World War.* Toronto: University of Toronto Press, 1982.

Morton, Desmond. *When Your Number's Up: The Canadian Soldier in the First World War.* Toronto: Random House of Canada, 1993.

Morton, Desmond, and Jack Granatstein. *Marching to Armageddon: Canadians and the Great War, 1914–1919.* Toronto: Lester and Orpen Dennys, 1989.

Mosby, Ian. *Food Will Win the War: The Politics, Culture, and Science of Food on Canada's Home Front.* Vancouver: UBC Press, 2014.

Oppenheimer, Melanie. *All Work No Pay: Australian Civilian Volunteers in War.* Walcha, NSW: Ohio Productions, 2002.

Pariseau, Jean, and Serge Bernier. *1763–1969: Le spectre d'une armée bicéphale.* Vol.1, *Les Canadiens français et le bilinguisme dans les forces armées canadiennes.* Ottawa: National Defence, 1987.

Patrias, Carmela. *Jobs and Justice: Fighting Wartime Discrimination in Wartime Canada, 1939–1945.* Toronto: University of Toronto Press, 2012.

Penlington, Norman. "General Hutton and the Problem of Military Imperialism in Canada, 1898–1900." *Canadian Historical Review* 24, 2 (1943): 156–71. https://doi.org/10.3138/CHR-024-02-04.

Pickles, Katie. *Female Imperialism and National Identity: The Imperial Order Daughters of the Empire.* Manchester: Manchester University Press, 2002. https://doi.org/10.7228/manchester/9780719063909.001.0001.

Potter, Simon. "The BBC, the CBC, and the 1939 Royal Tour of Canada." *Cultural and Social History* 3 (2006): 424–44.

Preston, Richard. *Canada and Imperial Defense: A Study of the Origins of the British Commonwealth's Defense Organization, 1867–1919.* Durham: Duke University Press, 1967.

Preston, Richard. "The Military Structure of the Old Commonwealth." *International Journal* 17, 2 (1962): 98–121. https://doi.org/10.1177/002070206201700202.

Pulsifer, Cameron. "The Great Canadian Machine Gun Mania of 1915: The Public, the Press, and Government Decision Making in Procuring Machine Guns for the Canadian Expeditionary Force." *Histoire Sociale/Social History* 46, 1 (2013): 91–120.

Radforth, Ian. *Royal Spectacle: The 1860 Visit of the Prince of Wales to Canada and the United States.* Toronto: University of Toronto Press, 2004. https://doi.org/10.3138/9781442628052.

Rutherdale, Robert Allen. *Hometown Horizons: Local Responses to Canada's Great War.* Vancouver: UBC Press, 2004.

Schagerl, Jessica. "The Tensions of Global Imperial Community: Canada's Imperial Order Daughters of the Empire (IODE)." In *Renegotiating Community: Interdisciplinary Perspectives, Global Contexts,* edited by Diana Brydon and William D. Coleman, 201–15. Vancouver: UBC Press, 2008.

Schurman, Donald, and John Beeler. *Imperial Defence, 1868–1887.* London: Frank Cass, 2000.

Shaw, Amy, and Sarah Glassford, eds. *A Sisterhood of Suffering and Service: Women and Girls of Canada and Newfoundland during the First World War.* Vancouver: UBC Press, 2012.

Sheffield, R. Scott. "'Of Pure European Descent and of the White Race': Recruitment Policy and Aboriginal Canadians, 1939–1945." *Canadian Military History* 5, 1 (Spring 1996): 8–15.

Sheffield, R. Scott. *The Red Man's on the Warpath: The Image of the "Indian" and the Second World War.* Vancouver: UBC Press, 2004.

Smith, David E. *Federalism and the Constitution of Canada.* Toronto: University of Toronto Press, 2010.

Stacey, C.P. *Arms, Men and Governments: The War Policies of Canada, 1939–1945.* Ottawa: Department of National Defence, 1970.

Stacey, C.P. *Canada and the Age of Conflict.* 2 vols. Toronto: Macmillan, 1971–81.

Stacey, C.P. *Six Years of War: The Army in Canada, Britain, and the Pacific.* Ottawa: Edmond Cloutier, 1955.

Stacey, C.P., and B.M. Wilson. *The Half-Million: The Canadians in Britain, 1939–1946.* Toronto: University of Toronto Press, 1987.

Steiner, Zara. *The Lights That Failed: European International History, 1919–1933.* Oxford: Oxford University Press, 2005. https://doi.org/10.1093/acprof:oso/9780198221142.001.0001.

Stevenson, Michael D. "Conscripting Coal: The Regulation of the Coal Labour Force in Nova Scotia during the Second World War." *Acadiensis* 29, 2 (Spring 2000): 58–88.

Strachan, Hew. *The Politics of the British Army*. Oxford: Oxford University Press, 1997.

Sugiman, Pamela. "Privilege and Oppression: The Configuration of Race, Gender, and Class in Southern Ontario Auto Plants, 1939 to 1949." *Labour/Le Travail* 47 (Spring 2001): 83–113. https://doi.org/10.2307/25149114.

Talbot, Robert J. "'It Would Be Best to Leave Us Alone': First Nations Responses to the Canadian War Effort, 1914–18." *Journal of Canadian Studies/Revue d'Etudes Canadiennes* 45, 1 (2011): 90–120. https://doi.org/10.3138/jcs.45.1.90.

Teigrob, Robert. "Empires and Cultures of Militarism in Canada and the United States." *American Review of Canadian Studies* 43, 1 (March 2013): 30–48. https://doi.org/10.10 80/02722011.2013.764914.

Teigrob, Robert. "Glad Adventures, Tragedies, Silences: Remembering and Forgetting Wars for Empire in Canada the United States." *International Journal of Canadian Studies* 45–46 (2012): 441–65. https://doi.org/10.7202/1009914ar.

Tennant, Paul. *Aboriginal Peoples and Politics: The Indian Land Question in British Columbia, 1849–1989*. Vancouver: UBC Press, 1990.

Thornton, Martin. *Churchill, Borden and Anglo-Canadian Naval Relations, 1911–14*. London: Palgrave Macmillan, 2013. https://doi.org/10.1057/9781137300874.

Titley, Brian. *A Narrow Vision: Duncan Campbell Scott and the Administration of Indian Affairs in Canada*. Vancouver: UBC Press, 1986.

Toman, Cynthia. "'A Loyal Body of Empire Citizens': Military Nurses and Identity at Lemnos and Salonika, 1915–17." In *Place and Practice in Canadian Nursing History*, edited by Jayne Elliott, Meryn Stuart, and Cynthia Toman, 8–24. Vancouver: UBC Press, 2008.

Trofimenkoff, Susan Mann. *Action Française: French Canadian Nationalism in the Twenties*. Toronto: University of Toronto Press, 1975.

Ungar, Molly Pulver. "Nationalism on the Menu: Three Banquets on the 1939 Royal Tour." In *Edible Histories, Cultural Politics: Towards a Canadian Food History*, edited by Franca Iacovetta, Valerie J. Korinek, and Marlene Epp , 351–58. Toronto: University of Toronto Press, 2012.

van Heyningen, Elizabeth. *The Concentration Camps of the Anglo-Boer War: A Social History*. Johannesburg: Jacana Media, 2013.

Vance, Jonathan A. *Maple Leaf Empire: Canada, Britain, and Two World Wars*. Don Mills, ON: Oxford University Press, 2011.

Vipond, Mary. "The Royal Tour of 1939 as a Media Event." *Canadian Journal of Communication* 35, 1 (2010): 149–72. https://doi.org/10.22230/cjc.2010v35n1a2217.

Waiser, Bill, and Blair Stonechild. *Loyal Till Death: Indians and the North-West Rebellion*. Calgary: Fifth House, 1997.

Walker, James W. St.G. "Race and Recruitment in World War I: Enlistment of Visible Minorities in the Canadian Expeditionary Force." *Canadian Historical Review* 70, 1 (1989): 1–26. https://doi.org/10.3138/CHR-070-01-01.

Winegard, Timothy C. *For King and Kanata: Canadian Indians and the First World War*. Winnipeg: University of Manitoba Press, 2012.

White, Richard. *The Middle Ground: Indians, Empires, and Republics in the Great Lakes Region, 1650–1815*. New York: Cambridge University Press, 1991. https://doi. org/10.1017/CBO9780511584671.

Wood, James. *Militia Myth: Ideas of the Canadian Citizen-Soldier, 1896–1921*. Vancouver: UBC Press, 2010.

Contributors

Mikhail Bjorge received a PhD in history from Queen's University. His primary area of expertise is economic and labour history, paying specific attention to race and gender. He has published on transnational solidarity movements, the role of song and poetry in multiethnic strikes, resistance to Japanese internment, and other topics germane to the experiences of common people. His current projects include fashioning his thesis, "The Workers' War: The Character of Class Struggle in World War II," into a book.

Eirik Brazier is an associate professor of history at the University of Southeast Norway. He holds a PhD in history from the European University Institute in Florence, Italy. His thesis, "Stranger in a Strange Land: British Imperial Officers in Canada and the Australian Colonies, ca.1870–1914," examines cultural aspects of military cooperation within the British Empire. His other fields of interest include Scandinavia, particularly Norway during the First World War; the intelligence history of Scandinavia before 1945; and the legal purge in Norway after the Second World War.

Claire L. Halstead is a postdoctoral research fellow at Saint Mary's University. Her research focuses on the Sisters of Service, a Canadian Catholic community of religious women. Her doctoral research, on which she has published, focused on British children evacuated to Canada during the Second World War. Her other interests include digital history, immigration, and war and society, and she is the creator of three large historical digital databases that intersect with these themes.

Geoff Keelan completed a PhD at the University of Waterloo and is an archivist with Library and Archives Canada. He has published on Canada, Quebec, and the First World War, and has a book titled *Henri Bourassa's War* forthcoming.

Steve Marti received a PhD from the University of Western Ontario in 2015. He has published articles in *Histoire sociale/Social History; Itinerario; History Australia;* and *Australian Studies,* and he wrote the entry "The Dominions' Military Relationship to Great Britain, 1902–1914" for *1914–1918 Online: International Encyclopedia of the First World War.*

William John Pratt is a postdoctoral fellow at the University of Alberta. He received a PhD from the University of Calgary in 2015, and his dissertation examined the medicalization of Canadian army morale in the Second World War. He has published articles and book chapters on Canadian military history and western Canadian history.

Amy Shaw is an associate professor in the Department of History at the University of Lethbridge. She is the author of *Crisis of Conscience: Conscientious Objection in Canada during the First World War* and co-editor of *"A Sisterhood of Suffering and Service": Women and Girls of Canada and Newfoundland during the First World War*.

R. Scott Sheffield is an associate professor of history at the University of the Fraser Valley. He is the author of *The Red Man's on the Warpath: The Image of the "Indian" and the Second World War* and co-author of *Indigenous Peoples and the Second World War: The Politics, Experiences and Legacies in the United States, Canada, Australia and New Zealand* (with Noah Riseman).

Robert J. Talbot is the manager of research at the Office of the Commissioner of Official Languages of Canada. In addition to publishing and presenting on the history of anglophone–francophone relations, he served as the English-language secretary of the Canadian Historical Association (2013–18) and won the Manitoba Historical Association award for scholarly history for *Negotiating the Numbered Treaties*.

Index

Action nationale, 94

Africa, 23, 26, 70, 125, 127, 187; African immigrants in Canada, 5; North Africa in Second World War, 61n18. *See also* South African War

Albert I, King, 132

Alberta, 145, 169, 172

alcohol, 56, 57, 60

American Federation of Labour (AFL), 146, 162n27

Angers, François-Albert, 95–96

animals, 26, 29

armistice, 48

Article X of the Covenant of the League of Nations, 86, 89, 100n4

Asia, 11, 70, 125, 187

Asian Canadians, 4, 5, 15n27, 145

Asselin, Olivar, 127

Atlantic Ocean, 52, 53, 96, 131

Aurora, Ontario, 112

Australia, 56, 71, 84n64, 85n69

Austria, 40, 41, 147, 151, 156, 158, 162n28, 165n104

Austro-Hungarian Empire, 3, 41, 125

Avery, Donald, 159n8

aviation, 55, 171, 173

Axis powers, 3, 4, 146, 149, 153, 166

bacon, 55, 142

Balfour, Arthur James, 90

Balfour Declaration, 90–92, 100n15, 102n45

Bégin, Louis-Nazaire, 130

Belgian relief in First World War, 46

Belgium, 125, 129, 131–33

Bennett, Richard Bedford, 92–93

Berger, Carl, 4, 126

biculturalism, 44, 90, 95, 97, 125, 127

bilingualism, 89, 97–99, 113, 125, 127

Bloc populaire, 99

Boer War. *See* South African War

Borden, Frederick, 21

Borden, Robert, 15n27, 88, 99, 128–29, 134–35

Bourassa, Henri: bicultural pan-Canadianist views, 90, 97, 126–28, 131; on Canadian independence from Britain, 126, 127; on conscription, 135, 185; and federal election of 1911, 128; and Ligue nationaliste, 127; and moderate Canadian contributions in First World War, 131–32; on Naval Service Act of 1910, 128, 136, 185; and outbreak of First World War, 132–33, 136, 185; role in Imperial Conference (1926), 90; and South African War, 127, 136, 185

Bowell, Mackenzie, 81n1

Boy Scouts, 46, 111

British army, 11, 44–46, 70, 73, 78–80, 82n13, 184

British Broadcasting Corporation (BBC), 58, 59, 106

British Canadians, 9, 11, 86, 88, 92–93, 186

British Columbia, 41, 104n90, 115, 145, 158, 168, 170, 171

British monarchy: Canadian admiration of, 105, 106, 111, 113, 116, 144; Canadian loyalty to, 106, 107; Crown as political body, 11, 76, 90, 101n28, 166, 184, 186; and imperial officers in Canada, 76–81; and Indigenous peoples, 9, 12, 166–67, 168, 169, 172, 175, 176–77, 186; on 1939 royal tour, 81, 105–18; as symbol, 9, 79, 166, 168, 180n10, 184

British Pathé, 114

British world, 5–6, 117

Britishness, 5–6, 9, 13n9, 38, 43, 52, 81, 103n61, 158; inclusion of German Canadians and French Canadians, 3

Brown, George, 83n45

Buchan, John (Lord Tweedsmuir), 107

James Wood, *Militia Myths: Ideas of the Canadian Citizen Soldier, 1896–1921*

Timothy Balzer, *The Information Front: The Canadian Army and News Management during the Second World War*

Andrew B. Godefroy, *Defence and Discovery: Canada's Military Space Program, 1945–74*

Douglas E. Delaney, *Corps Commanders: Five British and Canadian Generals at War, 1939–45*

Timothy Wilford, *Canada's Road to the Pacific War: Intelligence, Strategy, and the Far East Crisis*

Randall Wakelam, *Cold War Fighters: Canadian Aircraft Procurement, 1945–54*

Andrew Burtch, *Give Me Shelter: The Failure of Canada's Cold War Civil Defence*

Wendy Cuthbertson, *Labour Goes to War: The CIO and the Construction of a New Social Order, 1939–45*

P. Whitney Lackenbauer, *The Canadian Rangers: A Living History*

Teresa Iacobelli, *Death or Deliverance: Canadian Courts Martial in the Great War*

Graham Broad, *A Small Price to Pay: Consumer Culture on the Canadian Home Front, 1939–45*

Peter Kasurak, *A National Force: The Evolution of Canada's Army, 1950–2000*

Isabel Campbell, *Unlikely Diplomats: The Canadian Brigade in Germany, 1951–64*

Richard M. Reid, *African Canadians in Union Blue: Volunteering for the Cause in the Civil War*

Andrew B. Godefroy, *In Peace Prepared: Innovation and Adaptation in Canada's Cold War Army*

Nic Clarke, *Unwanted Warriors: The Rejected Volunteers of the Canadian Expeditionary Force*

David Zimmerman, *Maritime Command Pacific: The Royal Canadian Navy's West Coast Fleet in the Early Cold War*

Cynthia Toman, *Sister Soldiers of the Great War: The Nurses of the Canadian Army Medical Corps*

Daniel Byers, *Zombie Army: The Canadian Army and Conscription in the Second World War*

J.L. Granatstein, *The Weight of Command: Voices of Canada's Second World War Generals and Those Who Knew Them*

Colin McCullough, *Creating Canada's Peacekeeping Past*

Douglas E. Delaney and Serge Marc Durflinger, eds., *Capturing Hill 70: Canada's Forgotten Battle of the First World War*

Brandon R. Dimmel, *Engaging the Line: How the Great War Shaped the Canada–US Border*

Meghan Fitzpatrick, *Invisible Scars: Mental Trauma and the Korean War*

Geoffrey Hayes, *Crerar's Lieutenants: Inventing the Canadian Junior Army Officer, 1939–45*

Frank Maas, *The Price of Alliance: The Politics and Procurement of Leopard Tanks for Canada's NATO Brigade*

Patrick M. Dennis, *Reluctant Warriors: Canadian Conscripts and the Great War*

Richard Goette, *Sovereignty and Command in Canada–US Continental Air Defence, 1940–57*

Geoffrey Jackson, *The Empire on the Western Front: The British 62nd and Canadian 4th Divisions in Battle*

STUDIES IN CANADIAN MILITARY HISTORY
Published by UBC Press in association with the Canadian War Museum

Printed and bound in Canada by Friesens
Set in Minion and Helvetica by Apex CoVantage, LLC
Copy editor: Lesley Erickson
Proofreader: Lauren Cross